SEX AFTER THE
SEXUAL REVOLUTION

SEX

AFTER

THE

SEXUAL

REVOLUTION

by

HELEN COLTON

ASSOCIATION PRESS/New York

International Standard Book Number: 0-8096-1853-2
Library of Congress Catalog Card Number: 72-8863

Library of Congress Cataloging in Publication Data

Colton, Helen.
  Sex after the sexual revolution.

      1. Sex customs—United States. 2. Sexual ethics.
I. Title.
HQ18. U5C625   301.41′7′0973   72-8863
ISBN 0-8096-1853-2

Printed in the United States of America

This book is dedicated with joy

To my husband	Irvin E. Good
To my teacher	Dr. Charles L. Conrad
To my son	Corey Field
To my daughter	Mona Field
To my comp-kin	Marvin Werdesheim

CONTENTS

Preface

This preface is written in anger, in compassion, and in hope.

I was born in Newark, New Jersey on January 4, 1918 and started school there at the age of six. I am, at this writing, fifty-four years old. I never in my life have had anything that could be called sex education. What I thought about sex came from gossiping and conjecturing and wondering with my equally curious, guilt-ridden, and misinformed peers in the school playground, from occasional disrobing and playing doctor with young neighbors and relatives, and from reading "dirty" books with four-letter words that I sneaked from older relatives and would read surreptitiously in bed at night.

I am angry because I was permitted to go through the early part of my life—a lover of knowledge, a constant reader, a devotee of libraries, valedictorian of my high-school graduating class—without ever being taught, or without my ever coming across in my wide reading, the proper names for the parts of my own body. It was with great shock in my early twenties that I heard for the first time in my life someone at a family party use the words "penis" and "vagina." Some instinct told me that *those* were the proper words for the male and female sex organs and not the scatological ones I had known until then.

I am angry to have been deprived of my birthright to know about human sexuality and of having to find it all out with a great deal of trauma, disappointment, psychic pain, and shame. I am angry that

9

the society and the culture in which I was reared could have taken the ecstatic pleasure of sexual experience and so tarnished it for the first half of my existence.

André Maurois, the biographer, once said that he selected as subjects to write about, those people whose lives he hoped would hold a solution to some of his own problems. In a sense, this is what many of us unknowingly do when we select a profession in which to spend our lives. Since my early twenties when I started my free-lance career by writing articles for magazines, I have written mainly about family and personal problems and the ways in which we might solve them. With my words I have always hoped to calm troubled waters. I am sure that I considered myself to be the number-one student of the knowledge I garnered and dispensed in my writings.

It is significant to me, too, that when, in 1966 during a divorce after twenty-two years of marriage, I chose to start an organization around which to structure my work as a writer, teacher of adult education, and public speaker, I called it "Family Forum" and set as its theme: "The gathering and disseminating of information and ideas to help us gain insight into our own natures and the nature of the society in which we must cope with social change."

"My goal," I wrote then, "is to save others from the heartaches and trauma I experienced through lack of up-to-date information and attitudes."

The compassion I am feeling as I write these words is for the great number of people today, especially young people, who are still back where I was nearly a generation ago, deprived of their right to know, victimized for not knowing that which we refuse to teach them, experiencing, so needlessly, the same kind of pain.

I feel compassion for all young women, such as those described by Hariette Surovell, a New York high-school senior testifying before the National Commission on Population Growth and the American Future who said of her female peers and their uninformed sexual activity: "Most girls just pray that they won't get pregnant because they know nothing about how not to get pregnant."

I feel much compassion for the despairing young father who, at age 17, experiences the interruption of his life and his education, possibly never to be resumed, because of the forced parenthood and unwanted marriage he feels honor-bound to enter into because of having made a girl pregnant.

I feel real compassion for the many married women whose sexual orientation has been so rigid and depriving that they are uninterested or uncomfortable about entering into sexual experimentation with their husbands; also, I feel compassion for the husbands who, in order to experience the full range of their sexual desires, guiltily carry on affairs with women outside of their marriages so they can complete their sexual selves.

And I feel compassion for the young mother full of self-doubts over whether she did the right thing by letting her small son, when he asked to see the "hole I came out of," see her vagina. And for the elderly widower, alive and vital with life's sensory juices, who is called "a dirty old man" when he makes a sexual overture to a woman friend.

It is for all of us that I have written this book.

My hope is that my anger and compassion will turn out to have served humankind.

At this point in evolution, no species kills its own kind in such great numbers as does the human species. We are capable of such behavior because, in the words of my beloved friend and teacher, Dr. Charles L. Conrad, "we are not down out of the trees long enough yet to have become human." We are not yet human beings, we are human *becomers,* engaged in the long slow evolutionary process of *becoming* civilized.

Freeing our sexual selves is one of the obligatory steps humankind must take in order to move closer to a civilized state. And it is the Sexual Revolution which will bring us closer to that civilized state. The Sexual Revolution and its excesses may be likened to a child that is a burden and a nuisance because it soils itself but then grows up to be a beautiful human being.

I like to think that this book may make us aware of the potential beauty of the Sexual Revolution and that it may ultimately make a contribution by giving each of us individually more joyful sex lives and all of us collectively more humane beings with whom to share the planet.

HELEN COLTON

West Hollywood, California

Introduction: Our Changing Sex Philosophy

The human personality is one of our remaining frontiers for exploration as we approach the 21st century. In the words of Erich Fromm, we are "learning to look inward." What, we are asking, are we *really* like and how do we *truly* behave, in contradiction to what the mythology of the past told us human behavior *ought* to be? We do not yet know why we behave as we do, what needs we have in order to function at our optimum, and how to stop killing each other in such numbers.

As part of our search inward in this burgeoning age of insight, we are learning much new information about human sexuality. And more and more we are demanding our right to experience that sexuality, unwilling any longer to allow archaic laws, dogmas, customs, shibboleths, superstitions, myths, and thou-shalt-nots tell us what we may or may not do with our own bodies. We are beginning for the first time ever to own our bodies.

No longer will we permit our bodies to be the possession of the state, which has historically told us where, with whom, in what position, with which parts, with what kind of contraception, if any, we could exercise our sex drive—a drive so powerful in our personality that it is exceeded only by our drive for food and water.

As we free ourselves from history's shackles, the human race is in the process of evolving and of living out a whole new philosophy about the sexual part of human experience. Through the ages man's sexual ethic (the word *man* is used advisedly; this happened largely

13

before he began to stop blackballing woman from acceptance into the human fraternity) considered his sex drive to be a base and evil part of himself, a reflection of his carnal nature, the lowliest part of human personality. Sex was noble and beautiful only when it was experienced for purposes of procreation and within marriage. Otherwise, this same ethic said, sex whose primary motivation was pleasure and the avoidance of procreation was sinful and licentious—a weakness of the flesh which good men resisted and to which weak men fell prey.

But *whuman* (man and woman joined for the first time) is now embarking on a new philosophy which says that sex is not a negative force to be denied and hidden, but, rather, it is a positive force which can release and enrich the vast potentialities of the human personality to heights as yet only dreamed of.

To synopsize the existing and the emerging new philosophies: We have been equating sexuality with genitality. Now we are beginning to equate sexuality with the total personality.

In one sense we may say that the human adventure is only just beginning. Humanity has not yet experienced the wholeness of which it is capable. We have never yet been free to be either persons or sexual beings who could enjoy our sensory natures without conditions and guilt imposed upon us from without. Moreover, the joining at this juncture in time of our two concurrent revolutions—the sexual revolution and the gender revolution which is achieving women's liberation—means that for the first time the two genders, male and female, can bond together as equally free, equally sensory, halves of the human whole.

The sexual revolution is freeing us to explore whole new questions: To what heights might human personality soar when we throw overboard the sandbags of repression and it becomes acceptable to admit, among many other admissions, that we parents do get erotic feelings about our own children; to admit that most of us, even the happily married, may yearn for sexual varietism occasionally; to look squarely without blanching at the latent opposite-sexness we all have? What will it mean to human nature when our mass psyche receives approval to enjoy this exquisite pleasure of sex untarnished with guilt? In short, what can this ecstatic experience, no longer burdened by any societally imposed need to procreate, do for the human spirit individually and collectively?

Our emerging sex philosophy has come about as the result of many factors: modern technology; the invention of the pill; the emergence of a new ism, *equalism,* through which human beings are beginning to experience equality regardless of the shape or style of their genitalia; the exposure of Americans to the mores and manners of other cultures during and since World War II; the cross-cultural experiences of youth throughout the world who attend schools and spend vacations traveling in each other's lands; the increased longevity of human beings which makes monogamy less satisfying; our concern for the planet's depleting resources; and the changing values and antimaterialism of young people everywhere who hate the wars and false words of their elders and who are forcing us to scrape away some dry rot of human obsolescence.

In just a few short years the sexual revolution has brought forth the greatest amount of new knowledge and honesty about our sexuality that humankind has ever known. The changes being wrought by this information-and-truth explosion are evident in our laws, our mass media, our cultural customs, our language, our changing attitudes, codes, and practices. We are not only experiencing increased frankness and candor in public discussion, but as an inevitable concomitant we are also experiencing acceptance of a variety of sexual behaviors and life-styles. It is strikingly evident that we are going through a qualitative change in humankind's acceptance and enjoyment of its sexual nature. The truth of life is demanding out.

Once-taboo topics, such as abortion, homosexuality, adultery, transvestism, mate-swapping, group or "social" sex, sex language, vasectomy, impotence, frigidity, and premature ejaculation, oral-genital sex relations, out-of-wedlock parenthood, are all discussed without reticence by individuals and by couples who are experiencing them.

Biographies now routinely include material on the sexual lives and especially the sexual problems of their subjects, such as the impotence experienced by Ernest Hemingway and theatrical impresario Billy Rose; the football heroes, Jim Brown and Joe Namath, talk openly in their biographies about their swinging sex lives. Actor Orson Bean tells in his autobiography, *Me and the Orgone, One Man's Sexual Revolution,* how he conquered his sexual problems. James Baldwin, the novelist, asked by the *Los Angeles Free Press* if it were true that he was homosexual, replied: "I'm bisexual." Gore Vidal, playwright, novelist, and essayist, writing a review of a sex book for *The New York Review of Books,* tells of his own bisexuality.

Theatrical personalities have begun routinely to tell interviewers about their companionate living arrangements and trial marriages. A Broadway press agent, commenting on the decline of the gossip columnist in American journalism, says: "Look, you have glamorous stars now openly living with each other. You get people talking on TV about the most intimate things. You get magazine articles that are incredibly blunt. What's left to gossip about?"

During those same few years, films have been made in the United States and imported from other countries with increasingly explicit scenes of sexual activity—heterosexual, homosexual, and bisexual —and bluntness of language. A successful American play, later a film, about homosexuals, *The Boys in the Band,* used words such as the four-letter slang word for the female genital that had hardly been spoken out loud in polite company since the days of bawdy Restoration theater. "We appear to be overcoming obscenity by incorporating it into polite conversation," *New York Times* drama critic Clive Barnes has commented.

The truth of life began to out even in short stories and novels in popular magazines in which, something never done before, couples about to make love first checked with each other as to whether they were "prepared" with contraception.

The change has come with dizzying rapidity. In 1969 a public speaker elicited gasps of disbelief and cries of "No" from audiences when she said that a question many of us would one day face was whether to permit our children, living in companionate arrangements on college campuses, to stay with their companionate-mates in their own bedrooms when they visited home. By March 1971 *McCall's* Magazine was featuring in a full-page ad this question of protocol: "When my nephew and the girl he's living with visit us, should we put them in the same bedroom?" By May 1972, *The New York Times* was reporting that "Some [Parents] Accept Sex at Home for the Young" permitting unmarried children to cohabit with their partners in their own bedrooms at home.

And some of the change has come from astonishing sources. When a communal family of 270 men, women, and children moved from San Francisco to Tennessee, it was amazed to be invited to speak to the local Methodist Women's Club on its group marriage arrangements and to find the rural women "friendly and interested" rather than disapproving on the subject.

Concurrent with society's growing acceptance of the emerging sex philosophy being lived by humankind approaching the twenty-first century, there has also been acceptance from government agencies and officialdom, as they respond to the needs and wishes of the majority of the citizenry.

For the first time, social workers have been legally permitted to discuss birth control with families on welfare. Widespread existing rules had said that workers might answer questions of women who initiated a discussion on contraception, but that they could not initiate the discussion or urge the use of birth control. In Maryland, a social worker was fired because she could not resist the humanitarian urge to tell a harassed mother of the existence of contraception. In December 1966 the State Board of Social Welfare of New York revised previous rules and allowed caseworkers to give birth control information to welfare recipients.

As of January 1, 1967, the Defense Department began to issue birth control devices, free of charge, to the wives of all men in the armed forces. During 1970 the Department began to permit wives of American military men to have free abortions at military hospitals. The following year these rules were liberalized even further to provide that the Government would pay for abortions at civilian hospitals in any state where abortion was legal.

It was during this period that the United States Supreme Court wrestled constantly with definitions of the word "obscenity," satisfying neither those who wanted more censorship nor those who wanted less. "Obscenity," said Stanley Fleishman, Los Angeles attorney, "is a matter of geography." The geography apparently extended not only from national region to national region—the Bible Belt versus the big cities—but even from inside a house to outside a house. In a landmark decision the Supreme Court ruled that an Atlanta man had the legal right to possess and show stag films inside his own apartment, a bachelor pad. Out in the community, however, it was still illegal.

A major result of the sexual revolution is that the day is probably closer at hand than we realize when there will be no laws of any kind against any human sexual behavior unless there is a victim.

This is, in fact, the sexual code proposed by the Southern California chapter of the American Civil Liberties Union and by many legal and judicial groups. In a statement entitled "Sexual Civil Liberties" it proposes that no form of human sexual expression be legally proscribed unless it is done with force, violence, without the consent of both parties, to the mentally retarded, or to minors incapable of knowing the consequences of their actions. The American Assembly, an august body of opinionmakers, has made essentially the same proposal following its meeting, *The Health of Americans,* held in 1970. Point number fourteen of its report states in part: "To diminish mental anguish and improve the mental health of segments of society we recommend . . . the abolition of all existing laws concerning sexual behavior between consenting adults, without sacrificing protection for minors or public decorum."

During these same past few years institutionalized religion has been learning, at the high cost of losing millions of its congregants around the world, that in order to keep pace with the new philosophy approving of sex for recreation not procreation it must relinquish long-held taboos and proscriptions against premarital and extramarital relationships, masturbation, and homosexuality and update obsolete clerical attitudes that modern sexually liberated man and woman refuse to abide by.

Increasingly, as the late philosopher, Dr. Karl Jaspers, put it, organized religion is accepting that "there is no such thing as an absolute and finished truth that we can hear and learn in a single place at a single point in time."

Theologians of all faiths have joined in urging that truth be considered an ongoing process and not an eternal absolute. The Reverend Angelo D'Agostino, S.J., a Catholic physician writing on *Catholic Doctors in a Changing World,* declares: "A certain few absolutes are immutable but they are getting to be fewer and fewer." Agreeing that there can be a variety of religious truths, the Reverend Colin W. William, dean of Yale Divinity School, has said: "I'm not afraid of a plurality of truths." Leslie Dewart, noted lay theologian at St. Michael's College of the University of Toronto, has said: "Theology will have to get accustomed to an environment in which there is no certitude and no perennial religious truth." In his book *For Whom the Rabbi Speaks,* Dr. Joseph R. Narot said of Judaism's changing attitudes: "Religion must not deny or suppress the life forces of human nature, nor should it teach concepts about these forces which are contrary to human experience. Religion developed the notion that the human body is sinful, wicked, shameful, and that its needs and desires must be crushed or the soul will burn in hell."

Dr. Joseph Fletcher, theologian and professor of medical ethics at the University of Virginia Medical School, one-time Dean of St. Paul's Cathedral, Cincinnati, urges humankind to adopt the "new morality" of *Situation Ethics*, the title of his book, not only in sexual matters but in all human behavior. Dr. Fletcher maintains that time, place, and situation should define our morality and that what is moral and ethical at one time, place, and situation may not be relevant morality at another time, place, and situation. He advocates an ethic of love which extricates contemporary man from rigid, archaic rules and codes.

Summing up religion's changing attitudes brought about by the sexual revolution, Daniel Callahan, theologian, has written in *Commonweal* Magazine: "It is true that theology is no longer happy with the earlier Christian belief that man lives in an unchanging cosmos, possesses an immutable nature and is subject to fixed moral laws. . . . Truth is to be created more than discovered by man, *self-fulfillment* rather than *self-denial* should be the mark of the Christian's relationship to his body and his world."

Traditionally, all new freedoms in human behavior bring with them periods of license. Our new sexual freedom is, at this moment in time, freedom that is often widely abused, resulting in the birth of unwanted and unneeded humanity both inside and outside of marriage, epidemic venereal disease, the commercialization and brutalization of sex that demeans our humanness, and the exploitation of others for sexual relief. It is freedom without responsibility.

But all experience has its negative and its positive sides. Just as we need our failures recorded on our nervous systems to provide us with experience to learn from and to help us to know what we do not want, so too we need to experience the excesses of the sexual revolution on our cultural nervous system to help us choose what we do not want sexual freedom to be.

Traditionally, periods of license have always diminished as new freedoms become implemented into human existence. And this seems already to be happening with sexual license in the present. One indication that we are already changing may be seen in the fact that 50,000 people attended the first Danish pornography fair in 1970. The second year, 1971, the fair was a dismal failure, drawing only 5,000 people. Another indication that we are already in the early stages of integrating these new freedoms into our lives is the report in *Variety,* the show-business trade paper, that many movie houses which showed only "skin flicks" (sexy movies) a short while ago, no longer find them profitable and are switching to family film fare, often at lower prices, to draw audiences once again. "U.S. Filmmakers De-emphasizing Sex," reports a *New York Times* front-page headline of April 20, 1971.

As Erasmus, the fifteenth-century Dutch philosopher, pointed out, times of tumult always turn out to be times of transition to calmer periods of history. While irresponsible, depersonalized, and exploitive sex can be said to be the negative value of this traumatic time of turmoil, the growing truth about human sexual behavior may be said to be the positive value.

How exciting it is for us, how enriched and privileged our contemporary generation is, to be the first people to get a look at the "compleat man" of human history. Because we are newly entering a time in which it is acceptable to write and to speak honestly about our heros and antiheros of the past, we are enabled to make an interpretation that comes closer to truth than the mythology about human behavior with which we have been regaled since recorded history began. In a sense, humanity's history, like humanity's wholeness, is just now beginning.

Is humankind demeaned or inspired to rise above intolerance when we are permitted to know in our new age of candor that achievers like John Gorton, former Australian prime minister, singer-poet Rod McKuen, writer-critic Kenneth Tynan, German premier Willy Brandt were born out of wedlock?

Are we diminished or are we able to achieve new heights of understanding and compassion when this age of candor enables us to learn, in a book like *The Uninhibited Byron, An Account of His Sexual Confusion,* of the tortured bisexuality of the poet Byron? Or to read in a poignant *New York Times Magazine* article by novelist Merle Miller "What It Means to Be a Homosexual"? Or to know of writer F. Scott Fitzgerald's concern about the size of his phallus, a problem that worries millions of men, but which we never dared to mention right out loud in public before?

Are we closer to a core of truth when we can say, again right out loud, that the drive which caused George Washington to be known as the Father of His Country may have derived not only from self-lessness but also from his need to compensate for feelings of inadequacy from the sterility which prevented him from physically fathering a child of his own?

Are we human beings diminished or are we enhanced if, for the first time in human experience, women are permitted increasingly to own their own bodies as new laws regarding abortion are passed throughout the world?

Are we not more diminished when we deny a person the right to citizenship because he admits to having sexual relations with his fiancee? Late in 1971, citizenship was denied to a thirty-year-old man for this sole reason by the United States legal-sexual code—an example of the kind of irrational remnant of the prurient past which the sexual revolution is helping to free us of.

Is not human love more diminished when a doctor in Spain is threatened with a six-month jail sentence for having circulated an anonymous questionnaire among students at the University of Madrid as part of a study of sexual attitudes and practices? "I get patients . . . who have never so much as kissed anyone," he reported sadly in defending his research.

Is not the human right to pleasure enhanced when we acknowledge our need for sex as part of physical and mental and emotional well-being by beginning to provide rooms in which prisoners can have sexual relations and in which sequestered jurors can enjoy conjugal visits with their mates?

These are rhetorical questions. It is better for us to grow up knowing of the humanness of us all, poet and peasant, king and kook, alike. We did not fare better when many of us grew up so believing in the deification of public figures that we thought that folk heros like movie stars never needed to use the bathroom. We were not better off when prurience did not permit us to know that ennobled forebears who decided the fates of generations of human beings by passing repressive laws which we still live by had minds ravaged by venereal disease or engaged in orgies while severely controlling sexual expression of the common citizen. Or when potentates today can enjoy their several wives while their lowlier citizens can be condemned to death by hanging or be publicly stoned to death for acts of adultery in a legal standard of monogamy for the masses but polygamy for the politicians.

Despite some pain that inevitably accompanies truth, the net effect of an honest interpretation of human behavior of the past and of growing candor about it in the present will be healthy.

Truth gives each one of us subliminal psychological permission to experience our own humanness without guilt and doubts and self-recriminations. Every one of us is a freer human being when we need less of a facade to maintain our psychic equilibrium with each other. As a man in an audience called out, almost with hysterical relief, when a speaker on sex discussed the fact that teenhood homosexual experimentation is now considered to be a normal stage of psychosexual development: "You've just freed me from nagging doubts and guilts I've been carrying around for thirty years."

How victimized and how deprived we all were by the Puritan past in which, incredibly, a highly respected book of sex education, which was used only by those parents considered to be the most liberated and advanced, who would even discuss sex at all with their children, told them this: "One caution: As with practically everything having to do with sex, it's usually best to suggest that the child use his new words (accurate ones for parts of his body) only in the home. Each family in a neighborhood usually has its own way of handling sex questions, and your child may be scolded for using proper terms openly."

We were not freer people when Nicholas Murray Butler, then president of Columbia University, could singlehandedly remove the novel *For Whom The Bell Tolls* from consideration for a Pulitzer Prize because he considered its scene of lovemaking inside a sleeping bag to be "lascivious." We were not freer people when Mark Twain's bawdy writings and Pablo Picasso's erotic art works, "pulsing with the juices of life," were considered to be unpublishable in the United States.

We were not freer people when a group of American adults in a public hall in Wellesley, Massachusetts, hysterically screamed, "Kill him! Kill him!" about a young man who was attempting to discuss the origin of the word *fuck* with townspeople who had protested its use in Leroi Jones's Play *The Slave,* presented in the local high school. This happened in June of 1968, nearly three hundred years after the witchhunt in another Massachusetts community.

The information the young man wanted to give to them, which evoked threats on his life? He wanted to inform them that the word derives from an archaic German agricultural verb *ficken,* meaning "to plant seeds." Over the years the word gradually became *fuck,* meaning "to plant human seed."

We are not freer people nor is the human capacity to express love in a variety of ways enhanced when we have laws throughout the land criminalizing a form of sexual expression that many of our citizens engage in—oral-genital lovemaking.

At a conference on marital therapy, Dr. Aaron Rutledge, one of the country's leading researchers into marital problems, said that many doctors and counselors were reluctant to discuss sexual matters with patients for fear of violating such laws. Asking the California legislature to remove "oral copulation by consenting adults in private" from its criminal code, the Pasadena Bar Association stated: "This amendment will cause the law of the state of California to conform with logic and common sense. The section as it presently stands is an anachronistic medievalism."

"When we look at the whole sweep of man's history on Earth," said anthropologist Julian Huxley, "we see that everything that properly deserves to be called progress has depended on new knowledge and new organizations of knowledge in the shape of ideas."

For some among us, joint tenants of Earth at this point in time, the shape of new ideas casts a fearful shadow. But each of us has no choice about whether we like or agree to accept evolutionary change. Evolution's inevitability forces us all to grow forward into the future together. Whether or not we like the facts of social change, the facts are here to stay and we will soon find ourselves accepting the new ideas and techniques that are useful to us.

Out of deep social need and personal suffering resulting from overcrowded and unpleasant conditions of life, more and more of us are already coming to consider a whole new ethic of existence: shall people have unlimited right of reproduction or shall the community have the right to set limits on procreation?

This major social debate has already begun. Involuntary limiting of families is repugnant to many as not in keeping with the democratic ideal of free choice in such matters. If we legally limit a woman to two children, what do we do if she gets pregnant with a third or fourth child? Do we order her to undergo abortion and/or sterilization and carry her protesting into a hospital room to perform it? To many people, such a procedure smacks of the enforced sterilization of "undesirables" practiced by the fascists of Nazi Germany.

But the pressure for change continues unabated. Dr. H. Bentley Glass, biologist at Johns Hopkins University, says: "No longer can we defend excessive reproduction by saying, 'Well, they can afford it.' The question now is whether society can afford it." "Freedom to procreate equals freedom to starve children," says biologist Garrett Hardin, who points out that freedom to procreate could mean a form of infanticide similar to nineteenth-century mores when it was common practice to drown or to starve unwanted infants.

One school of thought believes we can successfully educate people to voluntarily limit the size of their families. Anthropologist Margaret Mead says: "The age of marriage, the age of parenthood, spacing of children, the number of children, are all matters of cultural style and they are all subject to change."

Another school of thought believes it is too late for that. We need parenthood-by-permission, and the question, they suggest, is no longer: "Should we have it?" but rather: "How do we best carry it out?"

Whatever form it takes, parenthood-by-permission in some form is likely to be a part of our future. When enough of us feel strangled by the umbilical cord of human fertility, our need to take a deep psychic breath unfouled by too many fellow people will probably make us say: "Yes, we're for sterilization. Yes, we're for abortion. Yes, we're for mass contraception. It is inhuman to turn out so much humanity."

"Abortion Gains Favor as Population Grows," says a newspaper headline reporting that in the three years of 1968 through 1970—that's thirty-six months, about a thousand days—there has been "a dramatic change in public acceptance of abortion." In less than two years the change in social attitude toward vasectomy as a form of birth control went from its being an unmentionable hush-hush to thousands of men wearing vasectomy pins on their lapels to show that they have joined men's liberation and made their contribution to population control.

Even those who now object to parenthood-by-permission—when they have experienced enough fear, anger, and discomfort from the "concrete madness" many of us seem to have because we share too little space and too little greenery with too many other human bodies—may one day find themselves, to their own surprise, coming out for legally controlled procreation. Our nation, says scientist René Dubos, will be compelled by events to accept social change.

These changes may not come easily. Most new ideas seem shocking when they are first proposed. Indeed, longshoreman-philosopher Eric Hoffer says that we can never be really prepared for that which is wholly new. "We have to adjust ourselves, and every radical adjustment is a crisis in self-esteem. It needs inordinate self-confidence to have drastic change without inner trembling."

For many of us who keep rejoining the future every day, the trembling is of brief duration. Others choose to go trembling to their graves, quivering and catastrophizing before the winds of social change. Catastrophizers are afraid to learn freedom.

For freedom is something we have to be taught. Never having before experienced full freedom of choice and control over our own bodies and our procreational destiny, we have to be taught how.

We have to be taught how to use the glorious freedoms available to us through contraception, how to be a woman forever freed from the tyranny of monthly tension as to whether she might be accidentally pregnant, how to be a male freed from the economic burden of having to support unplanned children. We have to learn what to do with these new freedoms.

We have to be taught how to use our new genetic knowledge and our ability to determine genetic defects prior to birth. Ask a couple who have spent $60,000 in hospital expenses during the brief three-year life-span of their mongoloid child how they feel about the human race being forever freed from this kind of experience.

Or ask a mother like Beverly Sills, American opera star, what she would have done if she had known through genetic testing that she would give birth to a mentally defective child. Miss Sills said poignantly to a newspaper reporter about her son, who was then ten years old and institutionalized: "Bucky is severely retarded. He doesn't speak and he's also epileptic. Last May he died—his heart just stopped beating. He had a grand mal seizure. They revived him with mouth-to-mouth resuscitation. I think that if I had known I was going to have a severely retarded, epileptic child, I would have had an abortion."

When we have humanity "telling it like it really is" about human sexuality, humanity unafraid to learn freedom and unafraid to consider the benefits of new ways of relating to each other in marriage, in parenthood, in fellowship, then we are all freed from the prison of our past to take one giant step forward together. Playwright Lillian Hellman urges that we give youthful bearers of social change "credit for their interest in the quality of life, not blame for possible excesses of language or imprecision of thought."

Instead of dreading what lies ahead, why not welcome it as a new and exciting adventure, with much pain but also with much promise? Alfred North Whitehead said: "It is the business of the future to be dangerous." It is the obligation we owe to this experience called Life to make our futures different from our pasts.

Not long ago, as world history goes, man learned to harness atomic power for the greater good of humankind. Today, humans, freed by the sexual revolution, are beginning to harness their procreative power as part of their new sex philosophy. That, too, will be for the greater good of humankind.

PART I

SEX AND YOUR PERSONALITY

1

How We Get Our Sexual Attitudes and Behavior

Every one of us is born with sex drive. This is the electrode that sparks Nature's transmission belt of relentless fecundity. It has long been recognized by science that the human sex drive is second only to the hunger drive. Only one thing can keep man from sexual functioning, and that is starvation. Nevertheless, so powerful is the sex drive that even in Nazi concentration camps where man lived as close to starvation as was physiologically possible without dying, and despite the inhuman penalty women prisoners paid for engaging in sex and becoming pregnant (their legs were sometimes tied together during labor and they died in screaming agony), the sex act still occurred.

This powerful sex urge is actually derived from a complex combination of body chemistry (sex hormones) plus a variety of visual, auditory, olfactory, lingual, verbal, and tactile stimuli. The release through orgasm of this powerful urge—that pleasurable tension in the groin which many of us confuse with being in love—activates a pleasure center in the brain. This process is exactly the same for male and female.

Sexual arousal and orgasm are largely functions of our *involuntary* nervous system, one of our two basic nervous systems. Our *voluntary* nervous system is the one we can control. We can at will bend an arm, move our fingers, tilt our heads. Our other nervous system, the autonomic or involuntary system, is the one we cannot control. This handles our heartbeat, pulse, blood pressure, eye movements and dilations, physical sensations, digestion and elimination, glandular secretions, metabolic rate, body temperature, erection in the male, clitoral tumescence in the female, and orgasm.

At this point in evolutionary development, humankind has not yet achieved control over the functioning of its involuntary nervous system although current research on brain waves promises one day soon to give us the thrilling new ability to control our involuntary body actions and thus perhaps to solve many of our physical problems. At present we have no control over whether or not our bodies experience the sex urge. However, we do have control over how we choose to act out the sex urge—where, when, and with whom we may satisfy, or choose to defer satisfaction of, our sex urges.

It is an indication of how little we know about our sexual functioning and how much we need research when we learn that there is much uncertainty as to which sexual stimuli are innate and which are taught to us by the culture in which we are reared. Only a limited amount of research has been done so far because of lack of funds for, and public acceptability of, such projects. It is due to the sexual revolution that we find growing acceptance of such research work as that being done by Masters and Johnson and others. The early pioneering work of Kinsey was considered by many to be salacious and dirty. Funds for Kinsey's work were denied to him after some legislators, shocked by the questions Kinsey researchers asked people about their sexual behavior, held hearings on foundations whose grants had supported the Kinsey studies.

And so we are not yet able to give a definitive answer to the question: What may be said to be truly physiological stimuli and what may be said to be culturally conditioned stimuli? To cite one example of the confusion: In our American Mr. Clean culture, underarm hair is taboo and is considered to be unpleasant, sexually and esthetically. Elsewhere, underarm hair is considered desirable olfactory and tactile sexual stimuli. When a European actress like Sophia Loren makes a film in the United States, her underarm hair is shaved off. When she makes a film such as *Two Women* in her native Italy, the hair remains.

The effects on our sexual functioning of such stimuli as light, heat, food, chemicals, and drugs are also matters of conjecture. Some nutritionists and physicians believe certain foods will increase sexual vigor. Others believe that foods considered to be desirable for human sexuality are exactly the same foods desirable for human sustenance: milk, meat, poultry, fish, eggs, enriched bread, fruit, and vegetables. Claims have long been made by some nutritionists that sesame seeds, honey, oysters, snails, nuts, buckwheat, beer, and wheat germ oil all have special aphrodisiacal properties. The hops of beer, which nursing mothers are often advised by doctors to drink, is said to contain estrogens, the same group of hormones produced by the ovaries. Sea foods have also long been rumored to be a high-virility food. The reputation that the French male has had for sexual prowess may be related to the national custom of eating snails, which contain glycogen in pure form, a sugar important in the manufacture of male seminal fluid.

Darkness and light and their effect on the body's biological rhythms may also influence our sexual activity. A study by Dr. R. J. Wurtman, endocrinologist at the Massachusetts Institute of Technology, suggests that the natural cycle of day and night, light and dark, influences our body rhythms and the production of hormones by our sex glands.

The effect of darkness on human sexual behavior has been the subject of much speculation as the result of the large crops of "blackout babies" born in New York City and in Venice, Italy, exactly nine months after those two areas had prolonged power blackouts. The obvious questions are: Did darkness stimulate people sexually? Did they turn to sex because of boredom due to the unavailability of other outlets such as reading, movies, television, theatergoing, and so on? Did the blackout evoke heightened perception in which people, groping in the dark, found themselves "turned on" by unusual tactile experience?

This human circadian rhythm—the twenty-four-hour body cycle related to day and night, awakeness and sleep—is undoubtedly responsible for some of our sexual frustrations. According to a study at New York Medical College, we have a higher level of sex hormone, as much as 40 per cent more, in the morning than we do at night. Thus, sexual activity should ideally happen in the morning. Unfortunately, our physiology (not only in the sexual area) is constantly at war with our sociology. For good sex lives we ought not to have to get up in the morning and rush off to work, school, or other pursuits. Gay Gaer Luce, author of the book *Body Time,* says that modern society requires a pace "that is dissonant with our inner needs. We no longer act in harmony with natural cycles."

The monthly cycle of the female is certainly related to sexual desire or indifference. The study cited above also found that the male emits sex hormones in a steady pattern while the female produces them in a cyclic pattern related to her menses. This probably helps to explain some sexual dissonance many couples experience—why the male seems more quickly ready for sex while the female, as some partners complain, "needs to be worked up to it. It takes her so long to be ready."

It is possible that even the season of the year and our terrestrial location may turn out to be sources of physiological stimuli to our gonads. The National Demographic Institute in Paris reports that Europeans conceive more babies during June, July, and August—the summer months. While the higher number of births during the summer months in many American cities—the Los Angeles County–University of Southern California Medical Center, for instance, reported a high during August 1970—would indicate more conceptions during the fall and winter months in the United States.

There are many myths surrounding drugs and alcohol as sex stimulants. Alcohol, rather than stimulating, actually depresses the nervous system. "It provokes the desire, but it takes away the performance." Those who boast of sexual prowess after getting drunk may be covering up failures and disappointments.

Similarly, the "increased sex drive from LSD and other drugs are [*sic*] in the user's mind," according to Raymond A. Neff, former public health official in New Jersey. Mr. Neff reports that "one man who claimed phenomenal sexual prowess while under the influence of drugs was observed during his entire trip crouched in a corner." While some smokers of marijuana claim to experience heightened sexual perceptions, a *New York Times* survey of college students reports "that heavy users of marijuana have less interest in sex than do nonusers."

Periodically we hear of aphrodisiacal properties in drugs being used experimentally, but such reports often are later found to have been exaggerated, much to the embarrassment of scientist-researchers. In recent years a drug called Levodopa, known as L-dopa, used experimentally to treat Parkinson's disease, and a compound, PCPA, used experimentally at the National Heart Institute in Bethesda, Maryland, both provided such news stories. Later, it was reported that "a minor effect of L-dopa, increased sexual drive, occurred in less than 2 per cent of the patients but received 98 per cent of the publicity." Cortisone is believed to increase sex drive, while diabetics on insulin are believed to have decreased sex drive. The insecticide DDT has been reported to have adverse effects on sex organs of rats and conceivably could also affect human sex organs.

Oriental peoples have traditionally used herbs as aphrodisiacs for centuries. One such herb, ginseng, has been enjoying a vogue in the United States, especially among theatrical people, for its claimed properties as an aphrodisiac and life prolonger.

It is apparent that we are not now sure what nature's innate sexual stimuli are. The Kinsey Report and many sex researchers since agree that the sense of sight seems to be the primary stimulus for the male—looking at females or pictures of them. Thus the popularity of pinup pictures and of magazines like *Playboy* and *Esquire*. Whereas women reported to Kinsey researchers, and this too has been confirmed by many researchers since then (among them the noted Dr. John Money of Johns Hopkins University) that they responded more to the sense of touch—tactile stimuli—as their primary incitement.

What all of this suggests is that we have a great deal yet to discover about our powerful sex drive, and that the research done so far merely skims the surface of what we will some day learn.

Whatever the biological and physiological stimuli may be, they are controlled by our minds and what was recorded in our brains early in life by our cultural conditioning. Certain stimuli—a woman's pleasant flagrance, for example—may make us respond to that person with genital throbbing or warmth, but if our cultural conditioning has taught us that sex with that person is not acceptable, for one or a variety of reasons, then our brains will likely send a message that this is forbidden. The sex urge passes, denied by the disapproving cultural conditioning. Men and women who daily deal with attractive, well-groomed, physically appealing people may frequently experience this sensation. Should they have the opportunity to attempt the sex act with such "forbidden" persons, they may find themselves unable to function. It is a truism among sex counselors that the location of most sexual incapacity is 90 per cent above the neck and 10 per cent below the waist.

Where does this cultural conditioning begin? What has happened in our early lives to make us feel as we do about our sexuality, about our maleness or our femaleness, and about the sex act? Answering these questions for yourself will give you insight into some origins of your sexuality and personality.

What were the sleeping arrangements in your home when you were a child? Babies who sleep in their parents' bedrooms and observe and hear the sex act often think its sounds and motions are acts of violence. "Daddy was hitting Mommy," one child reported. Other children have reported the sounds of orgasm as of parents weeping.

What was your sibling and gender sequence in your family constellation? A boy with a sister is more likely to be familiar with menstruation than a boy with no sister. A small boy whose mother died when he was four was reared by older sisters whose bossiness gave him a "script of life" calling for him to punish women for what his domineering sisters did to him. He acted out a sexual pattern of "love 'em and leave 'em." A female homosexual, who had been reared by brothers and her father, early determined that she had been made a slave to male demands on her domestic services and that when she grew up she would have nothing whatever to do with men but instead would try to *be* a man.

Do you think your parents were satisfied with your gender or would they have preferred the other gender? Studies have shown that throughout the world, men prefer that their firstborn be a boy to carry on the family name. In some cultures there is a special festive ceremony attendant upon a firstborn boy. Some men feel their masculinity is in doubt should they produce only female children. When an Australian woman, who already had two daughters, gave birth to nine children at one time, she said she had taken fertility pills to have more children because her husband wanted a boy.

Such antifemale attitudes derive, of course, from the historical tradition that a girl baby was a liability, another mouth to feed, one for whom a dowry would have to be provided in order to get her married off; while a boy child meant another hand to help with the hard work of an agrarian existence. Some women suffer subliminal rejection all their lives by their fathers, beginning that instant when a doctor or nurse announces: "It's a girl."

How did you think babies were born? Gay Talese reports in *The Kingdom and the Power* that, as a small child, Arthur Ochs Sulzberger, publisher of *The New York Times,* would explain the mysteries of birth to friends this way: "The male inserts his organ into the female and then the baby inside grabs hold of it and is pulled out."

How did you believe babies begin? It is a common misbelief among small children, who pick up an idea about liquidity being related to conception, that a baby is made by a male urinating inside a female.

What happened when you asked sex questions of parents? Many of us never dared to and we felt dirty and guilty for even being curious. Nor did we ever hear proper words for our body parts. The very use of nice-Nelly euphemisms—the word "tassel" is a euphemism for "penis" in some families—gives us a double-level, below-the-surface message which says that our bodies and sex are unmentionables for which we have to use substitute language.

What happened if you used "dirty" words? In Philip Roth's novel *Portnoy's Complaint,* young Alexander Portnoy had his mouth washed out with horrible tasting lye laundry soap for calling his sister a "cocky doody." A similar real-life incident is reported to have caused the death by suffocation of an eight-year-old boy: A bar of soap was shoved into his mouth and became lodged in his throat.

What do you remember about how you were toilet-trained? Many of us associate sex with bathroom functioning. That is why, says psychoanalyst Judd Marmor, so many of us are phobic about sex; we were taught to be phobic about elimination by harsh toilet-training.

What messages did you get about sex? How would you finish the sentence: "Sex is ———"? Such messages need never have been spoken in words; they are feelings we pick up via "radar rearing"—from the atmosphere in which we are raised. That sex is dirty, animallike, indecent, are common parental messages passed down verbally or nonverbally from generation to generation. Some women today still act out the message they received from the whole society via their mothers which said, in effect: "Nice girls don't enjoy sex. Sex is mostly for the pleasure and accommodation of a husband. Sex is a price a woman has to pay in order to be married and have a husband."

What messages did you get about the opposite gender? How would you complete these sentences: "All women are ———" "All husbands are supposed to ———" "All men are ———" "All mothers have to ———". When we have such messages we often take life actions, consciously or subconsciously, to make them come true. Men who blithely engage in sexual intercourse without concerning themselves about contraception might be acting out messages from their fathers to the effect that "women are nothing. It's okay for a man to use them for his pleasure. Let the women suffer the consequences."

What was your experience at your first menstruation? Your first nocturnal emission? Boys often get panicky because of telltale yellow stains on their bedsheets. "That's when I first began to clean up my room myself and to stick my own bed linens in the washing machine myself," one adult wryly remembers.

Some religions have considered a menstruating female so unclean that she was ostracized from the community during her menses. She was told she could not bathe, wash her hair, touch stainless steel cooking utensils for fear that acids in her body would blacken them, handle cut flowers because they would wither and die at her touch, and so on. Imagine what messages women have received about their femaleness from such injunctions. It is not surprising that the act of menstruating was often described by girls as "having the curse" or "being unwell" or "sick."

What was your early conditioning about nudity? Many families are uncomfortable about the nude human body. Even in homes where nudity is commonly practiced, children are often uneasy, worrying that mommy and daddy will appear nude in front of visiting friends.

Feelings about physical touching among members of our family also condition our attitudes toward sex. The fact that so many of us have grown up in environments where touching each other was not acceptable is undoubtedly related to common complaints of husbands and wives in marital relations. Husbands say that wives are ashamed to fondle their genitals. Wives complain that husbands engage in little or no sexual foreplay or precoital affection.

Each of us is born with intense skin hunger, the need to be fondled and caressed. For many of us, that hunger goes unfed throughout our lives. We have given touch an exclusively sexual meaning. By inhibiting the affectionate touching and hugging and stroking among parents and children, we are deprived of a major form of good communication in family life.

All children do these four things: masturbate, play doctor, suck their thumbs, pick their noses. What happened if your parents caught you doing these things which are sources of pleasurable sensual experiences?

Probably the single most powerful area of cultural conditioning affecting our attitudes towards sex is that of masturbation. Infants as young as six months have been observed happily rubbing themselves. The child's early pleasurable feelings in touching its own body and genitals, and how the people in its environment react to this usually provide a child's earliest antisex messages.

"If you do that you'll go blind—or insane" . . . "you'll never be able to have children" . . . "you'll go to jail" are a few of the warnings and threats made to children, often accompanied by the parental pulling-away of the offending hand, a slap on it, or a spanking. Physicians report cases of parents who punish for such activity by tying children's hands together or by pressing the offensive exploratory hand down on a hot stove.

Many of us, because of such threats, spankings, and parental anger, have grown into adulthood with guarantees of being sexually maladjusted. These reports by a husband and wife to their counselor of their early masturbatory experiences are typical of what happened to many of us.

The wife said: "Mother would tell me I'd better be good. If I didn't quit, terrible things would happen. I'd be put away in an institution. Or she would have to be put away because I was driving her insane. I'd never grow up normal. I'd never be able to have children normally. I'd never lead a normal, happy life."

Her husband said: "I remember at the age of perhaps four,

Mother told me that if I played with my teapot [a parental euphemism for penis] it would fall off. I have no memory of the act, only the constant warnings. As a clincher to her admonition, she cited the cases of the daughters of a neighboring family. They had lost their teapots for this very reason. Nonetheless, I continued to do what I was warned not to do. I'd sneak the forbidden act in and finish it as quickly as possible. Every time I did it, I was afraid the fateful day of losing my teapot would eventually dawn."

It is not difficult to make a connection between this early anxiety to achieve completion quickly before being discovered and that common problem in marriage: premature ejaculation.

What are our concerns about masturbation? What are some of the questions debated about it?

How much masturbation is too much masturbation? Whose standards do we use to judge—the repressed parent who thinks even one such act is wrong or the glandularly and gonadally charged teen-age boy who experiences the need to masturbate several times a day?

If we can even agree on what excessive masturbation is, would it then be an indication of personality disturbance or glandular imbalance. Some people believe that frequent masturbation at a time in life when one is highly sexually charged may help *prevent* the personality from being disturbed by providing release from sexual tension when sex experience is not socially acceptable.

Will masturbation hamper sexual adjustment later in life? Some believe that it will, others say that masturbation actually helps sexual adjustment because the masturbating youngsters have conditioned their nervous systems to experience climax frequently and thus it becomes easier for them to experience climax in future relationships with partners.

Our antimasturbatory feelings probably derive from the biblical injunction against onanism, "spilling one's seed upon the ground" instead of using that seed to fulfill divine intention of "begatting and begatting," of sex only for procreation. To foil that divine intention through contraception or masturbation was to commit a sin.

Man, as is his wont in many areas and not only the sexual, takes a stricture like this biblical one against onanism and then, generation after generation, musters up rationalizations to keep that stricture alive. In another context, the late play critic, John Gassner, once said that we decide, based on a feeling or "gut" level, what we like or do not like, and then we start casting about for reasons to justify those feelings. In the same way, man keeps casting about for reasons to justify archaic thou-shalt-nots which have, through fear, been conditioned into him at gut level down through the ages.

In reasoning through our taboos against masturbation, we may find help in dealing with a common problem in marriage—disparity in their individual sex drives between a man and a woman who love each other and do not wish to go outside their marriage to fulfill their sexual capacity. Shame about masturbation keeps such spouses from meeting their body's requirements and thus in a frequent state of sexual tension. Advice to such people to "go take a cold shower—a fast walk—or play a hard game of tennis" to sublimate the sex drive doesn't resolve the sex tension that may arise an hour after they have taken a cold shower, a fast walk, or played a hard game of tennis.

It has also been suggested that an effective way for a woman to overcome frigidity is to learn, guilt-free and with pleasure, to bring herself to climax, thus conditioning her nervous system to the experience of orgasm which would then be more likely to happen in her relations with a partner.

As a matter of fact, for some sexually satisfied people, masturbation provides one more additional source of sexual gratification. Orgasm in a variety of ways is the reason for their feeling sexually satisfied. Some women in the Kinsey study said that besides having satisfactory relations with their husbands, they also masturbated sometimes because that provided even more intense and pleasurable orgasms.

"An activity which should be benign, if not beneficial, has become a source of much human suffering and anguish," writes lawyer-psychologist David Cole Gordon in his book *Self-Love*. "The problem derives not from anything inherent in the nature of the practice itself but from the way man has historically thought about it."

Finally, we might ask ourselves as we seek insight into our early conditioning about sexuality: "How did our parents learn about sex? What information was available to them?" If we are having so much difficulty with it, what was it like for our parents, reared in a less fortunate time when open sex discussion was unthinkable? What sexual deprivations and guilts might they have experienced due to their own early cultural conditioning? Pondering these questions may help some of us to forgive our parents for their acts of commission and omission in our early sex education.

Today, many of us, because of the antisex recordings made on our nervous systems during our early years, find that we need at some point in our lives to seek sex counseling. A sex counselor who is a candid, unembarrassed, and warm human being serves the psychological purpose of reparenting. He or she helps to remove the effects of the repressive parents of long ago and gives approval to the counselees to enjoy their sexuality. Even a single session with a skilled counselor may be highly effective as it dredges up and ventilates long-hidden fears, guilts, angers, and anxieties.

Some of the factors that effective counselors deal with include sex vocabulary, the sounds of orgasm, comfort in discussing sex with another person, tactile sensations which may be pleasurable or uncomfortable—many people feel that manual pressure is too heavy or too light at the wrong times, most of them preferring a light feathery touch at the beginning of the sex act and stronger pressures after arousal—the acceptability and even the asset of sexual fantasizing, and so on.

Talking especially about early traumatic experiences can be of enormous help in freeing a sexually uncomfortable or repressed person. The little girl who received a merciless spanking when her mother found her playing doctor with a neighboring child, or the little boy whose hands were slapped with a wooden stick whenever he touched himself, find psychic relief as adults in telling how they felt when such things were done to them.

Our sexual patterns throughout life often repeat our earliest sexual experiences as they were first recorded on our nervous systems. As suggested earlier, the masturbating child who hurries to finish before being discovered may become the prematurely ejaculating adult. The child playing with himself knows there's less chance of providing visual evidence of his pleasure if he doesn't have an erection and so he learns to become aroused and yet not erect, the possible start of impotence. The girl whose parental message says that her primary responsibility in sex is to satisfy the male does satisfy him and never herself, becoming the nonorgasmic adult she was taught to be.

The counselor's work goes far beyond sex matters. The relationship of money to sex, or the need to finish the unfinished business of anger or punitiveness towards a person in one's past which is being projected onto a spouse in the present—these are common problems which are not overtly sexual but which affect sexual functioning.

The goal of counseling is to free our personalities to enjoy the human being's most intense source of pleasure—our sexuality. This often depends upon freeing ourselves from the prisons of our pasts. The free personality has no difficulty uninhibitedly expressing, in whatever position, with whatever parts of the body, with whatever sounds, whatever joy and pleasure and well-being and exaltation he or she feels in the sex act.

The good and beautiful act of sex may be described as one in which the partners, free to enjoy their sexuality to the fullest, non-exploitive and responsibly aware of the consequences of the act, both experience psychical growth and ego enhancement. In effect they are saying to each other: "I am an enriched person for having had this exquisite experience and having contributed to your having it, too."

Abraham Maslow in his study of the elite of the mentally healthy, *The Self-Actualizing Person,* described the orgasms of such persons this way: "There were the feelings of limitless horizons opening up to the vision, of being simultaneously more powerful and also more helpless than one ever was before, the feeling of great ecstasy and wonder and awe, the loss of placing in time and space with, finally, the conviction that something extremely important and valuable had happened so that the person is to some extent transformed and strengthened even in his daily life by such experiences."

For many of us, such exquisite experience requires that we first revise our pleasure ethic. The Christian-Judaic code has seemed to say that the pursuit of pleasure is sinful and slothful. But the sexual revolution and the leisure being brought to us by technology are bringing us to a time in human evolution in which the heretofore scorned ism of *hedonism*—the doctrine that pleasure is the highest good—will become acceptable and desirable.

Such a doctrine is en route right now to becoming the hallmark of sexual attitudes and behavior of the future. It could turn out to be a healthy doctrine for individuals and nations alike, if humankind, reared to glorify pleasure, should refuse to fight wars that bring pain. Thus a new ethic might become: Pleasure to the peaceful, pain to the warmakers, as exemplified in this poem:

> If there is right in the soul, there will be beauty in the person
> If there is beauty in the person, there will be harmony in the home.
> If there is harmony in the home, there will be order in the nation
> If there is order in the nation, there will be peace in the world.

2

Sexual Health and the Healthy Person

As research into human sexuality proceeds, the relationship between our sexuality and our mental and physical well-being becomes apparent. Dr. Daniels Hansen, professor at UCLA Medical School, speaking to the American Medical Association on "Physical Manifestations of Sexual Conflicts," has said he believes that at least one third of the patients who consult a physician for a physical ailment actually have a sexual maladjustment.

A study on *Sexual Problems in Medical Practice,* made by Dr. Donald W. Burnap of Harbor General Hospital, Torrance, California, and Dr. Joshua S. Golden of UCLA, reports that about 15 per cent of a family physician's practice and about 77 per cent of a psychiatrist's practice deals with problems related to "normal" sexual intercourse, with patients telling of their fears, inhibitions, shame, guilt, inadequacies, failures, and disappointments. The five most frequently reported complaints were lack of orgasm, lack of desire for intercourse, concern about frequency of the sex act, need for general sex information, and impotence.

The first question: What happens to us when we experience the pleasant tension of sexual arousal which is not subsequently released through orgasm? The physical symptoms of prolonged unrelieved sex drive often manifest themselves as backaches, headaches, depression, temper tantrum, irritability, insomnia, lassitude, fatigue, and absentmindedness. An attorney, newly separated from his wife, pleaded with a client to forgive him for his absentmindedness by

43

saying: "I just can't concentrate on anything today. I haven't had sex for a couple of weeks and I feel as if I could jump out of my skin." The heroine of the Tennessee Williams play of the same name, denied sex, felt as jumpy as a *Cat On A Hot Tin Roof.*

It is likely that there is a correlation between satisfying sex experience and every aspect of our mental and physical health. Dr. Richard Seiden, a behavioral scientist at the University of California at Berkeley, renowned for his suicide studies, urges us to use sex therapy to help the mental state of the would-be suicide. "Traditional methods of treating suicides are failing," he says. "What might help is sex therapy. Sex is an affirmation of life over death." Sex therapy has even been suggested as a possible deterrent to obesity. Dr. Eugene Scheimann, a New York physician, believes that sex, stimulating glandular functions and meeting a desire to have one's body feel the sensation of being filled, can keep one from overeating. "Don't reduce—seduce," he advises his patients, only half in jest.

One wonders if the crying spells and mental depression of some menopausal women might not be caused as much by their being sexually frustrated as by the fact that they are in the empty-nest stage of life and no longer as needed or valued by society as they were while rearing children. The male sex drive peaks early in life —usually during the teens and twenties. The female often peaks in the thirties and forties. A great number of women experience their most intense sex drive after menopause when their fear of pregnancy has ended. At exactly that same time they find themselves with sex partners in whom desire or capacity to function has diminished.

The wife of an impotent man describes her feelings when her husband was unable to satisfy her genitally and was indifferent about doing so manually, orally, or frictionally:

"When we'd attempt sex and he couldn't do it, my first feeling was rage. I could almost have lashed out at him with a punch. Then I felt frustration. My genital area was throbbing. Then I felt depressed. Then I became angry again and I thought about punishing him by divorcing him so I could find a man with whom to have sex. I was obsessed with a desire to have a firm penis inside me. Then I was depressed again. I felt hopeless about the situation and I began to have crying jags."

A therapist wonders whether patients, male or female, who cry easily, giggle nervously, or are extremely talkative, may not be suffering from unmet need for orgasm. "It's as if the orgasm were coming out in their tears or talkativeness or nervous laughter," she says.

The inability of a man to experience erection and orgasm, known as impotence, has been described as the most hidden mental health problem in our country, affecting the self-image of millions of men and their relationships on the job, as husbands, and as parents. Impotence affects not only those directly suffering it but probably has an indirect influence on all the rest of us as well. There is hardly a person whose life may not be entwined, as wife, sweetheart, date, employee, child, friend, sibling, student, with a person experiencing the frustration, irritability, depression, and even self-hatred of a man unable to function sexually. It is a myth that impotence affects only older men. Young or old, many experience temporary or prolonged periods of impotency, which one man describes as "sexual bankruptcy."

Here is a report of the effect on a man who is impotent:

"Psychologically, impotence can be either a cause or an effect of a man's loss of prestige and self-respect. In either case, the onset of impotence gives rise to a generalized anxiety that not only perpetuates and aggravates the condition itself but causes deterioration in other dimensions of the male personality as well. A loss of sexual potency frequently poses either a challenge or a threat to the femininity of his partner. If the woman sees it as a challenge, she often becomes more aggressively seductive, which only intensifies the man's feelings of inadequacy. If the man's impotence is seen as a rejection, an already insecure female may become hostile and accusing and thus arouse even greater guilt and anxiety in the male. The emotional problems most frequently associated with impotence are depression, castration anxiety (my wife is emasculating me), homosexual panic, and generalized hypochondriasis."

So terrifying is the idea of impotence that when a researcher in Great Britain asked men to list their greatest fears, the majority said that the thought of ever becoming impotent ranked just below their fear of cancer as a source of worry.

Several methods are currently being used to treat impotence. These include psychotherapy, medication such as male hormones, massage, surgery (in which silicone is implanted in the penis), relaxation techniques, and behavior modification. Brain-wave research promises especially to be a revolutionary boon to impotent men. Teaching him how to control brain waves would give the man the remarkable ability to have an erection at will.

Behavior modification is a mode of therapy that works to recondition the nervous system and is being widely used in conjunction with psychotherapy and relaxation exercises to treat impotence. Such therapists have a strict rule. A patient must not attempt coitus unless two factors, strong erection and powerful desire, occur simultaneously. Should these two factors not happen concurrently even for weeks at a time, the patient is forbidden to attempt intercourse. If he tries and fails, he is recording one more failure on his nervous system. The goal is for him to achieve success even if it is infrequent, and thus to record on his nervous system only successful experiences resulting in climax.

This method, which has a good rate of success with patients who follow instructions, requires a highly cooperative and loving sex partner who while helping the male may herself undergo denial of her own needs because of the intervals between coitus. Men undergoing behavior modification treatment are urged to put their own condition out of their minds and to concern themselves with their female partner's gratification, meeting the woman's needs during this reconditioning period using digital, frictional, or oral methods. In concentrating on thus pleasuring their female partners and with erection for themselves no longer the goal, many men find themselves becoming aroused, once the psychological pressure of having to perform is removed.

To help the process, some marriage counselors recommend a visual aphrodisiac, such as looking at books of erotic art together, as an aid for a couple working to cure the man's impotence. While the words "erotic art" in the minds of many conjure up cheap pornography (a librarian in West Orange, New Jersey, delighted his community by labeling a shelf of sex books "GOODNOGRAPHY"), there are fine printed collections of such art that has lasted for centuries, created by painters and sculptors from Michalengelo to Picasso. We in the United States with our Puritan inheritance are only beginning at this point in time to accept such facts of sexual life as erotic art, but other cultures have had them around, comfortably, for a long time. They consider us Americans to be silly, immature children about the whole matter.

Reconditioning of the nervous system is also an effective method used to treat premature ejaculation. The patient with this common problem is taught to masturbate or to have his wife masturbate him, and to stop physiological sensation just short of climax by gently clamping the head of the penis. Each time the man does so he is, by slower manipulation, to prolong the time it takes him to go from arousal to near climax.

Physicians and therapists believe that nine out of ten cases of impotence are essentially psychological. Only one in ten is organic. "The organic causes may be divided into systemic illness, disease of the nerve or blood supply, drug effects, and local conditions of the genitourinary tract," according to Dr. Joseph J. Kaufman, professor of surgery and urology at UCLA, writing in *Medical Aspects of Human Sexuality* (September 1967).

The female version of impotence has traditionally been called frigidity, a word ascribed to women who are either unable to experience sexual arousal or those who do experience it but lose desire prior to orgasm. Frigidity is a put-down word that hopefully is en route to becoming extinct. It has long been a negative label implying a cold woman. But many warm, loving women have difficulty achieving climax. There is nothing frigid about these human beings who may be victims of inhibitory messages about sex which they received from their mothers and from society. The more accurate phrase, the one used by those who are updating their vocabulary to this emerging era of equality, is *nonorgasmic* women.

Although being nonorgasmic certainly affects the physical and mental well-being of a woman, it does not carry quite the same psychological burden as impotence does for a man. A woman does not suffer decreased self-esteem to the same extent as a man who carries the cross of a societal evaluation that he is not fully a man if he is not making it sexually. So drastic and ego-destroying a threat does not hang over a woman. On the contrary, until recently a subliminal societal message implied there was something pure and good about a woman who didn't enjoy sex.

As a matter of fact, a nonorgasmic wife often imposes an even greater burden on a man. A common but erroneous saying has been: "There is no such thing as a frigid woman, there is only an unskilled lover." No matter how sexually skilled the husband, that alone is not enough to free a wife who grew up with a strong message that nice girls shouldn't enjoy sex.

It is cruel that the label of frigidity is applied to many nonorgasmic women whose difficulty is entirely physical, not mental. At least half of the nonorgasmic women are suffering from urethral or vaginal cysts, vaginal infections, painful surgical corrections after childbirth or hysterectomy, loss of elasticity of muscles, loss of hormone nutrients related to menopause, enlargement of the vaginal opening because of childbirth, decrease in the size of the vaginal opening due to aging, the atrophying of the pubococcygeus muscle inside the vagina, dyspareunia—pain during intercourse—and other problems.

It was as recently as the 1940s that Dr. Arnold Kegel of the University of Southern California School of Medicine first identified the part played in sexual perception and pleasure by the pubococcygeus muscle, a thick, wide band located about an inch and a half inside the vaginal opening. While doing research into bladder incontinence, the involuntary leakage of urine from a woman's bladder triggered by exertion, coughing, sneezing, or rapid movements, Dr. Kegel found a relationship between poor tone in this muscle and sexual dysfunction. Patients for whom exercises were prescribed for bladder incontinence reported that they were experiencing greatly increased sexual enjoyment. Dr. Kegel instructed such a patient that she was to repeatedly contract the vagina in rapid movements, both at its outer surface and deep inside; and also, while urinating she was to keep her legs apart and rapidly stop and start the urinary process, thus developing elasticity and strength in the pubococcygeus muscle.

Other treatments for nonorgasmic women at present include hormone therapy; stretching, by physician, of the vaginal opening; surgery for a condition that is known as "hooded clitoris," in which a fold of skin makes the clitoris unavailable to physical touch; and psychotherapy. Dr. Sophia J. Kleegman of the New York University School of Medicine urged medical schools to train students to locate and identify physical causes for nonorgasm. "Some doctors," she said, "have never been taught to identify causes of such sexual dysfunction and wouldn't know if it was staring them in the face."

Most of us who experience sexual frustration manage to cope, with only occasional snarls at our fellow humans. But for some persons with low tolerance levels for frustration, unrelieved sexual tensions may lead to sublimation of the sex drive into acts of physical violence to themselves, to others, or toward society.

Guns and knives often have sexual significance in acts of violence. Dr. Karl Heiser, a Cincinnati psychologist, calling them "psycho-gun addicts," declares that some men use guns as sex symbols to feel sexually potent. It is significant that as a child Clyde Barrow, the 1930s gangster whose life was portrayed in the film *Bonnie and Clyde* was called a sissy. A man who knew Barrow as a young man in prison has said that in his infamous life as a wanton killer, Barrow kept trying to prove to himself and to the world that he was not the sissy his family and friends had labeled him. Another film, *The Hunting Party,* portrayed an impotent hunter who, each time he failed at the sex act, would take out his rage by going hunting with a high-powered rifle.

A soldier returning from Vietnam has reported that at the moment he slit the throat of a young Vietcong he experienced erection and orgasm. This real-life incident was suggested in a movie, *The Sergeant,* in which "during a World War II patrol, the sergeant comes upon a German soldier. When his gun jams (his symbolic penis doesn't fire) the sergeant pursues the soldier, finally strangling him in what is really the reverse of an act of love."

In another movie, *The Boston Strangler,* based on an actual case, it is made obvious that the act of strangling his victims brought orgiastic relief to the deranged man. Similarly, one of the young women convicted in the Sharon Tate murders in Los Angeles in 1971 testified on the witness stand that while frenziedly stabbing a victim, she experienced an orgasm.

Those who start fires and those who make obscene phone calls are often erotically motivated. Setting fires is one of several acts people perform "to relieve or produce an excitement that has an erotic overtone," says Roderic Gorney, professor of psychiatry at UCLA. Fire departments in training new personnel routinely include information on spotting possible arsonists who may be standing among onlookers and apparently enjoying the flames with mounting sexual excitement.

Many obscene phone callers masturbate while talking "dirty" over the telephone; often they are acting out anger against strict parents, subconsciously saying by their behavior: "You wouldn't let me touch myself but, oh, boy, am I putting something over on you now!"

Dr. David Hubbard, a psychiatrist who has done studies of the personalities of plane hijackers, reports a pattern common to nearly all of them. The typical hijacker, he says, "is a failure in business, in sex, in marriage, in friendship. He worries about possible impotence. He can stand up and display his manhood by ordering the captain of a multimillion-dollar airliner to do his bidding."

Even our high automobile accident rate is undoubtedly caused partly by sexual frustrations. Many auto accidents, according to Dr. Robert Litman of the Los Angeles Suicide Prevention Center, are actually suicide attempts. "The typical suicide-prone driver is a man between the ages of twenty and forty-five who has had a put-down relationship with women, such as a fight with his wife, a broken marriage, or an unhappy love affair."

However, sexual sublimation is not always violent. The manner in which we drive and the style of car we buy, even our styles of humor and our modes of dress, may all be giving clues about how we feel about our sexuality.

George Basalla, University of Delaware historian, says that American men have a highly emotional and erotic relationship with their automobiles, long sleek styling often giving them the phallic-like power they wish they had. According to the December 15, 1970, issue of *Look* Magazine, Harvard psychiatrist Armand M. Nicholi found "an unusual emotional investment in their motorcycles" on the part of male students who also had fears of impotence and homosexuality.

People who tell jokes that rely on detailed sexual descriptions to make their points are probably not having good sex lives, according to researchers on the psychology of humor. Dr. Donald Spiegel and his wife, Dr. Patricia Keith-Spiegel, of the Veterans Administration Hospital in Brentwood, California, say that such people talk the sex they are not having. A flamboyantly and sexily dressed female may be giving out through her wardrobe a double-level message, one part of which says "I can be had," while the second level says she is afraid of sex and doesn't want the world to find out.

As we become more knowledgeable in the field of mental health, the more it is confirmed that when a human being is enabled to *talk* about his feelings and thoughts, he is less driven to *act* them out. Professor Michael J. Goldstein of UCLA, who directed one of the several research studies commissioned by the Presidential Commission on Obscenity and Pornography, found that most sex offenders, such as rapists and child molesters, seem to come from families in which it was taboo ever to discuss sex. As long as we retain a Puritan culture which does not provide opportunities for people acceptably to ventilate their sexual curiosities and thoughts in conversation, and as long as we have a government for which violence is an extension of national policy, it will be easy for us to be acculturated and conditioned to sublimate the powerful sex drive into powerful acts of violence. "Destructiveness stems from an unlived life," says Erich Fromm. Freed by the sexual revolution to live life more fully, we may find ourselves feeling less destructive. Certainly the sexual revolution means we now have less reason to sublimate sex into antisocial behavior.

What about those among us who have reasonably happy sex lives and are comfortable with their sexuality? What attitudes contribute to the sexual health of such people, who might be described as being "sexually mature"?

One factor in the personality of the sexually mature person would certainly be the realization that some sexual frustration and unfilled desire is inevitable. Given the conditions of modern life we cannot always fill the rising urge for sex at the moment we have it. But we experience frustration with many of life's physical processes. We cannot always eat at the onset of hunger. We cannot always eliminate at the instant of need to do so. And so it is with sex urges; we accept the fact that they must sometimes go unheeded.

Another factor contributing to sexual maturity is an acceptance of man's mammal nature. No person will ever be sexually free until he or she recognizes, admits, and feels guilt-free and unashamed of the fact that the human being is part animal. As Dr. Alexander Lowen says in his book *Love and Orgasm:* "Man is a placental mammal. If he cannot accept his animal nature as part of his biological heritage, he will struggle all his life with guilt and shame about his sexual function." Accepting our mammalian nature, the sexually mature person, should he or she be unable to satisfy sexual need with a partner for a period of time for whatever reason, would be able without paying any penalty in feelings of inner rejection or guilt to masturbate with pleasure and a total acceptance of the need to do so.

Another factor in sexual maturity is an understanding that we are all combinations of male and female. Genetically we have male and female components. Disagreeable and shocking though the idea may be, many of us are probably capable of homosexual response if we are deprived too long of heterosexual contact and if the only warm human being available is a person of the same gender. Heterosexual men in military service, in prison, or away on scientific expeditions, have found themselves engaged in homosexual behavior, despising themselves for it, and dropping it completely once heterosexual contacts were again available. Our primary need is for the physical contact, to be close to another human being.

Still another requisite is a recognition of the fallacy of the double standard. Implicit in the male-female relationship has been the idea that the female "services" the male. To be sexually mature means to know that there is no innate difference in capacity for sexual enjoyment between male and female. The differences have been taught to us.

One more indication of sexual maturity is to free oneself from what has been called "the tyranny of simultaneous orgasm." Some couples feel like failures if they do not always achieve climax together. Marriage manuals often set unrealistic goals which make couples feel inadequate. It is an exquisite and ecstatic experience when it does happen, but for many couples it does not happen regularly. Orgasm has been described as "a supremely selfish moment." Once this function of the involuntary nervous system has begun, it is impossible to turn it off or to stop it. To experience your own climax to its greatest height, you should not at that moment have to be concerned about your partner's climax.

"Think of that unknown number," write two researchers from the Institute for Sex Research, "who still grimly, remorselessly pursue simultaneous orgasm as the additional element that may well elevate them from the realm of the repetitive to that of ecstasy. And all the while they are unable to match their experience with anyone, not even a familiar partner, except to grunt from between clenched teeth: 'Are you ready?' Or to ask with the kind of nervousness that coerces: 'Was it good?' "

To be sexually mature is also to be aware that teen-agers' developing sexuality sometimes provokes envy in their parents. Teen-aged sons are usually in a period of rising sexual prowess and virility at exactly the same time their fortyish fathers are in a period of sexual decline. A study by the British Medical Association confirms that a male parent often envies a son's sexuality.

Knowing the difference between *sensual* need—for touching, stroking, caressing—and *sexual* need—for orgastic experience—is an important part of sexual maturity. Our human need to be touched is so deep that studies of babies in orphanages have shown that those who are well fed but not handled enough are more likely to die of a disease called marasmus than babies who are less well fed but who are stroked and fondled. Los Angeles County-U.S.C. Medical Center has an infant rehabilitation room for "failure-to-thrive" babies, and volunteers are sought to come at any hour around the clock to cuddle infants. The stroking sets up electrical impulses from the surface of the skin which stimulate the brain.

People who live alone report intense physical longing to have a person around to touch and be touched by. Newly divorced men and women who have been conditioned by a steady source of skin-to-skin contact in bed during marriage similarly report that one of the deprivations they feel most keenly early in their separation is the sensory deprivation of not having their skin touched by another. Lacking a human being to fondle, many people settle for the next best thing, a warm, pulsating household pet.

Touching between strangers and acquaintances, and between people of the same gender, have been among the strong taboos in our culture until the sexual revolution. In other countries men hug and kiss without shame or sexual meaning. In the United States we have associated hugging and kissing between men with homosexuality.

Inhibitions against touching children are much less strong in other cultures. American women living in Europe told an interviewer that the major difference they found in child rearing was that "parents in Europe show much more physical affection toward their children." Some Eastern cultures have the "reprimand hug" in which the child, while being gently bawled out, is held close or his back is rubbed to give a nonverbal, double-level message that he's still loved despite his behavioral blunder.

Touching is especially vital at times of stress. Author Theodore White, in the hotel when Senator Robert Kennedy was shot, has told how he went to the room of David Kennedy, thirteen years old, and held the boy in his arms to give him "bodily comfort." Many people turn off touching and say they are not comfortable with it. They laugh off sensory awareness groups as "the touchy-feely groups." But that is because they have been taught not to be comfortable with touching. By denying this human need, we keep ourselves sexually immature. Recognizing this, the World Council of Churches at an annual meeting in Uppsala, Sweden, in 1968 included in its program a sensuality seminar in which worshippers participated in a "touch and tell" service, clasping hands, touching each other's faces, and then telling what they liked about each other. Some churches now include such experience in religious services in which parishioners walk around and shake hands with each other.

So deep is our sensual need for physical contact that it may not be too farfetched to suggest that if it is not acceptable to touch in friendship, we will find a way to touch through fighting. A pioneer in sensory awareness, Bernard Gunther of Esalen Institute in Big Sur, California, suggests that if every person in the world gave and received a loving half-hour massage every day, there would be no war.

Certainly there would be less war within a family if its members were more comfortable with skin-to-skin contact. The Freudian Oedipal concept that if we touch our children we are being sexually seductive does great harm to family life, denying us our most effective warm, loving, supportive nonverbal communication—hugging, stroking, back rubbing, holding hands. One family calls this "kin-to-kin contact."

Facing the fact that we have erotic feelings about our children and they about us, that we have no intention of doing anything about it, and that it is nice for all members of a family to hug and kiss and hold hands is a major sign of sexual maturity. Guilt over fantasies of sex with parents or with brothers and sisters plagues many young people. How much less guilt ridden we would all be if we said: "Yes, we have such feelings. They come with the condition of being human. We have no intention of doing anything about them. Now let's get on with being comfortable about hugging each other."

If we have sexual health might we then reasonably expect there to be a relationship between that and our creativity and productivity? This is one of those questions that has been debated down through the ages.

Many of us know from personal experience that having satisfying sex on a regular basis with reasonably few unmet longings contributes much to our creativity, mental well-being, and physical energy. However, there are also those who believe that orgasm drains the body and the mind of some of its energy and drive. Great athletes, boxers, and others are forbidden to have sex prior to an athletic event. Some performers like musicians choose not to have sex before a public appearance in the belief that their sex drive, unexpressed in orgasm, is then converted into a more dynamic performance.

Historian Arnold Toynbee believes that the involvement of a nation's youth in early sex is a practice that can affect a nation's creative vitality. He urges that we discourage premarital sex because "part of the modern West's creative energy has sprung from the ability to postpone adolescents' sexual awakening to let them concentrate on the acquisition of knowledge."

On the other hand, in the study of human personality mentioned earlier, *The Self-Actualizing Person,* Abraham Maslow concluded that meeting physiological needs of food and sex is the first step up "the hierarchy of human needs," and that the person who becomes self-actualizing, thus making the greatest use of his abilities in many different areas, is likely to first have physiological needs, including sex needs, well met.

It is undeniable that there are among us some few mortals who seem comfortably able to sublimate their sex drive into dedication to work or into causes and beliefs they hold dear. Throughout history, clerical men and women, scholars, mystics, gurus, and other dedicated souls seem to have been able to live celibate lives and maintain sweet natures untormented by unmet sex need. Some sects today believe that divinity may be achieved by eschewing the pleasures of the flesh.

Whether they are asexual and have no sex drive, or whether they are content to release their drive solely through masturbation, a small number of such persons in any one generation seems able to achieve inner peace with no interpersonal sexual experience. Perhaps peak psychological experience—great joy in their work—replaces peak physical experience for them. But for the vast majority of mammalian man, some sexual expression seems necessary in order to achieve a peak of health and happiness.

Sex, as Dr. John E. Eichenlaub points out in his book *A Minnesota Doctor's Home Remedies for Common and Uncommon Ailments,* adds boundlessly to our energy, tranquility, and contentment. "It is the best and most natural tonic for good health," he says.

3

The Sexual Double Standard

Traditionally, woman's role has been defined for her and thrust upon her by the male. Woman has been told what her intellectual abilities were supposed to be, how high she could aspire to achieve, how far from home and hearth she could venture in her journey through life, what laws, rules, and codes she was to be governed by.

Those characteristics and traits which best filled the male's needs, she was taught to value as desirable ones. Those characteristics and traits which might fill her own needs, she was taught to think of as emasculating and unfeminine. Should she exhibit drive because her body had energy and her mind a high I.Q., she was told that she was being aggressive. Should she exhibit strength, she was told that this deprived the male of his masculine priority to lead and to decide. Should she exhibit the frailty the male ordered her to, she was told to stop being a clinging vine.

Man has been marching through the centuries, while woman has been permitted to crawl. If the theme of female existence until the sexual revolution could be summed up in one sentence, that sentence would be: Femininity has been equated with servility.

Nowhere has this been truer than in the sex relationship between the genders. Inherent in their relationship has been the idea that sex is something a male "does" to a female who "services" him. Woman's body parts were designed in the service of man—a vaginal orifice to accommodate his physical pleasure and a uterus to bear his children. Women going through the pain of countless pregnancies and childbirths believed this was their punishment for having committed the sin of being born female, a view that was buttressed by the statement of psychoanalyst Sigmund Freud that "anatomy is destiny."

This philosophy of male-female relationships did not always prevail. "Pre-civilized women," according to Dr. Mary Jane Sherfey, writing in the *Journal of the American Psychoanalytic Association,* "enjoyed full sexual freedom." The suppression of female sexuality began when primitive man evolved from his nomadic, hunting, food-gathering economy into the agricultural revolution in which he began to acquire and hold on to property.

Acquisitive man, needing a large family to work the soil of an agrarian existence and wanting to identify his own offspring for purposes of maintaining a family unit and for inheritance, began through laws and dogma to deny the female her sexual expression except in the service of that male who had "ownership" rights. The idea of ownership extended from the owning of land and coin of the realm to "owning" that person—the female—whose baby-making apparatus was needed to sustain acquisitive man in power.

And so over the centuries there has evolved the idea of the female servicing the male, but with little or no concern about orgasmic satisfaction for herself. The idea of sexual pleasure for the female, long dormant, achieved a renaissance about the time woman began to be educated. Until then, the female often did not expect to reach sexual climax, and, if she did, she was taught to feel ashamed of this animal side to her nature. William Acton, author of a nineteenth-century medical textbook, wrote that "the belief that women had a sexual appetite was a vile aspersion." William Hammond, the surgeon-general of the United States during the Civil War, wrote that "nine-tenths of the time decent women felt not the slightest pleasure in intercourse." Only prostitutes and depraved women enjoyed it.

Such heritage is undeniably a basic cause for so many women being nonorgasmic at present. Not enough generations of women have yet been freed from the double-standard injunction, passed down through the years, that they not enjoy their sexuality.

But while woman's behavior and ease with her sexuality are becoming freer, our laws and customs have yet to follow suit. The inequities of the double standard are pervasive and often quite subtle.

While a man can walk into a drugstore and buy male contraceptives, the female often does not have a comparable freedom. Because the use of the pill requires medical supervision, she first must pay for a visit to a doctor (usually male) to get a prescription. An unmarried woman, especially one under eighteen, sometimes has difficulty even in finding a physician willing to give her a prescription for pills. Should a female prefer to use a diaphragm as her form of contraception, that too requires a visit to a physician to fit the device. Few females want to risk buying a diaphragm with an improper fit off the counter at a drugstore. Should an overburdened mother wish to be sterilized in a hospital, her request must first be approved by a board of doctors, mostly male, obeying a male-designed rule, common in American hospitals, that no woman may be sterilized unless she already has five children.

Should a teen-aged girl become pregnant, many school systems drop her from classes and send her to a separate facility or tutor her at home alone. The boy who made her pregnant suffers no such penalty. Should a girl have sex experience with many males prior to marriage, she is considered to have been cheap and promiscuous. Should a boy have similar experience, he is considered to have been manfully sowing his wild oats. Indeed, a sixteen-year-old girl can be designated a juvenile delinquent and placed in a reform school for promiscuous behavior because promiscuity in girls is considered "ungovernable and unmanageable," but a sixteen-year-old boy who is equally promiscuous would not be punished.

Even that most female of experiences—childbearing—has been dominated by male pronouncements and regulations. Declaring that expectant mothers in contemporary America have been short-changed, Dr. Niles Anne Newton, associate professor of psychology at Northwestern University, says that women's opinions about what is best for them and what can make them more comfortable during pregnancy and giving birth has been ignored or countermanded by male obstetricians "who often make the expectant mother miserable by telling her to gain no more than 14 pounds when an average weight gain of 24 pounds is commensurate with the most favorable outcome"; who still use flat delivery tables when the physiology of childbirth enables a woman to be more comfortable and less pain-racked if she is in a sitting or squatting position—as other cultures have long known and practiced—and whose common obstetrical practices permit a woman laboring in childbirth to go many hours without nutritional sustenance. Obstetrical practices at this point in time are often more geared to the convenience and time schedule of the attending physician than to the comfort and well-being of a woman laboring to bring forth a child. It is not unknown for a nurse to be ordered by a physician who finds it inconvenient to rush to a delivery room to delay the imminent birth by holding the woman's thighs together so that the doctor can be "legally" present when the baby's head emerges.

An unmarried woman, until recently, was considered a spinster or old maid; a man, a gay bachelor playing the field. Female prostitutes are often arrested; their male customers rarely are.

The divorce law of the state of Nebraska deprives women who commit adultery of all but their personal property, a law which is presently the subject of an American Civil Liberties Union test case. The law of the state of Georgia says it is a felony offense, punishable with a one- to three-year sentence, for a man to steal a dog. In this same state it is a petty offense for a man to abandon his pregnant wife. In many states, if a man has a gender-based condition such as prostate trouble that affects his ability to work, he may collect disability funds; while, in these same states, should a woman have a gender-based condition such as pregnancy which prevents her from working, she is not eligible to collect disability funds.

An authority on the legal status of women and juveniles, Norman Dorsen, professor of constitutional law at New York University, has said: "The legal concept of women is essentially that they are children and wards of the state who can be punished for deviating from a strict moral code that is not applied to men."

"Behind all the pious pronouncements and lofty statements of concern runs the unmistakable reluctance of our white, middle-class, male-dominated society to relinquish the last vestige of control over the sexual activity of females," says Lonny Myers, a woman physician at Michael Reese Hospital in Chicago.

One wonders if there may not be an epic resentment of man against woman because she can function sexually at any time, whether or not she is desirous of sex, while the man needs first to experience erection? Does this physiological fact of life contribute to man's historic put-down of the female? Does man need to punish woman for this by controlling her sexual activity?

The defensiveness of maledom is woven into every strand of the tapestry of our times, determining and promulgating not only our sexual double standard, but our laws, customs, politics, education, mass media, work opportunities, and so on. Our media constantly run ads, headlines, and news items such as these:

"Little girls don't cope nearly as well as seven-year-old men." (An ad for children's wear.)

"Just like a woman, the *Queen Elizabeth* sailed into town late."

"New York City, Like Woman, Ignores Birthday."

"Women Don't Like to Look at Women." (An explanation for why we have so few women newscasters on television.)

A citizen, describing the newly built Verrazano-Narrows Bridge in New York, tells a reporter, "It's like a two-faced woman. At this distance she's beautiful but up close she's ugly." An auto mechanic at an automobile show is quoted: "These little foreign cars, they're sweet as hell but temperamental sometimes. Like a woman."

The Latin motto on the Great Seal of Maryland, *Fatti Maschi, Parole Femine,* translates to: "Deeds are masculine, words are feminine" or "Let women talk, men act."

A newspaper cartoon shows a woman saying blankly to her husband: "Oh, I didn't know an account could be overdrawn as long as there were checks left in my checkbook."

We have been taught both overtly and subliminally that man is stronger, has greater endurance, is physically larger, is more logical, and can deal better with abstract ideas, talks less, is punctual more often, handles money more prudently, and needs sex more than woman. How much of this is a bill of goods that women have been conned into buying?

Based on what we know at present, the physiological and biological differences are that the male bone structure is generally larger than the female, and the male is capable of lifting heavier weights than the female. In physical structure, women generally have shorter heads, broader faces, shorter legs, longer trunks, and smaller lungs. But woman has a larger stomach, kidneys, liver, and appendix than the male. Her heart beats more rapidly, eighty beats per minute versus seventy-two beats for man; her basal metabolism rate and blood pressure tend to be somewhat lower than the male's. Man has larger outer ears and these are better collectors and transmitters of low-frequency sound. Woman seems to be more adept at hearing high-pitched sound, perhaps prepared by Nature so that she can hear the wail of a hungry infant.

Physiologically, the female is capable of more orgasms than the male. And, as mentioned earlier, she is capable of functioning sexually at any time while the male is limited by his need to have an erection first.

In most cultures of the world, the female has greater longevity and can endure greater pain. The highest recorded pain on a pain-measuring scale is childbirth. The physical endurance built up by the female through childbearing may be among the reasons for her greater longevity.

And yet, despite the greater strength of the male, in many cultures today, the heavy work is done by women. In Thailand, Indonesia, parts of India, and elsewhere, women do the hard physical work of constructing buildings, carrying hods of wet cement on their shoulders as they climb ladders, and breaking rocks for construction projects. It is the men who do the fine handiwork of embroidery and crafts that is sold to tourists, or who staff the stalls at the market, while the women do the hard labor of homemaking, such as carrying buckets of water across their shoulders, beating rocks with their laundry, hoeing the fields, often while packing babies on their backs.

In 1967 the International Social Council, an agency of the United Nations Educational, Scientific and Cultural Organization (UNESCO), reported the results of a study it made in fourteen countries on how men and women spend their time. In every country, socialist as well as capitalist, woman's lot was found to be physically harder and more time-consuming than man's. A man's workday often ends when he comes home, but the second part of a woman's long workday often begins then. So that even if the man is innately stronger than the female, she has been acculturated to turn out the work as if she were the stronger.

Actually, the new knowledge being made available to us because of research motivated by the sexual revolution reveals that men and women probably have more similarities than differences. For example, recent researches confirm that all of us have male and female chromosomes and hormones in our genetic makeup. Each human cell contains twenty-three pairs of chromosomes—forty-four nonsex chromosomes and two sex chromosomes. The female sex is determined by the presence of two sex chromosomes known as X chromosomes and hence is denoted as XX. A normal male has one X and one Y chromosome and is denoted as XY. Female ovaries produce minute quantities of male sex hormones and some males produce enough female hormones to have fleshy femalelike breasts. Women past menopause, when the female body produces less female hormones, often find themselves developing hair around their upper lips and chins like men needing to shave.

Several years ago when female winners in the Olympics athletic competition were thought to be more male than female, a rule was passed requiring gender tests for female competitors. Such tests are made with skin scrapings from the lining of the mouth and the saliva. The International Amateur Athletic Federation withdrew ratification of all victories, medals, and records achieved by a Polish woman sprinter in the 1964 Olympics when a subsequent chromosome test determined "she" was genetically male.

A small percentage of men are born with a chromosome abnormality called the XYY syndrome. They have two Y, or male, chromosomes, instead of the usual one. Growing numbers of physicians and geneticists believe there may be a correlation between XYY males and criminality, the extra male chromosome being thought to make a person more aggressive and violent. Defense attorneys in murder trials have sought to make the XYY syndrome the cause for legal acceptance of insanity pleas. In Australia in 1968 a murder defendant was acquitted on the ground he was legally insane when he killed a woman because he had forty-seven chromosomes in each cell instead of the normal forty-six. That same month, a similar plea in France failed to free a self-confessed murderer who claimed to have an inherited chromosome imbalance.

The fact is that we are all part male and part female. It is one more benefit of the sexual revolution that we have not only become aware of our opposite sexness but that we can acknowledge it without guilt or shame. We could almost define "oppo-sex" as a kind of third gender of *Homo sapiens:* a male or female with their "oppo-sex" components and characteristics.

Indian Prime Minister Indira Gandhi has said that she doesn't think of people as being men or women, "Every person has some male and female in them." Dorothy Thompson, the journalist and political columnist, wrote that "the real woman looks for the man whom she feels to be her male self." A priest, pleading for the right to marry, said: "I seek my other half as I wander through life half a man."

It can give us insight into ourselves and our choice of marriage partners if we ask: "What about my spouse completes myself? What do I subconsciously seek in that person to make me complete?" Many of us undoubtedly select spouses to act out our opposite sexness. A passive man who likes to have a public image as a sweet-natured, gentle, obliging do-gooder selects a tougher, aggressive, "masculinized" spouse whom he subconsciously maneuvers to do his interpersonal dirty work, such as telling off people, disciplining the children, chasing nonpaying customers, and so on.

Our growing awareness of our opposite sexness provides us with a whole new area to explore in dealing with marital problems. Underlying many troubled marriages may be the very basic root cause that the two spouses' maleness-femaleness makes them behave in certain ways while our culture keeps saying they should be behaving differently. A wife who has drive and energy needs to express herself with great activity and executive-type behavior, but when she does, her husband complains that she is emasculating him by taking over his male prerogatives to lead, make decisions, and be the head of the house. In common parlance, she "wears the pants." But such a woman may not be emasculating a man at all. She may merely be expressing the male characteristics of her hormonal makeup.

Or a woman with a sentimental husband easily moved to tears may feel contempt for what she believes is a feminine weakness, almost a sissiness in him. Yet he may be expressing the feminine side of his nature which clashes with her cultural conditioning that it is unmanly for the male to cry.

As a matter of fact, much harm is done to American men by the cultural conditioning we, male and female alike, undergo that says it is a weakness to shed tears. Crying is the body's necessary catharsis at times of stress or sadness. Turning it off may well build up psychic and perhaps even physical scar tissue in men. Some day we may establish a relationship between this early injunction to the American male not to cry and his high death rate from heart attack.

Philosopher Alan Watts says that the male can arrive at his own true self only when he permits the flowering of his feminine characteristics, such as gentleness and tenderness and sentimentality. In the sexual area, a great many men who feel comfortable with their feminine selves admit they occasionally enjoy the traditionally passive feminine role and like to have their female partners do the pursuing and make the sexual overtures.

Writer Elizabeth Janeway, discussing Marya Mannes's autobiography *Out of My Time* in which she tells of her "hermaphroditism" —her masculine-feminine parts—sums up what might be a hopeful augury for all of us: "Some day, let us hope, no one will have to divide (and so cripple) the self in order to accommodate private abilities to public judgment." We can all cherish our "hermaphroditism," allowing it to be part of our humanity and our growth.

Creatively, legally, humanistically, only one gender—the male —has existed throughout much of human history. Now humankind is experiencing two genders who are equally free to strive and to be. Women around the world are on the march demanding their right to sexual pleasure, unlimited access to contraception, to abortion on demand, and to a single standard of sexual behavior and mores. In many countries, prominent women have been signing their names publicly to advertisements which say: "I have had an illegal abortion." The right to control her own body will be among womankind's freedoms achieved as the result of the sexual revolution.

Freedoms are contagious. None of us frees a slave without becoming freer in the process.

Man is beginning to learn that a single sexual standard in which women are liberated will increase the sum total of pleasure for him, too. A glorious reward in the sex act is the pleasure one derives from the sight and sound of one's partner enjoying climax. Having a nonorgasmic sex partner is frustrating and ego-assaulting. For many men whose women are throwing off the shackles of shame about sex, this whole new source of pleasure awaits them.

The willingness of many young people around the world today to obliterate the lines of demarcation between male and female is among their beautiful traits. More and more of them are refusing to abide by the destructive genderizing of the past in which human characteristics, chores, opportunities, and privileges were designated as being either male or female. The unisex clothing and hairstyles of contemporary youth are manifestations of a growing democracy between the genders. It is their way of saying, "We are emphasizing our similarities, not our differences." Ending the genderizing of chores and of opportunity, young people are en route also to ending the sexual double standard.

velopment referred to by Dr. Heersma as the homosexual stage, and then we grow out of it, going on to heterosexual behavior. But an increasing number of males remain locked into this stage of growth. Whether they do so because of psychological, social, and cultural factors in their early lives, such as the absence of an adult male figure on whom to model male behavior, or whether they do so because of genetic, constitutional, or glandular factors, is the subject of a major debate in the medical and mental health fields. Dr. Martin Hoffman, San Francisco psychiatrist and author of the book *The Gay World: Male Homosexuality and the Social Creation of Evil,* says: "The truth is we really know very little about the origins of homosexuality."

Those who consider cultural factors among the major causes for the rise in homosexuality among our population cite these reasons:

1. Pressure on young people to perform sexually well and early in life, leading some boys to avoid heterosexual encounters because they are afraid they will be inadequate, afraid their physical endowments will be ridiculed, afraid of making a girl pregnant, and because it is easier and less threatening to make a homosexual contact than to seek out a girl.

2. The $1-billion hard-core homosexual pornography industry and the proliferation of homosexual movies. "For the vulnerable male," says Dr. Lawrence Hatterer, author of the book *Changing Homosexuality in the Male,* "it's very stimulating and may be the thing that pushes him over the line."

3. The growing public tolerance of homosexuality which sees the gradual ending of put-down language such as "fag" "homo," "queer," "pansy," and manifested by many noted persons openly admitting their homosexuality or bisexuality.

4. The blending of traditional male and female roles that confuse a male child as to what is male and what is female.

5. Social values which equate masculinity with being physically aggressive, competitive, assertive—gung-ho personalities. The esthetic boy who prefers quiet or artistic or solitary pursuits has been scorned in a culture that places higher value on brawn than on brain, on sociability than on solitude. Such boys may be saying, in effect: "Part of me is feminine and wants feminine expression." What the culture answers, in effect, is: "In order to exercise your feminine side, you have to be homosexual."

6. The high rate of divorce in which more children are raised in single-parent families, most often by mothers. Thus the male child's life has little to do with adult males, since child care centers, nursery and elementary schools, and other institutions to which the child is exposed during his formative years are staffed mostly by females. To counteract this, males are beginning to train to be baby nurses in hospitals and nursery school and kindergarten teachers, another of the changes wrought by the sexual revolution.

Usually cited as the most common environmental cause of homosexuality has been that of an absent or domineering father and the presence of a seductive mother. However, the more we learn, the less parents are being blamed. Why some children become homosexuals while others with similar environmental and familial influences do not, is a question to which we do not yet have an answer. "It is by no means easy to turn a child into a homosexual," says a researcher, "and most children seem able to resist even the worst combination of influences."

Far fewer medical and health workers believe the causes of homosexuality to be physiological or genetic. Biologically, the homosexual is considered to be a normal male. To test whether giving a homosexual extra doses of male hormone might make him more virile and more desirous of female sexual outlet, a UCLA researcher injected homosexual laboratory rats with extra dosages of male hormone. The rats did not seek out female rats; they merely increased the frequency of their homosexual encounters.

In 1971 a controversial study on the biochemistry of the homosexual challenged this belief that homosexuals are biologically normal. Dr. M. Sydney Margolese, a Los Angeles endocrinologist, and two confreres who made the study with a grant from the National Institute of Mental Health, suggested that the male sex hormone, testosterone, broke down differently in the urine of homosexuals and hetrosexuals, indicating possible biochemical causes of homosexuality.

Later that year, a study made at the Reproductive Biology Research Foundation at Washington University in St. Louis and reported in *The New England Journal of Medicine,* said it had found levels of the male sex hormone, testosterone, to be lower in homosexual men. Such studies, begun because research funds have become available as a result of the sexual revolution, promise to give us a wealth of new knowledge in the future that will further free us from the prejudice and prurience of the past.

Along with uncertainty and controversy as to what causes homosexuality, another major dispute revolves around whether or not homosexuality can be changed to heterosexuality. Here, too, there are two major schools of thought, the one stating, yes, the homosexual can be changed by psychotherapy but only if he is strongly motivated to do so, the other school believing that most homosexuals are comfortable with their sexual variancy, do not wish to change, and should not be pressured by society to do so.

Lawrence LeShan, a New York psychologist, sees homosexuality as less of a problem for those engaging in it than it is for a Puritanical disapproving culture. He says: "The Gay Liberation movement (which is bringing them civil and legal rights and social acceptance) is the best therapy the homosexual has had in years." Many agree and maintain that society should adjust to the homosexual, not the homosexual to society.

Many psychiatrists, psychoanalysts, and psychologists report, however, that they are having success in changing homosexuals to heterosexuals. A *New York Times* report of February 28, 1971, tells of successful changes guided by Dr. Hatterer, quoted earlier; by Dr. Samuel B. Hadden, Philadelphia psychiatrist and a pioneer in the group therapy approach to redirecting homosexuals; and by Dr. Joseph Wolpe of Temple University's Behavior Therapy Institute who uses the technique of reconditioning the nervous system by rewards and punishments (mild electric shock to create "aversive" reactions to undesired behavior). Dr. Albert Ellis, noted sex researcher and author, also reports success at his New York City Institute for Rational Living, utilizing his technique of rational-emotive therapy.

Whatever the mode of therapy, its goals are to adjust the homosexual to enjoying the social company and then the physique of the female, and to overcome fears of inadequacy and negative feelings about female genitalia. A National Institute of Mental Health study group on homosexuality has called for "an expansion of efforts to develop new therapies and to improve the efficiency of current therapeutic procedures. . . . We hope and expect that as treatment methods improve and expand, more persons will seek treatment voluntarily." Dr. Hatterer suggests a Homosexuals Anonymous in which former homosexuals who have successfully changed to heterosexual would counsel in sexual mental health clinics.

Female homosexuality—lesbianism—in contemporary life was apparently so rare that when the Postgraduate Center for Mental Health in New York sought lesbians for a study it was conducting in the late 1950s and early 1960s, it had difficulty finding enough women to participate. The Daughters of Bilitis, a national organization of lesbians, had fewer than five hundred members at the time. A decade later, emboldened by the openness of male homosexuality and by the women's liberation movement, lesbianism has surfaced. Many new organizations have been formed with chapters in most major cities.

Researchers into female homosexuality have found that its backgrounds are often similar to those of heterosexual women and do not present the kinds of family situations which were thought to contribute to male homosexuality. No parallels have yet been established between the early backgrounds of male and female homosexuals.

In addition to male and female homosexuality, yet another style of human sexual behavior seems to be on the increase—bisexuality —enjoying and seeking sexual contact with both genders. At one stage of their lives, some bisexuals may be entirely heterosexual, and at another stage entirely homosexual. As homosexuality becomes more accepted, it is believed that some bisexuals veer more frequently between the two, as in the case of a married man or woman who occasionally has a night out with homosexual friends.

Psychoanalyst Bruno Bettelheim believes that our high number of divorces contributes to growing bisexuality. People become disillusioned with the opposite gender, especially those who have been married several times, and they turn to their own gender for rapport, understanding, and sympathy. This social and psychological need being filled by a person of one's own gender often turns into the filling also of physical needs. Divorce laws of some states now specifically include "bisexuality" among legal reasons for divorce.

Among the questions raised by the fact that many creative people —writers, artists, designers, poets—are homosexual, is the one posed in the February 1972 issue of the magazine Sexual Behavior: "Is There a Relationship Between Homosexuality and Creativity?"

The consensus among the six physicians, therapists, and researchers who were asked this question is that there is no apparent relationship between one's style of sexual functioning and one's capacity for creative expression. It is true that many homosexuals are engaged in the creative professions, but that is likely to be related to the fact that they do not find acceptance in establishment occupations such as business or science and tend to seek out careers and develop occupational skills in the freer artistic world. Dr. John Money concludes: "By far the majority of homosexuals, or strongly homosexual bisexuals, are distinguished by neither creativity nor ability in the performing and decorative arts. Vocationally they are ordinary people, indistinguishable from anyone's husband or wife."

Still to be explored is the as yet unsubstantiated idea that creativity springs from the feminine part of human nature—the source of sensitivity, intuition, tenderness, sentimentality—and that a greater willingness to express their feminine nature may be a factor in the creativity of some homosexuals.

One day, given a freer and more enlightened mind, humankind will probably accept the fact that we do have more than one kind of sexuality and that varieties other than heterosexuality are probably part of the human spectrum and, as such, will always be with us.

At such a future time, we may have given up the sexual double standard among heterosexuals. But we are likely to be living with a new kind of multistandard, one in which there will be three styles of acceptable human sexuality—heterosexuality, homosexuality, and bisexuality. The late British scientist, J. B. S. Haldane, said that "the society that enjoys the greatest amount of liberty is the one that permits and respects the greatest amount of polymorphism, or variety in human forms."

Nevertheless, while homosexuals may before long have complete civil, legal, religious, professional, and human rights—including being permitted to marry and to adopt children, practices which have already begun in social custom if not yet in legal form, and they are already being chartered to have their own congregations under the aegis of some churches—they may be considered in some ways to be deprived people.

In this experience called life, the more people and the more personalities we can like and be friends with and be close to, the richer our existence can be. The homosexual leading a one-gender life-style is deprived of one of life's sources of riches—interacting with the personality and physicality of the opposite gender. Aging homosexuals often agree that their life-styles have deprived them of pleasures of heterosexual family life.

For this reason, a great many civil and legal libertarians as well as many who work in medical fields, while believing that homosexuals should have every right available to the rest of us, still feel that society should make all possible efforts to research causes for homosexuality and to do all it can to keep down the rising incidence of homosexuality through psychotherapy, education, and identification early in life of the potential homosexual.

Toward this purpose there are being set up Gender Identity Clinics, as there already have been at UCLA, at the University of Washington in Seattle, at Johns Hopkins University, the University of Minnesota, and elsewhere, to help parents who feel concern about early childhood behavior that might portend homosexuality. Whether to feel panicky or unconcerned over a boy child whose interest in wearing dresses goes on inordinately long is an example of the kind of worry that plagues many uneasy parents.

Moreover, one in every thousand babies born is an incident of "intersex" or anomalous sex in which genitalia are so indefinite that the doctor isn't sure if it's a boy or a girl. Intersex means that the appearance of the external sex organs is at variance with the chromosomal, hormonal, or genetic sex of the infant. Such confusion on the part of Nature is likely to be related to the fact that all mammalian embryos, male and female, are anatomically female during the early stages of fetal life. The differentiation of the male from the female form by the action of fetal androgen begins about the sixth week of embryonic life and is completed by the end of the third month. And so here, too, Gender Identity Clinics can help prevent the psychological problems of labeling as male an infant whose chromosomes and hormones may indicate a preponderance of femaleness.

The sexual revolution has brought us important new insight into gender identity. We find that in order to truly know what a person's gender is, we need to identify that person's *chromosomal* sex—the number of male and female chromosomes; *gonadal* sex—the development of ovary and testes; *hormonal* sex—the proportions of male and female hormones in a person's body chemistry; the development of the *external genitalia* such as vulva in the female, penis and scrotum in the male; and development of *internal sex organs* such as uterus and vagina in the female and prostate in the male.

It is impossible to calculate how much psychic pain will be spared untold numbers of human beings in the future by the new knowledge we are now garnering, nor what this freeing from psychic pain will ultimately do for human personality.

PART II

SEX IN MARRIAGE

5

Is Marriage Here to Stay?

During the late 1960s, a movie was released on the life of Isadora Duncan, free-spirited, iconoclastic dancer of the 1920s. Wherever it was shown, its opening scene brought spontaneous outbursts of applause, especially from youthful audiences. The scene showed an adolescent Isadora Duncan destroying her parents' marriage license. That burst of applause reverberating around the globe was a revealing critique of what many people were feeling about legal marriage. In almost every style of human society, no matter what its economic, political, and humanitarian persuasion, the institution of marriage was under attack, with a demand for its reexamination or abolishment.

Many people, public and private personages alike, were openly dismissing marriage both on the personal grounds that it had never worked for them and also on the philosophical ground that, ideally, no state should have any jurisdiction or say-so over a person's body or the living arrangements in which he or she used that body.

Distinguished novelists like Katharine Anne Porter of the United States, thrice-divorced, and Françoise Sagan of France, twice-divorced, along with many theatrical celebrities, students, lawyers, jurists, historians, philosophers, psychologists, mental health experts —a gamut of intellectual humanity—were saying that marriage as we have always known it is the cause of much human misery and it was time a free, enlightened humankind called a halt to the perpetuation of the institution in its present form.

Newspaper headlines reported such stories as these:

"Marriage May Become Irrelevant in Sweden." A judge in Stockholm, announcing the start of an inquiry into all aspects of family rights, said future legislation would be based on the principle that marriage is a form of voluntary cohabitation between independent persons. New laws would not permit the asking of any questions about one's marital status. Full rights and privileges and economic benefits would be given to children with no one asking whether a child's parents were married or not. It was predicted by some sociologists and historians that the institution of marriage in Sweden would eventually wither away.

"Experts See Great Changes in Institution of Marriage." A consensus of opinion among United States doctors, marriage counselors, psychiatrists, and economists was that marriage is likely to disappear eventually, especially as there are fewer children being born and less need for a man and woman to enter into or to maintain a legally constituted relationship.

"Psychology Association Asks Major Overhaul in Marriage Code." Dr. Harold Greenwald, then president of the National Psychological Association for Psychoanalysis, said that for centuries we have been forcing men and women to conform to the mold of marriage, when what we should be doing is to change marriage to suit the convenience and happiness of people. He proposed that marriage become a "nonlegal, voluntary association" between a man and a woman.

A research psychologist asked, "I wonder if marriage *ever* worked? Or has our marriage myth really added up to an incredible sum total of unhappiness that we haven't had the courage to talk about until now?"

Anthropologists Robin Fox and Lionel Tiger, wondering if marriage should even be considered a natural institution, point out that no animal except the human animal forces mates to remain together and combine the parent-lover role beyond their natural inclination to do so.

Certainly the institution of marriage in its traditional form is being dramatically challenged. Modern marriage has been defined as being like a romantic novel in which the hero and heroine die in the first chapter. Marriage repairpersons everywhere have been working hard to shore up the structure, but their efforts are mostly not working. We have had more marriage counseling in the past quarter-century and more divorces. In nearly every country, marriage is failing at an accelerated rate. We need desperately to reexamine marriage and family, to change their expectations and rules, to modernize their *modus operandi,* so that throughout the world we do not have such huge numbers of good human beings so miserable in these social structures.

Living through this upheaval of changing social institutions is painful for some people, but that's because they evaluate it as a breakdown. We can give positive rather than negative meaning to this reexamination. We can consider it not a negative breakdown but a positive "mating-updating" which can lead to happier marriage and family relationships. Happiness has been waiting in the wings too long; it is time that we auditioned it on the barren stage of joyless marriage.

"Before the escape hatch of divorce began to open up in the early 1920s," says Robert L. Tyler, professor of history at Southern Connecticut State College, "millions of persons had been chained to each other, hating each other's guts more and more each year, feeling the sad realities profoundly cheating them of their impossible - utopian hopes."

The sexual revolution frees us to drop the syllable *im* and to live with *possible* utopian hopes. By experimenting with ways of modernizing marriage and family, we can all aspire to add to the possible sum total of human happiness.

Our philosophy of marriage until now has said that ideally it ought to fill all or most of our needs. This philosophy is among the reasons for the growing failure of marriage. No one relationship ought to be asked to do that much for anyone. It is the expectation of so much togetherness that makes of marriage a stultifying, throttling experience for a great many.

It is one more indication of our need to redefine our marriage philosophy that our culture is pervaded by a provincial code of marriage in which one may not acceptably have friendships with people of the opposite gender without inviting jealous accusations, innuendos, and hints of sexual transgression. What sad deprivation each of us undergoes because our one-and-only marriage code says that once you get married you have to start being deprived of enriching, stimulating, rewarding friendships with those of the opposite gender. "No one woman can possibly combine all the virtues that are characteristic of women in general; no one man all the excellences of men in general. Every sensitive and completely alive person has something unique to give every other sensitive and completely alive person," says philosopher Corliss Lamont in *A Humanist View of Marriage*. People need and should have abundant friendships with people of both genders and all ages. Marriage will justifiably continue to fail until it encourages our right to such human riches.

Amelia Earhart, a noted aviatrix, while deliberating whether to marry publisher George P. Putnam II, wrote to him: "Please let us not interfere with the other's work or play. . . . I may have to keep some place where I can go to be myself now and then, for I can not guarantee to endure at all times the confinement of even an attractive cage."

The idea that marriage will provide us with a relationship that will be a steady source of supply of interesting conversation and intellectual stimulation is another myth contributing to its downfall. The practice is far different. Should a husband and wife even find time to read a book, the actuality of life rarely finds them sitting down leisurely and having an intellectually stimulating discussion about it, especially when there are children in the household also demanding a mother and father's time and attention.

If the quantity and the circumstances of intellectual stimulation in marriage were to be measured in a scientifically controlled study, it would inevitably be found that most intellectual stimulation and interesting conversation occurs not when a couple are by themselves but when they are in a social exchange with others. Recognizing this, a group of young couples in Washington, D.C., has started a "learning network" in which they exchange names of people who have recently read the same books so that they can get together and rap about what they've read.

Even the world's renowned intellectual couples, writers, scientists, historians, will admit that outside of the work they may do jointly, their most stimulating exchange on an average day is apt to be: "What do you feel like having for dinner, dear?" And yet marriage mythology leads many of us to expect a steady source of mental stimulation to come from tired spouses who are more likely to flop down in front of the television set and fall asleep than they are to ask, "What do you think of the day's news, dear?" Appropriately, a cartoon shows a husband and wife leaving a party with the wife saying: "How come you're never witty and amusing at home?"

Homebound women have been especially deprived by the absence of varied intellectual stimuli in their lives. Bruno Bettelheim says that one of the major causes for the downfall of marriage is that our society has traditionally permitted only the male two major areas of personal completion—family and work. Husbands at least get away from the home and have the opportunity to see new faces and to interact with different people during the course of a day. But it has permitted woman only one major area for personal completion—family. Technology, according to Dr. Roger Revelle, former director of Harvard University's Center for Population Studies, "makes it possible for a woman to run her own household alone, thus trapping her in the necessity of doing all the work and having no company but that of small children." Women are only now beginning to sweep themselves out from under the wall-to-wall monotony that has been among their marital furnishings.

The idea that intellectual leadership and opinion-making in marriage should derive from the male is a remnant from the time when women were not permitted to vote and to have a voice in politics. Women were expected to follow husbands' and fathers' political opinions. Even then, they couldn't do anything about it because they did not have the vote. This tradition is so strong that many women, still carrying out this archaic message that females aren't supposed to be thinkers, choosers, and deciders, do not bother to vote. The Gallup Poll reports that millions of eligible American females have not voted in recent presidential elections.

Besides this myth that mental stimulation and interesting conversation is supplied mostly by the male spouse, another important myth that burdens marriage is the one about love. Our culture has taught us to confuse a pleasant tension in the groin with undying love. A person crosses our path in life, something about him or her triggers stimuli to the arousal center in our brains, our groins get warm and palpitant and turned-on and we call it love. Such a pleasant tension is often a major reason for marital union. The relationship between many a man and woman doesn't really have much more than that going for it. The waning of that tension, in its time, is also a major reason for marital disunion.

What is truly love may not even *begin* until that tension abates. That's when we can take a real look at the person we are married to, uncolored by the rosy glow of sexual sunshine. And either mature unselfish love begins to grow or what was only a childlike, ego-centered infatuation begins to wane.

The mature love says: "I will do all I can to help you to grow to your optimum potentiality and capacity, even if that means you must sometimes be away from me and do things without me. Because I love you as a human being I want you to become all that you are capable of."

The childlike, ego-centered love says: "You have to be here to do for me, for me to lean on so I can feed on you. If you are not here to hold me up I will collapse. You and I need togetherness so I can keep you responsible for what happens to me."

Many of us have been defrauded in our marriage experience because what we were taught to believe was love was, in fact, dependency. A biography of playwright Eugene O'Neill reports that his third wife, Carlotta Monterey, said bitterly of their marriage: "He would . . . say: 'I need you, I need you'—never 'I love you, I think you are wonderful'—just 'I need you.' "

"Love," as defined by Dr. Solon Samuels, Los Angeles psychiatrist, "is respect for each other's equality"—equality to grow and, to coin a phrase, to "optimate ourselves." By this definition there is not much love abroad in our marital land. It may not be too far-fetched to say that human existence has not yet truly experienced love and it won't until women's liberation is a *fait accompli*. Equality not yet having existed so far in the human experience, we could say by Dr. Samuels's definition that neither has love. It may be a genuine new emotion awaiting us in our futures, not to be confused with the ersatz emotion so lauded in song, story, and poetry until now.

A prescient commentary by cartoonist Jules Feiffer has a man and woman talking about the crack-up of so many marriages they know and then deciding that the reason their own marriage survives so well is "because we don't love each other."

That woman needs marriage more than man does is another myth that needs updating in the light of new female freedoms. It may have been true when woman was not permitted to work, could not earn her own keep, or had little or no equality of employment. But now as more women become self-supporting and, in increasing cases, are the major support of the family, this notion, too, is having its ashes strewn over the coffin of chauvinism.

Actually, man needs marriage more than woman does. A study of human happiness made at the University of Chicago reveals that single men are twice as likely to be unhappy as are single women. Dr. Norman M. Bradburn, psychologist, who conducted the study, found this to be surprising "in view of the widespread impression that being unmarried is one of the worst things that can happen to a woman."

This is confirmed by the Los Angeles Suicide Prevention Center which reports the "highest rate of suicide is among divorced, middle-aged men living alone." A woman who is divorced continues responsibility for the chores she has always performed, such as meal planning, shopping, food preparation, laundry, and so on, especially if she has custody of children. The man, accustomed to having a wife do all this for him, must go through the painful adjustment of learning to do this for himself.

When Barbara Castle, a Member of Parliament, was asked why there weren't more successful women, she said: "Because a woman doesn't have a wife to come home to, who does all the dirty work and frees her to be successful, just like wives now do for men."

Woman in marriage has traditionally been the human garbage disposal for the trash of existence generated by all others in the household. It is thus the life-style for many men to drop their dirty linen on the floor and to leave towels strewn about the bathroom for the human garbage disposal to pick up and throw into the clothes hamper. It is the custom for the male to walk away from the table leaving the human-garbage-disposal wife to clear his dishes and wipe his crumbs. The wrapper from his cigarette pack or stick of chewing gum, the metal tab from his can of beer, his soiled handkerchief, his sweaty shirt, were all customarily left on the dresser or end table or floor, for the female beast of burden to dispose of. The male, who has been conditioned by having one female—his mother—do all of this for him when he was a small boy, continues in marriage the pattern of having another female—his wife—do the same.

No wonder that as women are freed financially, maternally, and sexually, through having paid jobs, fewer children, and sexual equality, more of them declare their disinterest in being married. Let man live through the ignominy of putting in a sixteen- to eighteen-hour workday and then having to come to another human being for his sustenance for food, shelter, clothing, and pocket money, and he may begin to get some small idea of the rage women are feeling at the indignity of the marriage dole.

It is not surprising that the National Health Center reports that "there has been a large increase in remarriage rates for divorced men," while the higher the educational level of a divorced woman and the more her capability of earning her own living, the less likely she is to remarry.

A cartoon shows a man and a woman looking at engagement rings in a store window. The woman is saying: "I *am* thinking of the thrill of being a wife and mother these days, Otis. That's why my answer is NO."

To further update marriage, another custom that ought to go is the joint checking account. Whatever the style of future pairing, it must inevitably see a woman keeping her own checking and savings account and all legal papers pertaining to herself—insurance, car ownership, passport—all in her own name. She would have absolute equal legal rights to purchase real estate, to go into business, establish a credit rating, without having to get permission from any male or having to use his name. Many states have laws considering a married woman a "legal incompetent." Marriage would have to guarantee to a woman that she would retain the same autonomy of her personality that she had as a single woman. A legal reason for divorce could be: Deprivation of autonomy of personality.

Should a woman stay home and not work, the law would provide compensation for her homemaking services, requiring that no matter what the male's income or on what economic level the family lived, a percentage was the wife's pay for her own use, unaccountable to anyone. What a commentary on marriage it is that millions of women, exerting hard physical labor as homemakers year after year, often do not have one single penny they can legally call their own when joint accounts and paychecks are in the husband's control. Imagine what it does to the self-respect and self-esteem of countless numbers of women who, in order to have a few cents they can call their own, are forced to siphon off dribs and drabs surreptitiously from household money and deposit it in secret bank accounts.

It is another of our many hidden injustices that divorced women are disfranchised from social security in their later years unless they had been married at least twenty years and continue to get more than half of their support from former husbands. We have a large segment of such deprived women who, having devoted their major productive years to marriage and motherhood, do not have one whit of social security in their senior years because they either divorced short of twenty years or their ex-spouses are not providing half of their support in their divorcehood.

In 1965 the Chase Manhattan Bank in New York estimated a housewife's labor as cleaner, gardener, plumber, repairperson, chauffeur, cook, handyperson, to be worth $159.34 a week in the labor market at that time. But a woman's housework is not counted in the national tabulation of goods and services. According to government statistics, the work a wife does around the house adds nothing to the wealth of the country! It is not considered part of our gross national product. Ask a woman who is mopping the kitchen floor, or lugging in hundreds of pounds of groceries per week, or driving a car pool full of noisy embattled youngsters, or being tormented by repetitive demands for "Mommy—Mommy—Mommy —Mommy" from small children how she feels about that.

Mother love has been history's most exploited emotion, the rationale for which woman was told she ought to be content in marriage despite its drudgery. Housewifing is the world's oldest unpaid profession. Marriage is the domain that sanctions her exploitation.

In California when a man asked for an annulment after a seventeen-year-marriage on the grounds that his wife's previous marriage had not been legally dissolved, she sued for and was awarded $29,100 for housekeeping duties performed during the alleged marriage. It is a fact that more women have money in their own names when they are divorced, as part of divorce settlements, than they ever did as wives. And that many people look upon alimony as retroactive pay to a woman, compensation for years of unpaid housewifery.

During a recent Christmas season, several young liberated California couples ran ads in the *Los Angeles Times* as a public service at their own expense, urging husbands to "Give Your Wife Equality for Christmas." Even though California has a community property law, the ad suggested, division of assets is usually more lip service than life-style. The husband still legally controls the money, often maintains it in his own name, and has exclusive power to decide how the community property should be spent.

"If you as a husband trust and respect your wife as a truly equal marriage partner," the ad declared, you can write to us and "get a simple form which you and your wife can execute yourselves, to give your wife an equal voice in deciding how to use the property which is hers as much as yours."

In effect, these couples were saying to husbands: "Put your money where your mouth is."

But despite all of the above, despite the many debits against marriage on the balance sheet of life, the institution is apparently not yet ready to be written off as bankrupt. Marriage failure may be at an all-time high, but so is the contracting of new legal marriages. Many intelligent people who know all about its pitfalls keep on entering marriage. Obviously, there is enough going for it to keep marriage a lively invalid.

While some deep inner core in the human personality likes variety and adventure and roaming, another deep inner core in us also craves a one-to-one, I-thou relationship with another human being, a "significant other" with whom we can be utterly, even disgustingly, ourselves, our dragged-out, unmade-up, occasionally unkempt, irritable, and irrational selves, and still find acceptance.

It is only when we are with a significant other that many of us let down our psychic armor and dare to reveal even those parts of ourselves we don't want to go around exposing to the world. Marriage can provide this.

Eric Berne, the late psychoanalyst and author of *Games People Play,* who devised the effective system of insight into human personality called Transactional Analysis in which he analyzed transactions between the parent-adult-child parts of all of us, believed that what we especially seek in a significant other is a steady source of supply of nurturing, to be babied throughout our lives, regardless of chronological age.

Actually we are all part roamer and part "homer." It is great to be free to roam around sampling many personalities, but it is also great to have a secure home base to return to. For most of us, life is one long teeter-totter of compromise between our sometime need for freedom and our sometime need for security and nurturing.

What most of us want psychologically is probably exactly what we would most enjoy sexually—ongoing security of a home base with freedom to roam occasionally. It is significant that the majority of never-marrieds or divorced people who have all the freedom in the world to constantly roam, ask their friends after a period of doing so: "Do you know someone to introduce me to? I've had it with free-lancing."

Knowing what the human personality desires and is most likely to enjoy, why do we not go about implementing it into marriage experimentation? Whatever the style of future marriage, individual or group, legal or companionate, a philosophy of marriage that would be a start toward improving it would be a relationship we expect to fill only *some* of our needs.

A future philosophy of marriage would allow two independent, constantly growing human personalities—in addition to those needs for socializing, intimacy, and nurturing that they have of each other —to have some interests, activities, and friendships that the other would not necessarily be part of.

The obvious question that comes to mind is this one: "How do we handle feelings of jealousy?" Jealousy stems from low self-esteem and feelings of inadequacy. Double-level feelings of jealousy say: "I am not sure I have enough to hold on to this person. Someone else can come along and take him or her from me."

When we have feelings of self-worth and we know we are filling needs for another person, we do not feel threatened by jealousy. As one career wife said when friends asked if she were not threatened by the fact that her husband went dancing without her when she worked at night: "If there is ever another woman who can fill his needs better than I do, then I would not stand in the way of his leaving me for that other person. That would be his human right, to get his needs met. But I know that we fill so many needs for each other that neither of us feels threatened when one is doing something without the other."

Such a marital style of the future would inevitably find many more men and women enjoying good self-esteem derived from their autonomy to grow and to achieve on their own. We will find that much of the damaging low self-esteem—which so many women have because they lean dependently on husbands and have had small opportunity to grow on their own—will be replaced by feelings of self-worth. For many, that will be a brand new experience.

A marital style of the future would probably also find some legally married men and women choosing not to live full-time under the same roof. A trend toward this has already begun among some professional men and women who have their own careers and their own apartments and who join together for socializing, companionship, and sex in a "week-end marriage."

The late novelist, Fannie Hurst, and her husband, pianist Jacques Danielson, lived in separate apartments during their long marriage and declared it to be a "happy arrangement." John F. Cuber, sociologist, has listed among his suggestions for future lifestyles: "The termination of the requirement that paired couples must share the same domicile."

Marriage that expected less togetherness would probably also see an increase in the idea of separate bedrooms so that each person would have an oasis of retreat entirely for himself or herself. Dr. Elizabeth Austin, a California physician, saying she believed strongly in separate bedrooms and bathrooms, if possible, for married couples, declared: "My own marriage might have persisted if we had had our own rooms and could meet when we felt like loving human beings."

Before a man and woman knock the idea of separate bedrooms for happier marriage, they ought first to go through the experience of dressing for an evening out and learning how much more exciting it can be not to see each other in various stages of getting dressed, groomed, and made up. There is something enormously tranquilizing about the couple meeting each other outside their respective bedrooms, attractive, relaxed, without the constant small interruptions of bumping into or crisscrossing space with each other which we experience when a husband and wife get dressed in the same room. As well as having clothing in separate bedrooms so that a husband cannot hassle a wife with cries of, "Where are my cuff links?" Only *he* would be responsible for knowing where *his* cuff links were because they would be kept in *his* own room.

Couples who can afford separate bedrooms also find it more sexually exciting when they have slept separately for a few nights and then crawl into one or the other's bed for physical affection. Lying next to each other night after night over the years often becomes a sexual turn-off. Sensory excitement with each other's body is much greater after a few nights of being apart.

Even the very architecture in which families live has contributed to the dissolution of marriage and family. Open-space houses without doors or even walls, as in kitchen-and-family rooms combined into one, have created a neurotic, noisy, tawdry togetherness in which it is impossible for the residents to escape from each other's blaring radios, television sets with their insistent haranguing commercials, voices, quarrels, cooking odors—a constant assault of jarring stimuli on our nervous systems. Families planning to build new homes ought to flee from any architect who suggests open-plan housing.

Middle-class residential architecture is one more aspect of marriage that disfranchises women especially. Many such homes are built with a den or some retreat for dad to relax in, but no such separate eyrie for mother. Her "retreat" is apt to be part of a workroom—a recipe desk in the kitchen or sewing room or service porch or laundry room—all of them designed to get her to work more but not to free her for relaxation. Each child, if it has its own bedroom, can retreat to that. Dad can retreat to his den. Mother doesn't even have her bedroom to retreat to for uninterrupted solitude because she shares that with dad.

Would a marriage style of less togetherness also call for less togetherness sexually? Would it require "genital fidelity"? That would depend on the marriage contract between the partners. Some of us would probably find this style of marriage in which we were free to fill psychological and intellectual and friendship needs with a variety of people so satisfying that our emotional and sexual feelings towards our own mates would be so warm and loving that we would not care to fill physiological need for orgasm with anyone else, but would joyfully share it exclusively with our "significant other." A man and a woman, living with such beautiful freedoms, are likely to become even more endeared to each other. Others would undoubtedly find that as they enjoyed filling psychological needs with others, they would also want to fill physiological needs as well.

Even these arrangements, which for most of us would certainly be less trying than marriage as we now know it, would not necessarily make for marital longevity. The most pleasurable of experiences can become tiring through repetition. The human organism needs a variety of changing stimuli and new experience to maintain itself comfortably and pleasurably in a condition of homeostasis.

As sex is separated from procreation, as women are freed from the bread-and-butter arrangement marriage now is for so many, as we have fewer children needing the protection of legally married parents, we may find ourselves caring less about a couple's pairing arrangements than we do about their right to pleasure. Increasingly, we will be living the philosophy of existence which makes hedonism (pursuit of pleasure) acceptable.

Our Christian-Judaic ethic has conditioned us to believe that in hard work and denial we achieve our nobility and goodness. But when 2 per cent of our population will produce 100 per cent of the goods and food we all need, as is anticipated, the philosophy of pleasure will perforce become an acceptable one. This will take an adjustment from a philosophy of existence that equated hard work with being a good person to a philosophy that says even the loafer, in pursuit of pleasure, is also a good person.

As marriage changes, so do its customs and rituals. Updated custom finds more women who are not giving up their names and identities when they enter marriage. Many American women are already tacking on, with a hyphen, their husband's names, as European women have done for years. In a precedent-setting about-face, a liberated groom has legally added his bride's maiden name as his own middle name.

We will also see the growth of another European custom, that of a child using in adulthood either its mother's or father's name. Dr. Jose M. R. Delgado of Yale University, one of the world's foremost brain researchers, uses his mother's maiden name, Delgado. We may even see anti-girl-child sentiment disappear among fathers. If girls can carry on a family name and not lose it to marriage, one of the reasons men prefer boy children may end.

Wording of the marriage service is also changing. Asking a woman to "obey" her husband began to be deleted several years ago. "Obey" implies the master-serf relationship modern women will not stand for. In England a bride insisted on walking alone to the altar rather than on her father's arm and would not permit the question: "Who gives this woman to be married to this man?" "Marriage is an equal partnership," she declared, "and I have no intention of being given away like a cooker."

"Do you take this person unto death?" is also disappearing. Reverend Angus Roderick of England says: "It is wrong for couples whose love has died to be held to this solemn pledge." A marriage service of the American Humanist Association has the couple dedicating themselves to each other "as long as it is a rewarding growing relationship for both of us."

Many young people today write their own marriage service or do favorite readings. The laws of most states permit couples to perform the rite themselves as long as it is in the presence of a legally constituted authority who can sign the marriage document. During 1972 the Inter-Lutheran Commission on Worship issued on a trial basis new rules for the marriage ceremony under which the couple can write their own marriage vows; the bride's father no longer will "give her away", the subordination of woman to man is "played down", and the prayer for fertility is eliminated on the ground that "we do not regard marriage as a matter primarily of child bearing." In France, Roman Catholic bishops and the French Protestant Reform Church have jointly issued a new wedding manual stating that a bride and groom may marry each other before a clergyman rather than being joined in marriage by him.

More couples today are foregoing traditional bridal finery and flowers. They may choose instead to wear identical robes or peasant garb, with sandals or bare feet. A well-to-do couple in Westport, Connecticut, was married barefoot in the woods outside the rough cedar home the bridegroom had proudly built with his own hands, All the guests were also barefoot. Everyone became a participant, not just an observer, by being asked to take part in group reading of poems of love and fellowship.

Increasing numbers of brides are also choosing not to wear wedding rings—early symbols of slavery when human chattels wore rings in their noses to identify their owners. Instead of the groom being asked to put the ring on his bride's finger, they are asked to clasp hands.

Someone has said of such new marriage rites: "All this is driving the caterers and jewelers of the world crazy."

Whatever customs humankind has designed, humankind can redesign. Just as we are changing marriage rites, so can we change marriage rights. If we can work to rid the world of terrestrial pollution, why can we not put as much effort into ridding human beings of their emotional pollution caused by the rot in the institution of marriage?

Surely a humankind which found itself able to endure the dropping of atom bombs on other humans should be able to endure the lesser upheaval of modernizing archaic human institutions.

6

The Search for Alternative
Life-Styles

Our worldwide pandemic marital misery has been forcing us during the past decade or so into a search for alternative marriage styles. Marriage theoreticians and repairpersons have become busy crusaders on a quest for the Holy Grail of marital harmony, a quest that has led half of America's marriage counselors themselves to end their marriages in order to seek more harmonious relationships.

Many of the ideas and suggestions of these theoreticians of new marriage styles are variations on the theme of companionate or trial marriage first proposed by Judge Ben Lindsey in his book *Companionate Marriage,* published in 1927, and by Lord Bertrand Russell, British philosopher, in his book *Marriage and Morals,* published in 1929.

Both men were excoriated by what Lord Russell described as a "howl of horror" for their outrageous suggestion that people cohabit without legalities unless they decided to have children. Judge Lindsey was hounded off the bench in Denver, Colorado, and Lord Russell was hounded out of his teaching appointment at the City College of New York in 1940 on the grounds that his espousal of "trial marriage" made him unfit to teach. Less than a generation later, Judge Lindsey's and Lord Russell's suggestions are mild ones —"you might even say old-fashioned by today's standards," a librarian says—in a world marked by frenetic marriage mobility.

Today, companionate arrangements, if their numbers were recorded in some archive, are probably pacing legal marriages. They have been mostly initiated by the young and are now an accepted life-style in many college dormitories; out in the "civilian" noncollege world, in growing numbers of minicommunes of a few couples who rent a house and share expenses; and in larger communes where the companionate arrangements may or may not also include switching of sexual partners.

Colleges which frown on such arrangements are finding their dorms going empty. *College Management Magazine,* a journal for college administrators, says the latest headache for colleges is "how to keep them happy down in the dorm." Students are moving out, preferring the greater freedom in off-campus living arrangements.

Companionate arrangements are finding many schools caught in a generational squeeze between students who are demanding their right to choose their own living styles and parents and alumni who are writing schools out of their wills and canceling contributions in protest over what used to be called, in the parents' time, free-love arrangements.

During 1971, the student-dominated housing policy board at the University of Michigan's Ann Arbor campus, one of the nation's leading campuses, voted to delete the wording in dormitory rules which barred "cohabitation, overnight visitation, and premarital sexual intercourse." Some parents and alumni registered strong protest and a minister excoriated the school in a sermon on its "rampant sinfulness."

But all this furore is transitional. It is likely that before many more years have passed, companionate living will be the norm in most American colleges and universities. The right to such lifestyles is among the demands of the powerful National Student Association, and they will achieve them in the course of human events and evolution, just as they are achieving their demands for dissemination of birth control information and devices without parental consent.

But besides that, companionate arrangements are now also increasing rapidly among older people as well, especially among those who have been divorced. And with good reason. So traumatic and sadistic is the adversary system of divorce—most divorce laws are traps of legal spears that goad fine human beings into the humiliation and indignity of ripping each other to verbal and legal shreds in order to end an unhappy human relationship—that, once having been bloodied by it, many are wisely afraid to enter that potential trap again.

Joan Longo, a divorcee who later married a former Roman Catholic priest, has said of their living together before marriage: "I did it because I had been divorced once and I didn't want to make another mistake." A distinguished corporation lawyer in Washington, D.C., a divorced man in his fifties, told a reporter who asked how he felt about his daughters' companionate arrangements: "How can I tell my daughters not to live with their boyfriends on campus? I myself am living such an arrangement right here in my apartment. If you knew the number of people in my subculture—professional divorced people—who live in arrangements, you'd be amazed."

One of the games of our times being played avidly by sociologists, psychologists, marriage counselors, and educators is the game of marriage-inventing. Professional journals and popular magazines, and publications devoted to futureship, are all having fun thinking up assorted concepts of marriage and family for the future.

Virginia Satir, noted family therapist, has proposed the five-year renewable marriage contract. She says that marriage is the only human contract in our society that has no time length, no opportunity for review, and no socially acceptable means of termination.

If a marriage goes well for the first five years, Ms. Satir suggests, the couple could renew the contract for another five-year period. If it fails, it would automatically be dissolved without undue stress, expense, litigation, or social stigma. Ms. Satir's further recommendation is that a couple go through an apprenticeship of living together before entering into the marriage contract.

Two women legislators in Maryland's House of Delegates have already introduced a bill that would allow three-year contract marriages with the option to renew. Humor columnist Russell Baker wonders if with such contractual arrangements, we may not soon see people trading spouses with other people, the same way baseball teams now trade players whose performance may not have been up to expectations.

Robert L. Tyler has suggested in *The Humanist Magazine* for November-December 1970 a "Two Marriage Revolving-Mate Generation-Bridging Plan to Save Marriage." He writes: "The plan is simple. At about 20 to 25 years of age a man would contract his first marriage to a woman of 40 to 45 who is leaving her first marriage. A woman of 20 to 25 years of age would contract her first marriage to a man of 40 to 45 who is leaving his first marriage. Presto! revolving mates. At 60 to 65 years of age both men and women would leave the system, to marry each other in third marriages if they wished, or to enjoy retirement in well-earned single bliss." Mr. Tyler believes that among the advantages of this plan is that it takes into account, more realistically than present marriage styles do, "Nature's heartless joke" in giving greatest sexual vigor to males in their teens and twenties and to females in their thirties or forties.

Leo Davids, sociologist at York University, Ontario, Canada, suggests that compound marriages, polygamous (having several wives), polyandrous (having several husbands), or group, will be among the commonly practiced future life-styles acceptable to a pluralistic society.

According to an article "The Future of Women and Marriage," which appeared in *The Futurist Magazine* for April 1970, Larry and Joan Constantine of Acton, Massachusetts, are already living a group marriage, based not on male or female dominance but on essentially equal and mutual bonds, including sexual and financial bonds, among all partners.

Psychologist Herbert Otto, in his book *The Family in Search of a Future,* compiles the opinions of fifteen experts who suggest one or another variation of marriage, including duos, trios, groups, "intimate networks" of extended families, progressive monogamy or serial marriage, and polygamy (to help take care of larger numbers of females than males in the senior years). Whether these arrangements would be legal or nonlegal, companionate or trial marriage, would not matter at a time when human beings are engaged in the higher philosophical goal of optimum human growth and pleasure and enjoyment. All that would matter in new marriage, suggests Dr. Otto, is that it must acknowledge and respect each person's human potential.

This growing trend of living together creates a need for new words to be added to the language. What to call the person with whom one shares a sleep-in arrangement trips the tongues of many such participants. The words, *companimate, apartmate, housemate,* have all been suggested. How much social acceptance there already is to the idea is shown by a column of advertising news which comments that a new product is being introduced to "housewives, house-husbands, and housemates."

The parents of young people living together are probably just going to have to get used to introducing what used to be called a son-in-law or daughter-in-law as a *Companimate-in-law* or, less unwieldy, a *comp-kin.* As a matter of fact, all of us of all ages are going to be learning new words as more *companimates* live together in *compan-unions,* or, more trippingly on the tongue, *comp-unions.* We may all experience at one time or another being *comp-mom-in-law, comp-dad-in-law, comp-broth-in-law, comp-sist-in-law, comp-aunt, comp-uncle,* and so on. Should companionate marriage prove to add to the sum total of human happiness, the names by which the relationships are known will soon be adapted comfortably into the common language.

But is *companimating,* by whatever name or style it goes, going to provide the cure for marriage malaise? It's doubtful. Companionate marriage as it is now being lived may be likened to erecting a building without a building permit. If the building is constructed with crumbling brick or wormy wood, it is just as collapsible with a building permit as without.

Two people living together and acting out the same old she-and-he curriculum of marriage are not really instituting any great advance over the same old failures.

It is ironic that a story about "The Young Unmarrieds" in *Look* Magazine, January 26, 1971, a couple who are supposedly living a "brave new world" kind of existence, reports: "Like any young housewife, she does most of the cooking, shopping, and laundry" while the male partner "fixes their car." One would like to project these unmarrieds ten years into the future and listen to the legally unmarried female complaining about how she is bored to hysteria doing "most of the cooking, shopping, and laundry," while her legally unmarried male partner cops out from sharing menial chores by being busy "fixing their car" or some other equally masculinized dodge of the future.

Writing on "The Unmarrieds on Campus" in *The New York Sunday Times Magazine,* January 26, 1969, Arno Karlen says that all those couples daringly "shacking up" together are living lives of ideology and activity amazingly similar to the lives of their parents, and no doubt destined for marital disharmony amazingly similar to that of their parents.

It is, moreover, certainly doubtful that trial marriage will inevitably prepare those companimates who later decide to have children and then enter into a legal marriage.

All human behavior is determined by three factors: time, place, and situation. How we behave in one particular time, place, and situation is different from how we will behave in another time, place, and situation. New and changing external factors and personalities entering our lives create new conditions and additional interpersonal dynamics. Each one of us is a constantly changing and mutating "congress of selves."

Thus a couple, living companionately and getting along fairly well, introduce a whole new set of dynamics into their lives by having a child. The male, now a legal husband, is probably working harder than ever to earn more money for the additional person; the female may now have given up her job and is no longer bringing money in. Instead of the two of them coming home from their respective jobs, husband now comes home to an exhausted and bored female who hasn't had time or desire to put on her make-up and is busy folding diapers and preparing formula or safety-watching an ambulatory toddler.

The good relationship of their companionate marriage is sorely tried and tested in this new time, place, and situation of a credentialed marriage, dependent child, and need for larger income, larger living quarters, disturbed sleep, and the male's inevitable loss of some time-and-attention stroking that he used to get from his wife, now going to this third human being. Virginia Satir says that in "the law of three—two are participants and one is an observer." Indeed, there is already some indication of growing divorce among young people who did live together and then later married in order to legalize their planned parenthood. The practice marriage involving two people just didn't apply to the parental marriage involving three human beings.

Companimating can be valuable if it is used as a time for acquiring psychological skills and know-how, not just for being a marital partner but for being a partner in humanity. What is needed are human relations skills that we use not only in marriage but in all relationships—spousehood, parenthood, jobhood, and humanhood. A person who functions well in interpersonal relationships with friends, on the job, in the community, will function well in any style of marriage. It is impossible to separate functioning in marriage from functioning in every area of human relationships.

Actually, contemporary companimating is offering less solution to marital problems than to *divorce* problems. Should companimates tire of each other or find that they cannot get along—and many of them do—the arrangement certainly makes the ending of a dissident relationship easier and less costly than old-style divorce. The psychic pain, for many, turns out to be just as great. And so, oddly, the living-together arrangement might be considered to benefit companionate divorce more than companionate marriage.

Dr. Sidney M. Jourard, professor of psychology at the University of Florida and author of *The Transparent Self,* has suggested that all couples, married or not, pay a regular sum into a federal fund that would take the place of alimony and provide interim support to a woman after the breakup of a relationship, until she could get on her own feet financially.

What it comes down to is that the rules, regulations, expectations, obligations, responsibilities, and genderizing of marriage need to change first. No matter in what kind of setting it takes place and by what name we may call their relationship—whether it is between two people "pair-bonding" in their own quarters, in a college dormitory, or as part of an extended family in a communal setting, whether it is credentialed by society or not, whether it's woodsy or citified, a man and a woman need to begin living the new ism of equalism for the institution of marriage to be entitled to a building permit.

It is less the *form* of a marriage than its *content* that determines its worth. Before two people join together in whatever style of living arrangements, the most important consideration in evaluating desirable traits for mates is to become aware that the other person is one who will not seek to "own" us or to tread on our freedom to grow. Once that pleasant tension in the groin indicating sexual arousal subsides and we get our heads back on straight, here are some things about a potential partner we might take a look at in order, hopefully, to enter a relationship which turns out to be ego-enhancing and not ego-assaulting.

Self-esteem. A person with low self-esteem feeds on a mate and expects the other person to provide the lacking self-esteem. A living companion who needs excessive reassurance of his or her worth becomes a drag on one's life. No one can give anyone else his or her self-esteem. We each need to establish it for ourselves. Women especially, who have been taught by the culture from birth on that they are inadequate, incapable, don't measure up, and that they don't need to develop their abilities because a man is going to come along and take care of everything for them, are apt to have few sources of self-esteem, unless they "get with" women's liberation and begin to realize how much they are capable of doing.

Sense of humor. Humor falls into several categories—man against man, man against nature, man against society, man against fate, man against underdog or minority. Beware of anyone whose sense of humor gets its kicks from remarks of sarcasm, cruelty, or other put-downs. The double-level message such a humorist is giving out says: "In order to feel good about me, I have to put you down, but I'll do my putting down in the guise of humor. That makes it okay." Sarcastic humor is deadly and ego-assaultive to live with day after day. Sarcasm is like a pinch of the psyche, the subliminal version of a cruel pinch of the body.

Pattern of apportioning or spending money. The myth is that well-to-do people will have no money problems. What really counts is not how much money there is but the psychological pattern of spending or apportioning it. The woman who thinks she'll have life easy because she marries a rich man is in for a shock if she learns that he is a player of a psychological game called Deprived in which he hoards money, saves all of it for tomorrow and enjoys none of it today. Some husbands, having control of the money, go out and buy whatever they like; the wife must first endure a financial cross-examination to find out if she really needs it or is merely being self-indulgent.

Pattern of apportioning or spending time. "He spends more and more time at the office. He comes home late from work. Sundays he sits in front of the TV set all day. He's never too tired to spend a night out with the boys, but he's too tired to go anywhere with me." These are common complaints about the apportioning of time in a marriage. Underneath the feeling that she is a neglected wife is often a woman who really wants some time-and-attention stroking and nurturing from a husband. If she got even a little, she'd be satisfied. But because she doesn't get even that little bit she craves, she keeps on feeling unhappy about how much time he spends away from her, in business, with male friends, etc. It is often not so much a block of time we seek from a mate; it is the psychological stroking and nurturing we really want.

In retirement, many men who are around the house all day make inordinate demands on a wife's time. One wife says: "I hate my husband's retirement. I have twice as much husband and half as much income."

Intellectual stimulation. As we have seen in an earlier chapter, our intellectual stimulation is apt to come less from a mate than from social occasions we attend together. Understanding this, we have more realistic expectations of each other and of our need to have some outside activities that bring us the stimulation we desire.

Sensual need as differentiated from sexual need. Every experience of touching and of physical affection need not wind up in the sex act, nor do many of us want it to. We often have great sensual need and want to be stroked and caressed and babied, even when we are not feeling sexual. It is a frequent complaint of spouses to marriage counselors that their mates absolutely do not understand this and seem to think that every physical approach must be sexual. "In our largely 'touch-me-not' culture we use sex as the coin to buy skin," says counselor Emerson Symonds.

Friendships. Do you like each other's friends or merely tolerate them? Are they relationships that elevate or drag you down? Friendships aren't worth maintaining unless they provide growth for all concerned. If one is always giving and the other always taking, that's not friendship, that's human usury.

Sense of exploration. It is the childlike parts of our personalities that find fun and wonder and awe in new experiences. Does your inner "fun kid" and your mate's "fun kid" have fun together? Or does one or the other douse this beautiful sense of excitement and wonder with that icy squelch: "Don't be so childish!"? One of the earliest signs of breakdown in a relationship is when the "fun kids" of the two people are not having any fun together any more as they did in the courtship stage.

Morning person or night person. We are learning more and more about our inner biological clocks, our diurnal rhythms. It is easy for a morning wife and a night husband, or vice-versa, to be frequently out of synchronization. Knowing this, solutions could lie in going to a party in two separate cars so the morning person can leave earlier and go home to bed. Or the morning person, anticipating a late night, could schedule a rest time or nap late afternoon or early evening. Adjustments in sex lives are necessary when the morning person is asleep by 10 P.M. and the night person is wide awake and reading in the living room until 1 A.M.

Auditory person or visual person. Some of us learn better through our eyes, seeing and reading. Others learn and enjoy more through hearing, such as listening to tapes, to music, to the radio, or to a lecturer. A visual mate may prefer to stay home and read a book while an auditory mate might prefer to go hear a lecturer talk about the same thing. An auditory person and a visual mate, having exactly the same experience, may each perceive it quite differently. They could then accuse the other of lying, distorting, or of not paying attention. Each of them has truly perceived it differently according to whether they are primarily "eye or ear" learners.

Memory. We remember what we *want* to remember. Do you find yourself constantly needing to remind a mate of appointments, social engagements, promises, anniversaries? Poor memory could indicate lack of commitment or of caring, or lack of a sense of responsibility or obligation. "You have to forgive me, I have a lousy memory," is a racket. The person who wants to remember and may have difficulty doing so, will write it down not once but in several places.

Dr. Solon Samuels says that the human organism has two basic needs which it seeks to have fulfilled in relationships with others, whether they be partners, parents, friends, relatives, or whatever: comfort and excitement. Comfort includes both the psychic comfort of being able to be relaxed and not having to be defensive, frightened, hostile, or resentful, and the physical comfort of creature pleasures. The excitement we seek is pleasurable excitement that evokes a feeling of "Whee, isn't this fun or great!"—not the excitement of fear or danger.

Should a relationship between two people lack this comfort and excitement, and should it also deny either one the freedom to grow, then the pair themselves and society should all look askance at their coupling. Courtship behavior gives enough clues to recognize such probability. Studies confirm that problems or boredom in courtship do not get resolved but only deepen and grow worse in marriage.

At the announcement of a pairing, instead of proclaiming our romanticized, fairy-tale-burdened idea of marriage from the past— "Ooh, how beautiful that these two people are joining together"— what society ought to be saying is: "How sad that these two people are about to get together and start depriving each other of the adventure of growing." Reversing what we do now, such marriages ought to be commiserated and the ending of them celebrated, by a humanistic society.

Free to experience and to enjoy growth, marriage, in the words of Los Angeles marriage counselor Allan Spotkov, "can become a continuous learning process, a relationship between two people who feel that by living intimately they can each accomplish and perform satisfying work in making this world a better place in which to live not only for themselves but for others."

Pairing rites of the future might well include this credo for companioning:

I Free You to Be You

Each freedom I give to you begins with me.

Each freedom I give to you—to be, to do, to experience, to think, to feel, to touch, to taste—I have first given to myself.

I grow and expand as a human being in proportion to how much I help you to grow and expand.

And because that to which we give of ourselves is dearer to us because we are a part of it, you are dearer to me because of the freedoms you are helping me to give to myself.

7

The Six People in a Marriage

No matter what the form of a marriage, be it legal or companionate, the difficulty in its content usually begins with the fact that there are actually six people who embark upon every marriage. The sexual revolution has not yet changed that fact.

These six are the husband, the wife, and their two sets of parents who reside in the heads of the couple no matter how distant in geography or chronology they actually may be, and who often rule in absentia the marital life of the pair. One marriage counselor calls these parents "the fearsome foursome."

These four parents have indoctrinated their children with messages and injunctions to do and don't, to must and must not, to ought and ought not, to should and should not, about husbanding, wifing, sex, money, child rearing, education, and housekeeping, which they absorbed in their childhood from their parents who learned it in childhood from their parents who learned it in turn from their parents. Thus there is passed on from generation to generation obsolete ideas and values—bits and pieces of antiwisdom—constantly repeated reflections from some dark, cracked mirror of the past.

The clashing ideas and values of all these parents with their varying backgrounds and ethnic and religious origins make many couples combatants on a battleground of marriage as they unceasingly try to bend a spouse to fit the mold of parental messages inside their heads.

Many husbands today were reared and indoctrinated at a time when the children, kitchen, church *(kinder, kuche, kirche)* philosophy of womanhood was the predominant one and they still carry into modern marriage this obsolescent message about what women are *supposed* to be. A wife who could be speaking for millions of women has said to her husband, "I feel as if I'm married not only to you but to your father, your grandfather, and your great-grandfather, and I'm supposed to please all of you."

American women perform an amazing amount of drudge work, keeping intact maternal messages about housekeeping. Millions of exhausting woman-hours are spent by females who regularly get down on hands and knees or wield mops to shine their floors, carrying out messages that worthy housewives have shiny floors. About forty million American women are full-time homemakers, still acting out their variation of that nursery rhyme, "Rub-a-dub-dub, scrub-and-scrub-scrub, this is the way we wash our floors, wash our floors, wash our floors, just like mother told us we ought to."

An Italian architect visiting the United States has commented that nowhere but here do housewives have such an obsession with shininess. All that dedication to shine doesn't do a thing for American housewives. It still doesn't earn them official government acknowledgment as contributors to the gross national product.

Early in life a script of marriage is prepared for us by what we observe in our parents' marriage. There is, says family therapist Virginia Satir, "an amazing parallel between the interactions of the spouses in the families of origin and the interaction between the present marital pair."

We are all casting directors on the stage of life, seeking players to cast in our scripts to help us carry out messages and injunctions. When we find ourselves attracted to a man or a woman, the first question we might ask ourselves is this one: "In what role am I casting this person, expecting him or her to help me act out my script?" The people to whom we are attracted and with whom we believe ourselves to be in love often are those whom we subliminally feel will help us to act out our scripts of marriage.

For instance, a boy child, observing his father stingily doling out money to his mother and making her account penny by penny for her expenditures—a common practice in past marriages—may seek out and marry a girl whose own script of marriage calls for a female to be browbeaten and who will put up with the demeaning way money is handled in her marriage, meanwhile stewing about it internally just as her mother did. Their neurotic life scripts will fit perfectly together.

Such a young man's message about women and money may be this common one: "Women don't know how to handle money. So a man has to control the purse strings and dole it out." This message has come down through the generations, derived from a time when women were not permitted to go to school and truly did not know how to handle money because they had never been taught simple arithmetic. Some generations later, a male marries while still carrying this parental message in his head. Trouble begins, of course, because the time is then the 1970s, not the 1870s, and the woman he marries has been taught the same arithmetic in school that he was taught.

Life With Father, one of the longest running plays in the American theatre, based on recollections by Clarence Day of his family in the gaslight-and-spats era of the 1890s in New York, made much capital of this message, depending for a good deal of its humor on the mother's idiocy about money and charge accounts. Millions of theatergoers chuckled appreciatively at mother's charming stupidity which reinforced their message about women's inability to handle money.

To help identify what your own script of marriage might be, ask yourself how you would complete these sentences:

All women (or all men) are ——

All wives (or all husbands) are supposed to ——

A male who would finish the first sentence by saying "All women are weak, whining, demanding, unreasonable, or vain" (a message he received from father) is likely to select as a spouse a woman who already fits this description or—if she doesn't—he will behave toward her in such a way as to program her to react this way, feeding her the right lines in their script of marriage to make it come out that way. He may withhold compliments when she looks pretty and when she asks, "How do I look?" he decides, "Father was right. All women are vain." He may withhold money and when she asks him for some, he can say, "Father was right. All women are demanding." Father is actively one of the six people in that marriage.

A male who would finish the second sentence by saying, "All wives are supposed to do the shopping, cooking, meal-planning, cleaning, to make love whenever a husband chooses to, to be economical, do the laundry, come to the husband for the weekly household money [instead of his giving it before being asked], and always put husband's and children's needs ahead of her own," enters marriage with such parental messages recorded in his head. He then finds that liberated women may hate shopping, cooking, cleaning, will refuse to make love unless they too are in the mood, often earn their own incomes, expect husbands also to press the buttons that run washing machines and dryers, and insist on their own needs being right up there on a par with needs of husband and children, *if* they choose to have children at all.

A wife whose message says "All husbands are supposed to carry out the garbage cans" will fret because her husband comes home from work too tired to do so. Her message derives from a past time when garbage collections were more infrequent and when garbage cans were often too heavy for a woman to handle. The updated facts of life would tell her that she can buy a hand truck or dolly and easily wheel the cans out herself. If her husband is reluctant to do this chore, which *all* husbands are expected to do, that must indicate some lack of feeling for her. Somehow this message from her mother about the man handling the trash cans becomes equated in a wife's mind with her husband's degree of devotion to her and to their marriage. Her mother is one of the six people running that marriage.

Many marriages are marked by the need of spouses to re-create family situations similar to those from which they came. The spouses are thus enabled to act out unresolved tensions and angers and to finish the unfinished business of their childhood. The marriage becomes a rerun of familiar scenes, cast, and script, and usually produces the same kind of pain their parents suffered in their marriages.

Dr. Ivan Boszormenyi-Nagy, director of family therapy at Eastern Pennsylvania Psychiatric Institute, says: "If you're a child and leave home with unsettled accounts, you may later punish your mate or children to settle that old account."

We may act out our script of marriage in either of two ways. In one way, we re-create the same conditions and personalities in our own marriages that our parents had. A woman marries an authoritarian tyrannical man and then goes through life submissively, quietly hating him, as her own mother did. A man marries a career-minded woman who spends a lot of time outside the home, as his mother did, and then constantly complains that a woman's place is in the home, as his father did.

In the other way, we cast in our script of marriage those people on whom we can act out the leftover unfinished business from our childhood. A boy who was enraged at his mother for divorcing his father and thus depriving him of his father's daily attentions and companionship grew up with a script of marriage calling for him to punish women because of what his mother did to him. Three marriages and three divorces later, he was still tyrannizing over women, attempting to finish his unfinished business of rage at his mother. In the same vein, a woman whose meek mother took a lot of harassment from her father, never standing up to his verbal abuse, in turn married a meek man whom she constantly berated and put down, doing to her husband what she wished her mother would have done to her father. It is the parents in the heads of such spouses who are among the starring players in the *dramatis personae* of these marriages.

In sexual relations, six people in a marriage make for a crowded marriage bed. Often "in bed" with a couple are four parents of varying degrees of prudishness, Victorianism, and inhibition, along with their antisex messages, both overt and below the surface, that the husband and wife have been bombarded with since infancy.

Even a family in which sex is never mentioned nevertheless gives out a strong message. Its subliminal message is that sex is a hush-hush dirty affair. A child in such a home may well conclude that those powerful pleasurable feelings he has are probably bad ones and that he's wicked for having them.

Transfer this to the marriage bed and you get such results as those reported in a study by sociologist Robert Bell of Temple University: that a fourth of American married women are dissatisfied with their sex lives. Or the revelations of some husbands to marriage counselors that the chief reason they go outside their marriages for sex is because their wives are unwilling to be experimental about sexual positions, the locale of the sex act, and use of different parts of the body. Many women carry into bed their parental messages that the only "nice" sex act is the customary one of male above female and they rebuff a husband's overtures for variations from that. Far more women than men still act out messages that oral-genital contact is perverted and many nonorgasmic women act out maternal messages that "nice girls don't enjoy sex."

Many men and women carry out parental messages even into old age. For example, we know now that the sex drive almost never ends. What does abate as we grow older is the frequency of desire; but people have sex urges as long as they live. The sensual pleasures of climax and of being stroked all over one's body may be just as intense in our seventies as in our twenties. But because of what we carry in our heads, some of us gradually cease to engage in sexual activity in our forties or fifties. Dr. Ralph Greenson, Los Angeles psychoanalyst, has found that a surprising number of older men believe their bodies are capable of only a limited number of sex acts and that they refrain from sex in order not to use up their life's quota! The exact reverse is probably true. The feelings of well-being from the hormonal activity and pleasure engendered by sex is a life-extender, not shortener.

All these parental messages and injunctions began way back in the superstition and ignorance of humanity's less enlightened past. They have come down to us through the generations as ennobled traditions. But since such traditions are often destructive of our capacity to grow and to enjoy, tradition must go. How to separate those traditions—which must go and which to retain—can be decided by a simple consideration. Any tradition which no longer contributes to humankind's physical, mental, psychical, and spiritual enhancement and which continues to genderize human beings' capacity has served its time and should be discarded.

Our society constantly works to update job and professional skills based on new information and new technology. We need to apply the same rules to marriage skills and demand that people take periodic courses in marriage-craftsmanship and "mating-updating." All education for marriage, no matter where given or at what age, should automatically include the updating to the present of archaic and obsolete data about marriage. Lesson number one could start with these questions: "What are the facts of husbanding, wifing, parenting, sex, money, in marriage today? How do today's facts differ from the messages in your head about them?" Homework assignment number one could be to write one hundred times Alexis de Tocqueville's statement from *Democracy in America:* "Amongst democratic nations, each new generation is a new people."

But tradition is a leech difficult to pry off the national body, and so it is likely that even after the sexual revolution has cleared away much other debris of the past, we will still find ourselves mired in the stresses imposed by the six people who enter every marriage.

8

Sex as a Weapon

As a result of the sexual revolution we are becoming increasingly aware of how important satisfying sexual expression is to our mental and physical well-being. As our new knowledge becomes woven into the social fabric, we may eventually stop fighting history's most unsung war—the one that men and women fight with their genitals.

Because so much of our sex tradition has been negative, denying us the right to fill this deep need except under stringently prescribed conditions, sex has often been a commodity in the marketplace of human relationships. Its bestowal or withholding has been the customary means by which many of us rewarded or punished. Underlying the sexual relations of many marriages has been a pattern in which one or the other spouse expressed this theme: "If you don't behave the way I want you to, then I won't let you have sex."

If we were to use the same behavioral dynamics with food, we would be permitting our spouses to eat only when we approved of their behavior and we would withhold food when their behavior irked us, saying in effect, "Go hungry."

Even pregnancy may become an expression of hostility in a relationship when a woman, knowing full well that the male doesn't want any more children because he already feels overburdened supporting the family, or doesn't want a child at all, has an "accident on purpose" with her diaphragm or neglects to take her pill, and creates one more mouth for him to feed. One wife, angry at her penny-pinching husband, became pregnant and offered him the choice of either paying for an abortion or supporting another child for years to come.

There is often an astonishing parallel between the way money is handled in a marriage and the way its sex is handled.

A penurious husband who tightly controls the money is apt also to be tight and hoarding in bed, concerned only with his own pleasure and denying his wife's physical needs the same way he denies her financial needs. An equally destructive pattern finds a male turning over his paycheck to his wife and then coming to her for carfare and lunch money, more like a child dealing with a mother than a man with his wife. Such a male may also come to his wife asking her to please dole out sex to him, the interpersonal relationship of their sex being exactly like the interpersonal dynamics of their money.

The "prostitute wife" using sex as a medium of exchange will withhold it unless her husband comes across with some "payment." In Los Angeles several years ago a man on trial for the courthouse slaying of his wife who was divorcing him testified that she refused on their wedding night to have sex relations until he agreed to buy her the expensive jewelry she craved.

As suggested in the previous chapter, it is usually not the amount of money that is available in a marriage but rather the pattern of apportioning or controlling it that is important. Since in most marriages, at least until the sexual revolution, the male is the primary or sole money-earner, he is also in control. Ostensibly, while the woman does most of the household purchasing and *seems* to be comptroller of the marriage finances, the existential reality is that the person who brings home the major share of the money, in this money-oriented society, is actually in control.

One of our society's most destructive ploys, as mentioned earlier, is the joint bank account which provides the vehicle, when the bank statement arrives, for a couple to play a monthly game of marital uproar in which one berates the other for carelessness in handling the checkbook, for neglecting to enter checks paid out, and so on.

In some marriages this has become routinized. The bank statement arrives. Husband goes over it and starts grousing about how the wife handles it. If he is dissatisfied with her handling of it, why doesn't he take on that responsibility himself, she asks. They quarrel and withdraw from each other verbally and sexually for several days, lying in bed with their backs to each other, careful not to touch. Then one or the other—and it is usually the same one in a repeated pattern of behavior—makes the verbal or sexual overture that results in temporary armistice until next month's statement when the routine is enacted all over again.

That money be in the name or in the control of the husband is a tradition that absolutely must go if women are to live with equality. No matter how minimal the balance a wife is able to maintain, even if it is just a checking account for which she pays fifteen cents per check and which enables her to maintain a low bank balance if that is what the family finances can afford, it is important that she have some of the financial autonomy necessary to feeling psychologically mature and self-responsible.

No person who has not had to do it can know how degrading and demeaning it is to *have* to come to another human being for one's wherewithal or to be expected to account for every expenditure as some archaic husbands demand of wives. Moreover, each of us is entitled to an occasional foolish or extravagant or unnecessary expenditure commensurate with family income. Making some such expenditure which we later regret is among the ways in which we learn to handle money. Certainly it is difficult to feel one's self a whole person if one needs constantly to come to someone else for money.

As more women go out to work and are contributing financially to their marriages, a new money-and-sex syndrome is emerging. It might be called "dough and drudgery." Such couples may have had good sex before marriage when the woman was not yet contributing financially or was not yet fully into homemaking responsibilities. But after marriage the woman begins to feel this way: "Here I am working, shopping, cooking, cleaning, doing the laundry, and paying my own way in this marriage. On top of all that you expect me to service you with sex, too!" Her constant resentment against her husband for his lack of cooperation with household tasks makes it hard for her to be aroused sexually by him.

One working wife who contributed financially was always burned up over her husband's expenditures for expensive sports and hobby equipment while she slaved away at work and at home and watched her own expenditures carefully.

Many working wives say that the one area in which they are finding it most difficult to get husbands to cooperate is with the drudgery of housework. These couples usually have to work out a satisfactory agreement about sharing not only the dough but also the drudgery before their sex improves. Any male who will not exchange some of his freedom from financial pressure by having a wife contribute monetarily, in exchange for helping her with some of the drudgery, ought to be labeled a marital illiterate.

The relationship between money and sex in marriage is beautifully summed up in this poignant shriek from the wife in the play, *Dark at the Top of the Stairs,* when her husband berates her for not responding in bed: "How can I fight with you all day about money and then feel like making love to you at night?"

One of the benefits of equality between the genders will one day see the end of money hassles in marriage. As women also work and contribute to what are called Dutch-treat marriages or living arrangements, money as reward or punishment for sex will get the burial it richly deserves.

(In another area of family relationships, that of giving allowances to children, some parents make the children ask them, week in, week out, for their allowances instead of dignifying the procedure and having the money, on time, in an envelope on a child's bed or desk. Children have pocket-money needs whether or not they've been "good" boys or girls; to reward a child for "good" behavior by giving it an allowance and withholding the money for "bad" behavior only teaches a child to place undue and unhealthy emphasis on money.)

Both male and female are capable of power plays in sex behavior. The female, choosing whether and when to insert her diaphragm or forgetting to take her birth control pill, can subliminally control the occurrence or frequency of sex. The male, subconsciously retaliating against his wife, is unable to get an erection or has an erection but goes limp upon entering, denying her the source of sexual pleasure she prefers to all others, that of having a firm male organ inside of her.

A husband-and-wife team of counselors who deal with sexual problems employ a psychodrama of the genitalia in which they have the penis and the vagina of a problem couple do the "talking."

Statements by the genitalia of many couples have a great sameness and familiarity.

"I'm too tired."

"I just had my hair done."

"You're an animal, that's all you want me for."

"After the way you behaved tonight, you expect me to reward you with sex!"

"I can't stand the sight of you, the kids, or the house. I'll run away if I see one more dish." (The person does "run away" sexually.)

"If you find the companionship of your friends so enjoyable, go to them for sex."

"You forgot our anniversary——my birthday——the children's birthdays——etc."

"You talk more to your girl friends than you do to me."

"You didn't even look up and say hello when I came from work."

"All you want me for is to bring home the paycheck."

"How come you weren't at your office when I called in the middle of the afternoon?"

"You danced so often with him that you made a spectacle of yourself."

"How do you expect me to look sleek like the girls at the office on the money you provide?"

"You forgot to pick up my shirts at the laundry."

"I will *not* go to your parents for dinner every Friday like clockwork!"

Nearly all such statements are variations of anger and hostility which result in denial of sex. Anger for being denied personal freedoms or finances; anger masquerading as hurt feelings of rejection or inattention; anger masquerading as depression over the monotony of housework and child rearing. One of anger's great masks is the one we call "depression"—which is often anger turned inward upon one's self.

Whether the sex in a marriage goes bad first, thus affecting other areas in the relationship due to the physical frustrations or disappointments, or whether the other areas go bad first, resulting in poor sex, is a perennial debate among marriage healers.

Dr. James J. Rue, Los Angeles marriage counselor, says that underneath the overt reasons couples give for marriage problems—child rearing differences, money problems, in-laws, personality clashes—are frequently two people who are unhappy with the sexual side of marriage. He believes poor sex causes many marriage differences. "You don't find two people coming in [to court] who have a happy, healthy sex life," he says. Similarly, the British Lawyers Council has said that it believes "sexual maladjustment to be the major cause of breakdown of modern marriages."

But Dr. John L. Schimel of the William Alanson White Institute of Psychiatry, Psychoanalysis, and Psychology in New York says: "It has long been believed by many that a gratifying sex life is the basis of a happy marriage. I believe that actually works the other way around: a gratifying sex life is the *result* of a happy marriage."

A good sex relationship is likely to be most determined not by what happens in bed but by what happens outside of bed, long before a couple gets to bed. When a couple's needs for empathy, affection, being listened to, for sensual and psychological stroking and recognition of individual worth, for the exercising of the autonomy of each personality in the marriage are well met, so, too, are their orgasmic needs likely to be well met.

When sex is not used as a weapon, a spouse's sex urge may sometimes be accommodated even if one is not in the mood at the moment, and it may also sometimes be turned aside without evoking hostile and punitive behavior or withdrawal. A spouse feeling the need could comfortably say, "I'm in the mood, how about it?" And the other could be equally comfortable either accommodating the spouse or saying, "Can you hold out until I'm in the mood, too?"

For mature people sex often is a healer providing release from the tensions of irritation with each other. A prescription to heal marital stress may well be, "Go to bed and make love not war."

9

How to Have an Affair
with Your Mate

It has been conjectured that possibly 90 per cent of all human endeavor goes into repairing deficiencies and breakdowns and only 10 per cent goes into new growth and creativity. We have been taught to accentuate the negative. A study by Earl R. Carlson, psychology professor at California State University at Long Beach, indicates that of all references to human emotions listed in the indexes of 172 textbooks on psychology published from 1877 to 1962, 69.1 per cent involved unpleasant emotions and negativism.

Applying this to the sexual, we might say that most research deals with repairing sexual negatives—impotence, nonorgasm, criminality, Puritanism. Much less concern is given to sexual positives, such as how to prolong the quality and pleasure of sexual experience for those who function fairly well, do not wish to go outside their marriages for variety, and yet who inevitably find some monotony in sex with spouses. Vast numbers of married people seek not to repair damaged or impaired sexuality but rather to keep alive sexual excitement with each other. Their goal, in short, is how to have an affair with their own spouses.

Pleasuring each other by massage is a method of stimulating sexual interest and excitement many couples have never tried. Achieving climax is not the goal, sensual pleasure is. If sex should result, that's fine. If it doesn't, it is not a cause for disappointment because orgasm was not the idea in the first place.

In pleasuring themselves, couples take turn massaging each other's bodies with soft cream, covering both front and back with long caressing slow strokes on legs, thighs, feet, abdomen, breasts, genital area, buttocks, knees, neck and shoulders. This may be done with a variety of positions, with one lying on the back and the other sitting between the open legs; or with one sitting against the headboard or the wall cradling the partner's back and massaging the other's body with one hand in the chest area and the other in the genital area.

The idea behind such massaging is to free our *sensual* selves as differentiated from our *sexual* selves. Sensual pleasure has been among our taboos, many of us having been taught to equate the sensual with the licentious. But one of the changes we are now experiencing as a result of the sexual revolution is the emergence of the Sensory Human for whom it is acceptable to have and to fill sensual needs. Not only acceptable but necessary. As we get deeper into brain research we learn that the stimulation of areas of tactile perception in the brain is necessary for us to have feelings of well-being, and that physical stress, irritability, and depressed moods may result from the denial of this sensual need. It is delicious throughout life to have this physical sensation of being "babied."

Engaging in such physical play can be a deeply satisfying new experience for many couples who have tended to rate themselves as failures unless every sexual overture ended in orgasm. Many people play a game that might be called Sexual Report Card in which they keep trying to attain standards of performance set in marriage manuals or by friends' boasts (frequently exaggerated) about how well they make it in bed. A couple may have a satisfactory and releasing sex experience but, accentuating the negative, they give themselves only a *B* or *C* grade. *If* they had done something differently or harder or softer or if a partner's orgasm was noiser, they might have earned an *A* on their sexual report card. But they never achieve that *A* because they constantly grade themselves against other people's alleged performances instead of what's comfortable for themselves.

Some couples find it helps to restimulate sexual excitement if they periodically re-create the scenes and activities they especially enjoyed during courtship, returning to the same motel room, or going out on dates right from work, or going on outings such as skiing, hiking, or ecology trips with groups of single people.

Our Noah's Ark theme of life which insisted that people go through life two-by-two-by-two has deprived us of the pleasure of being friends and associating with all kinds of people regardless of marital status. We need to start living a whole new social style in which people, single or married, participate in activities together. For married men and women it can be a rejuvenating experience to socialize with single people whose conversation is not about children, house repairs, and such domestic talk. The growing custom of calling women with the salutation of Ms. rather than Miss or Mrs. is a healthy one en route to removing human beings from the ghettoizing impact of "married" or "single." Living in a rich human mix undefined by marital status opens up whole new areas of enjoyment of life.

That truism, variety is the spice of life, is especially valid in revitalizing interest in sexually devitalized marriages. All routine and ritual, no matter how exciting at first, tends to become dull. The monotony of day-to-day routine, whether it be felt by the housewife who shrieks, "I can't stand looking at the same four walls," or the student who numbly feels as if he has been attending school "for a zillion years," may be among the early causes of mental and emotional disturbance. Human personality and physiology need a variety of experiences and stimuli to feel good. "Nature loves nothing so much as change," said Marcus Aurelius, Roman philosopher.

All of these ideas can bring variety into the sexual lives of married couples.

One is to engage in "pillow talk," a discussion of what you like or don't like in the sex act. The wrong degree of pressure at a particular moment is a common cause of turning a partner off. If a husband's pressure is too heavy or too light at the wrong time, take his hand and show him by applying pressure yourself, what feels good to you. Most people want pressure and finger play to be light and feathery at the beginning of the sex act and firmer after arousal. Not until they engaged in such pillow talk did one husband reveal to his wife that her heavy-handed pressure often made him lose desire. When he was a child, he had been scalded by boiling water. For months his mother and nurses had changed his bandages. Any pressure, except an extremely light one, set up in his nervous system the painful response of his childhood experience.

It is an anomaly that we live in a culture which is wide open in its blatant sexuality, but many couples have never once talked about their sex lives in the privacy and intimacy of their beds. Husbands have told counselors with some embarrassment that they are unaware of the location of the wife's clitoris; they report that they feel unmanly to have to ask her help in locating it. Never having been taught to engage in "pillow talk" and thus to verbalize their dissatisfactions, some women evade sex with such time-honored claims as: "I'm too tired." "It's my menstrual period." "My hair will get mussed." "The children might wake up." "My diaphragm isn't in." Because our sexual performance is so mixed up with our self-esteem, some men absolutely refuse to engage in "pillow talk" and become angry at wives who try to do so. They become defensive with an attitude of "What's the matter? Are you trying to tell me I'm not a great lover?"

When there are children and a husband has been coming home night after night, year in and year out, to a house with wife and clamoring youngsters, it is a great treat for parents to have the house to themselves once in a while on an unexpected occasion such as a school night. Children might be farmed out overnight to friends, relatives, or neighbors so that a mother and father can enjoy this unaccustomed pleasure. "In the seventeen years since our first child was born," a father of four exclaims, "I don't think I've walked into that house once after work and found it without children. I sure am ready for that experience."

It can also be a treat to have the house to yourselves for a whole weekend and to make love in different beds in different rooms. Or to use the unaccustomed privacy to shower together and to dance together in the nude to radio music. "We love," one couple says, "having no kids around and sex before dinner."

An exciting change in routine is also available if a couple has access to a private office where they can make love on the sofa or on the floor. A professional man whose small office building is empty on Sundays says that his office is the site of his best sex experiences with his wife. "There's a marvelous feeling of being in hiding from the world," he reports.

This same couple, who are innovative and experimental about

sex, like two children gaily exploring life's pleasures together, also occasionally pull their station wagon into the dark garage and enjoy having sex on the mattress pad on the rear floor. On a warm evening they also enjoy having sex on a blanket spread on the lawn of their enclosed private rear yard.

Varying the ritual by which couples tell each other they may be in the mood for sex also helps. Nearly all of us enjoy the process of being slowly and gradually wooed into sex. A frequent complaint of women is that the male makes love "like a jackrabbit, on and off, in and out, fast," and that what's lacking is ritual that would make the arousal gradual, prolong the pleasure of anticipation, and enhance the culmination of their act of love.

For one couple the question, "Feel like playing cards?" is an indication of sexual mood. This began unexpectedly once when they were playing cards with their feet bare. They found that rubbing each other's feet, legs, and thighs under the table as they relaxed over the game, was a delicious turn-on. One husband gets the message to his wife by hugging her from the rear and gently pressing his hands on to her breasts. The wife's signal that she "can be had" is to stroke the back of her husband's neck at the dinner table or to fondle the inside of his wrist or run her hand, under the table, along the inside of his thigh.

For a newly married couple who take turns setting the table and fixing dinner, the way one or the other sets the table provides a sex signal. If in the mood, they set the knife and fork together at one side of the plate rather than on separate sides. How urgent their desire may be, they communicate by a numbers game. "What number?" one asks the other. "Oh, two or three," which means "I'm pleasantly turned on but it can wait till later." "Six or seven" means "I'm getting close to wanting to go to bed now." "Ten" means "I've been thinking about it all day today, let's go right now, before dinner, okay?"

Fantasizing an ideal sex act, utilizing ritual and setting never before experienced and then acting out the fantasy is another way of revitalizing sexual pleasure. A wife describes her fantasy this way: "My husband and I would go for a leisurely drive on some backwoods road on a weekday when there aren't so many people around. We'd be relaxed, chatting, fondling each other's legs and thighs. Then we would to to a motel, have sex, fall asleep and then awaken and go dinner-dancing." Having formulated her fantasy into words, it was easy to carry it out.

Ultimately, under all human interactions, those relationships we enjoy the most are apt to be those which are our sources of three things:

1. Our greatest source of psychological and physical stroking.
2. Our source of interesting new knowledge and experience.
3. Our source of approval for the childlike part of our personalities that enjoys excitement, variety, exploration, and fun.

A "stroke," as psychoanalyst Eric Berne called it, may be any interaction between two people—word, act, look, gesture, touch, nod, gift, smile—whose double-level message below the surface is: "I acknowledge your personhood, your worthwhileness." Strokes may be for one's appearance, for accomplishment and achievement, for character traits, for one's presence, or for just *being*.

A teacher walking down a school hallway and nodding his head in greeting to a student has given that student a "stroke," acknowledging his presence and his existence. To pass that same student without acknowledging his personhood says, in effect, "You don't exist." A husband, returning home from work to a wife who is busy talking on the telephone and doesn't look up or nod or smile or wave at him in greeting, is getting this same you-don't-exist message when his wife doesn't acknowledge his presence in the house.

Again, accentuating the negative, we have been mostly taught to comment on those things in people which displease or irritate us and not to comment on the positive things worthy of stroking. A family counselor, asking a client, "What do you genuinely like about your husband, or wife, or children?" often draws a long silence or a blank stare. We have been so conditioned to report on what we *dislike,* the negatives, that we are often hard put to it to answer that question. Try it out yourself. Stop and think about what you like about spouse and children. Then ask yourself, "How long has it been, if ever, that I've told them?"

Feeling comfortable letting out the childlike part of our personalities is also related to continuing sexual pleasure in marriage. One of the early indications of breakdown in the marriage relationship is when the inner "fun kids" of the husband and wife cease having fun together any more because they have become mired in the marital meniality of hearth and home. Also, too often we confuse child*like* with being child*ish*. The child*like* part of a personality, the part that enjoys excitement, variety, exploration, new experience and adventure, is often the part that's the most fun to be with. Many husbands and wives turn each other off by saying, "Stop acting so childish," but it is our childlike parts that can keep the fun of sex alive.

And so these three factors—strokes, new knowledge and experience, and finding it acceptable to let out our "fun kids" without being put down for it as being child*ish*—are likely to determine whom we most enjoy being with. People can find in these factors a clue to a good sex life with their mates.

PART III

SEX OUTSIDE MARRIAGE

10

Premarital Sex

Among the major truths to out as a result of the sexual revolution is the one about premarital sexual activity. For thousands of years we have been preaching and teaching premarital chastity. For thousands of years the preachings and teachings haven't worked. In every culture, clime, and country, people have always treated themselves to sexual pleasures—premarital, nonmarital, legalized or not. A recent book on human behavior reports that premarital sexual relations are allowed in a clear majority of human societies today. We are now freed from the burden of promulgating one more hypocrisy.

Even the description *premarital* is in the process of change. Many sex alliances no longer end in marriage. Premarital is just one variation among styles of sexual relationships. To categorize relationships being practiced today we would need to define a maze of variations: premarried, nonmarried, comarried (as in companionate arrangements). Even these classifications will cease to have meaning as we stop labeling sexual experience as happening with or without the documentation of a marriage license.

During the sexual revolution a much debated question has been whether more people are engaging in premarital sex than ever before or whether we are just talking about it more openly.

In 1966 Dr. John H. Gagnon, then of the Institute for Sex Research at Indiana University, said he believed the percentage of those out of the total population engaging in premarital sex had increased only a little since the end of World War I when the so-called Flaming Youth of the 1920s sang this ditty about a popular writer of racy novels:

"How would you like to sin with Elinor Glyn on a tiger-skin?
Or would you prefer to err with her on some other fur?"

SIECUS (the Sex Information and Education Council of the United States) maintained in 1966 that it also believed there was a misimpression that a far larger *percentage* of people than ever before engaged in premarital sex. In a statement challenged by many who disagreed with its evaluation, SIECUS said that while we have a larger population and therefore a greater number of people engaging in premarital sex, the percentage of the total population is not much more than the percentage engaging in premarital sex after World War I. The 1920s, not the 1960s, said SIECUS, was the time of the greatest leap forward in permissive sexual behavior in the United States.

One of the ongoing conflicts in our culture is the one among some sociologists and psychologists who frequently engage in a numbers game in which sociology says: "Well, the *percentages* of those out of the total population involved in a problem is not so great"; while the psychologists say: "While the societal percentage may not be so high, the individual person to whom this may be a problem may be experiencing 100 percent of misery and anxiety."

Whichever side of the numbers game one chooses to play on, no matter what percentages one can cite, the undeniable facts are that there are far more human beings than ever before who engage in premarital sexual behavior and far more human beings than ever before who accept it. In the past, attitudes and behavior were divergent; now both attitudes and behavior are drawing towards the same common point.

This growing acceptance is largely divided by generations. In 1969 the Gallup Poll reported that the generation gap is dramatically evident in the views of Americans on premarital sex with a majority of people over thirty years old saying they were against it while college students approved it two to one.

A variety of polls among college students have indicated that about three-fourths of the women graduating from United States colleges said they were virginal when they entered school; only one-fourth were still virginal at graduation. The 1969 convention of the National Young Adult Conference of the Young Women's Christian Association has called for the dispensing of birth control aids to all women regardless of age or marital status. More than half of our college health services now provide contraceptives to students without parental consent. Throughout the world, doctors are prescribing contraceptives for unmarried teen-agers without parental consent; many have expressed willingness to make legal test cases if parents should object. In London in 1971 a physician making such a test was found "not guilty" of professional misconduct by Britain's General Medical Council for having told a sixteen-year-old patient's parents that she was taking birth control pills and he believed it was her right to have them. Among the recommendations to emerge from the White House Conference on Youth in 1971 was that all matters involving sexual behavior should be private ones, removed from the legal area.

There has been a gradual erosion of what sociologist Ira L. Reiss, author of *Premarital Sexual Standards in America,* labeled the "virginity paradox," in which young men once said they wanted to marry virgins, but then set about to render as many women nonvirgins as possible. More and more college men now say they no longer wish to marry virgins. Now they feel that girls who have had some premarital experience would make more gratifying sexual partners in marriage. The director of a computerized matchmaking service declares: "It's very hard to place a virgin these days."

The National Student Association has demanded dissemination of contraceptives, removal of housing restrictions so men and women can share living quarters, and removal of curfew and visiting hour restrictions in college dormitories. These newspaper headlines, typical of the sexual revolution, already seem to belong to an ancient age:

University of Pennsylvania to Let Coeds Spend Night
Dormitory Curbs on Women's Visits Ended at Columbia College
207 at Bennington College Defy Rules on Men in Dorms
Barnard Students Defy Curfew on Men in Rooms
Stony Brook to Establish Unlimited Coed Visiting
Students at Vassar Vote on New Hours for Men Visitors
Princeton Extends Hours for Women in Dormitories
Notre Dame Relaxes Policy on Women Visiting Dorms
Wellesley Group Proposes Dorms with No Male Curb

Many colleges have introduced these new freedoms into campus life, amidst a philosophical question that has never been resolved by American higher education: "What obligation, if any, does a college have to act *in loco parentis* (in the place of a parent) in the personal lives of students?" This question, much to the relief of college administrators to whom it had long been a thorny issue, is rapidly becoming moot, as more young Americans achieve adult legal status at the age of eighteen and as premarital sexual experience is joining the repertoire of human freedoms.

Not long after World War II, Sarah Gibson Blanding, then president of all-female Vassar College, said to her students publicly: "Vassar College is no place for a girl who indulges in premarital sex. Any girl who does so should remove herself voluntarily from school," a statement which she never lived down. Nightclub comics, taking up the line, would declare: "Ladies of Vassar College and your guests from Harvard and Yale: I would like to say that premarital sex is indecent, immoral, and wrong. Furthermore, I wish you'd stop doing it while I'm talking to you."

At that time, colleges had what were called parietal rules which said that when a college boy or girl visited in each other's rooms, the door had to be open a few inches and "all four feet on the floor at one time," a description which led to many hilarious bull sessions in which students would try to figure out ways of evading the rule by engaging in sex with "all four feet on the floor at one time."

Each year now colleges are instituting more coeducational dorms with no restrictions of any kind. Many students openly live in companionate marital arrangements. Far from adversely affecting the scholarship and the study habits of students, college administrators and parents are finding that such arrangements often inspire young men and women to work harder as they enjoy the intellectual stimulation and the availability of sex partners, and don't have to spend so much time on the logistics of the dating game. Educational institutions and housing arrangements which genderize humans beings into male and female living arrangements are headed for a niche in the history books.

What are the reasons for their attitudes given by holders of both pro and con views about premarital sex? Those who believe premarital sex to be acceptable cite these reasons:

1. The earlier physiological maturation of young people due mostly to improved nutrition and medical knowledge. A hundred years ago the average age at first menstruation of girls in the United States was seventeen. Today the average is twelve. "Today's teen-agers are a lot more grown up physically than their parents were at the same age," says Dr. S. A. Kaplan of Los Angeles, an authority on childhood endocrinology. Recent cross-cultural studies confirm that throughout the world the age of maturation for both boys and girls has steadily become younger during the past 300 years. In Bach's boys choir in Leipzig, boys stopped singing soprano because their voices changed at an average age of eighteen. London choir singers in 1959 showed the average age of voice change to be 13.3 years.

2. The invention of the pill, which social scientists report is having as profound an effect on human behavior as the invention of the wheel, freeing women from unwanted and unplanned consequences of the sex act, putting them more in control of their own destinies, pioneering their freedoms in all other areas of their lives, as well as the sexual.

3. Prolonged years of schooling for higher degrees in which more people than ever before are spending more years in higher education, thus delaying the time of earning a living and of marriage. College women are now marrying at later ages, taking time out first for careers and travel.

4. Intercontinental schooling with many of our young people spending semesters at schools in other lands and foreign students coming here, cross-acculturating the attitudes and mores of young people everywhere. For example, demands for coeducational housing on American campuses were spurred by the fact that American

students had enjoyed such living arrangements at Uppsala College in Sweden and the Free University in Berlin, among others.

5. The rejection of the strictures of institutionalized religion by young people who say: "Institutionalized religion does not fill any needs for me in the twentieth century, therefore I will not follow its injunctions against sex." At the same time, many young people are expressing religious belief separated from any formal institution. Dr. Cecil Hoffman, a United Presbyterian minister affiliated with the University Interfaith Foundation, says: "This is the most religious and socially concerned student generation in the more than thirty years I've been in the campus ministry. But students are probably less interested in institutional religion than at any other time."

Historian Will Durant has said that he believes the single most powerful idea to come out of the twentieth century will be the decline in institutionalized religion. By the twenty-first century he envisions that formalized religion will be practiced only in small pockets of the society, with services being held informally by people in their own homes. A similar view has been expressed by Dr. Gary Lease, young theologian at Loyola University in Los Angeles who predicts the crumbling away of institutional religion and the emergence of a "kind of polytheism," with each person taking the best from various religions, philosophies, and systems of thought, to give meaning to his own existence.

The concerns traditionally felt by those who prefer that we should teach and encourage premarital chastity include these:

1. Promiscuity of some young people. "The only way to avoid the damage done by casual sexual relationships is to be able to discuss freely the place that sex has in a serious relationship," suggests Dr. Lester A. Kirkendall, professor of family life at Oregon State University, one of our country's pioneer sex educators. The public image of youth who engage in premarital sex is that of carousing swingers. The fact is that the majority of them are engaging, or seeking to engage, in stable relationships, and that it is more likely to be some of youth's parents who are engaging in the kind of sex lives they ascribe to the young.

Dr. Ira Reiss, mentioned earlier, says that his wide study into premarital sex patterns reveals that a pattern of "permissiveness with affection" is practiced far more than "permissiveness without affection" among young people, but that it is the latter which gets sensationalized attention. Young people, like most of their elders, long for one "significant other" in their lives.

2. Rise in venereal disease. During the past twenty-four hours, it is likely that some 2000 people were infected with the microbes of syphilis or gonorrhea. Several persons are infected each minute. No communicable illness except the common cold afflicts more people than does venereal disease.

According to the American Social Health Association, an agency concerned with V.D. education and eradication, we are experiencing in the United States a pandemic, out-of-control epidemic. After World War II, because of the discovery of penicillin and other antibiotics, it was believed that man could forever wipe out this ancient scourge. In the 1950s, there was a drop in the number of V.D. cases. Much less need seemed to exist for research and education. Public health officials were comforted with the knowledge that a variety of antibiotics existed.

This began to change during the 1960s when V.D. rose sharply, due to a combination of causes.

● Intercontinental lives led by many people such as students on summer travels, or attending school in foreign countries; commercial travelers; airline personnel; and so on.

● Wide use of the birth control pill, resulting in vastly increased sex acts in which genital parts are not covered by contraceptives.

● Increase in homosexuality.

● The return to the United States of our military personnel from foreign countries in which many have been infected with stronger strains of V.D. resistant to existing treatments. During 1971 there was reported in California a virulent new strain of gonorrhea, known as Asian or Vietnamese gonorrhea, brought by men returning through West Coast ports. All known medications were proving ineffective.

● Lack of scientific knowledge about V.D. Gonorrhea in the female is almost undetectable. She has none of the symptoms experienced by a male: pus from the penis, frequent and painful urination. Women often pass on gonorrhea without knowing they have it. United States Public Health Agency researchers are now engaged in urgent research, hopefully to develop a method of detecting gonorrhea quickly in the female. Meanwhile, many physicians are recommending that all women, especially those under the age of twenty-five, be given routine V.D. examinations as standard medical procedure. Another research goal is to find a way to help dentists test quickly for V.D. should they see suspected V.D. lesions in the mouths of patients.

● The rising rate of divorce in which greater numbers of men and women lead sexual lives as single people with a variety of sex partners.

● The reluctance of doctors to report patients with V.D. to the U.S. Public Health Service, as required by law, because they do not want to embarrass patients with follow-up visits from health workers asking for names of their sexual contacts.

● More youth engaging in sexual activity, their lack of education about V.D., and laws which prevent them from getting treatment without parental consent so that some are denied treatment or choose not to get it, if that means they have to tell parents of their sexual activity.

About half of our states have now passed laws which permit minors to get treatment without parental consent. Some agencies are experimenting with programs in which minors may come for blood test and treatment and not have to give names of sexual contacts or even their own names. All that is asked is that they send in personally, without naming names, those with whom they have had sexual contact.

3. Aside from promiscuity and venereal disease, those who believe we should discourage premarital sexual activity are rightly concerned about premature parenthood through unwanted pregnancy. Margaret Mead has commented that it is not juvenile sex that's the problem; it's the risk of unwanted pregnancies.

We have more than a quarter-million babies, nearly all of them unplanned, being born out of wedlock each year to females from the age of eleven on up. In 1969 there were about 400,000 such births in the United States. According to population projections for the future, ten years from now there will be born out of wedlock each year in this country anywhere from a half-million to one million babies. One out of every six girls will be pregnant out of wedlock before she is twenty years old.

One school system alone, the New York City Board of Education, reported a 100 percent rise in pregnancies in the decade of the 1960s. Every major city in the country has inaugurated methods, such as tutors at home or on the telephone, special classes or special buildings, in which to educate pregnant youngsters. In January 1970 there was held in Washington, D.C., a conference which was described with the foreboding title of *First* National Conference on Parenthood in Adolescence.

What this says to us is that giving people sex education classes in reproductive biology, as many school systems have been doing, is not enough. Students laughingly call these "human plumbing courses." What is required as a result of the sexual revolution and what we are beginning to have in senior high schools is sex education in which contraceptives are shown to students and the discussion is therapeutically designed to bring them psychological insight into themselves and to help motivate young men and women not to be the victims of their own sex drives.

In 1971 a sixteen-year-old high school senior in New York, Hariette Surovell, testified before the National Commission on Population Growth and the American Future: "Our curriculum was severely lacking in a topic of vital concern to a large percentage of high school students: namely, contraception. . . . How can high school girls be expected to be responsible about using birth control when all knowledge is gotten on the streets? Many don't even have a clear picture of how babies are made. 'Oh, I thought you couldn't get pregnant if he only comes one time,' a girl once told me. 'You can only get pregnant right after your period,' said another. And then there are others who knew about the pill, so that they took their mother's, sister's, and friend's pills or they took a pill before they had sex or after they had sex. *Most girls just pray. . . .*"

All this makes us wonder what is wrong with us human beings that in a world approaching the twenty-first century, with all the freedoms that exist for the learning and the using, young women must assume an ancient posture of supplication to deal with their own bodies?

Some people cling to old ideas long after they have ceased to correspond to the facts. A segment of the population will always be cultural laggers, like the sole physician in a Texas town who "will not even discuss birth control." According to a news report, nine of the twenty girls in a recent high-school graduating class in that town received their diplomas pregnant.

For many cultural laggers there will come the painful dawn of awakening when they will look at the facts as *they actually are,* not fantasized facts they wish *would be.* Since we have each year more than a quarter-million babies born out of wedlock and more than that number of abortions of pregnancies of young women, there probably are anywhere from a quarter-million to a half-million American families—the families of all these young women—who each year are undergoing firsthand experience with the result of inadequate sex education, who are being catapulted out of their cultural lag into the realities of the present, and who are changing their minds about making contraceptives available to young people.

Sex education as we now know it is only a start. What we have, and there is not even enough of that, is bio-sex—biological—education. What we will inevitably have in the future is a combination of biological and psychological sex education, combined under some name such as "Sexological Education."

We have a great many people of all ages, not only teen-agers, who have had some sex education or access to sex information, who know about the fertility cycle and the reproductive process, who know about contraceptives and have access to them one way or another—through drugstores, family planning agencies, college health services, private doctors—and who still engage in acts of unprotected sex and become the losers in a game of Sexual Cops-and-Robbers—"Will I get caught this time; will I have an accident?" Lesson Number One in any class in sexological education might well get down quickly to the nitty-gritty of self-victimization. Why does this happen to so many of us?

In counseling sessions with pregnant teen-agers, among the reasons for unwanted pregnancy brought out with great frequency is a girl's subconscious wish to punish parents whom she feels have not been loving, supportive, or responsive enough. Girls often are testing the love of indifferent parents.

A report in the *American Journal of Orthopsychiatry* reveals that many pregnant girls "told of a new closeness and more attention from their mothers" than they had ever had before. One girl wept as she reported this. Her tears were not so much for her situation as an unwed mother-to-be; they were because the experience had shown her that her parents really cared about her after all. Testifying before the National Commission on Population Growth and the American Future in Los Angeles, a coed said: "I'll never forget what my father said when my mother told him I was pregnant. He said, 'I want you to know we don't love you any less than we did yesterday.'"

A seventeen-year-old boy became aware in group counseling of his subconscious anger at all women because he was angry at his mother, a social do-gooder who spent much time on civic committees helping abandoned children, but was rarely around when he needed to talk out his own feelings. He had made three girls pregnant before he realized he was using his sexuality to hit back at his mother. "Deep down I figured that one way to get attention from her was to make a few more abandoned babies for her to bother with."

Another common cause for premarital pregnancy, one that might be called the Snow White version—pure and innocent while having sex—is guilt, according to Dr. Addie L. Klotz, then the director of San Fernando Valley State College's Student Health Services in Northridge, California. Girls in this situation become pregnant because they feel it is a shameful public admission that they intend to engage in sex if they get contraceptives in advance. Sex is more romantic and they are basically nicer girls if it happens spontaneously without previous preparation for it. Secretly getting pills or being fitted with a diaphragm when they know parents disapprove carries a tremendous burden of guilt. Hiding the pills or diaphragms in purses and dresser drawers thereafter keeps feeding the guilt. It is almost a relief when they get pregnant and parents find out.

Dr. Samuel Black, a psychiatrist at the Florence Crittenton Home for Unwed Mothers in Los Angles, finds that some girls "block out" the risk inherent in unprotected sex acts and some even deny their own pregnancies until it becomes physically apparent, in a sort of "it-can't-happen-to-me disbelief."

Parents who unwittingly give out subliminal messages to their children can sometimes be the cause behind pregnancies. A father who had not been permitted much opportunity to date during his own teenhood would urge his son to get in all the "fun" he could before settling down. The father always talked in abstract terms of "fun" without ever mentioning the specifics of contraception to his son.

Margaret Mead believes that some mothers don't mind if their daughters become pregnant if that provides a way to get a daughter married, out of the house and off their hands so that the family doesn't have to worry about having an unmarried daughter around.

Wanting a girl out of the family nest may subconsciously motivate some parents who send seductively dressed girls off on dates and have never once talked sex education with them. The conflicting double-level message that parents may be giving their daughters is, "Be sexy but don't engage in sex." Not wanting to be thrust out of the family nest and to face growing up and making major lifehood decisions on her own may motivate a girl to get pregnant in order to switch dependency from one male (daddy) to another (husband).

Next to punishment and guilt, a common reason for premarital pregnancy is the need of the male to prove his masculinity. Reuben Pannor, a social worker at Vista Del Mar Child Care Center in West Los Angeles, author of notable studies on the young unwed father, has found that many of them came from homes that were female-dominated due to death or divorce or because the father had abdicated his responsibility, leaving the son with "weak or distorted masculine identity." Such boys often become involved in sexual relationships "to prove their manhood."

At one time the climate of social opinion said that the male was almost solely responsible for such an unfortunate occurrence as accidental conception. Should a woman become pregnant it was the male's obligation to help find and pay for an abortionist or to marry her and to assume all moral and financial responsibility for the child.

This climate of opinion is changing as a result of the sexual revolution and the growing equality of women. At a time when females, too, have access to contraception, they are also considered culpable for unwanted pregnancy. A girl wanting to hold on to a boy and thinking he will marry her if she becomes pregnant used to be a common reason for accidental conceptions, one that is no longer so prevalent as a single standard emerges and fewer men feel any such obligation. A UCLA student expresses the viewpoint of many males when he writes the following to the college newspaper:

"As things are, the burden of responsibility for pregnancy has clearly shifted. Before the pill, it was the male role to assume the precautions and the male responsibility to help with any undesired consequences. Now the girls have all the knowledge and the necessary wherewithal to prevent 'accidents' and so must accept the results as their own doing."

A girl who tells a boy nowadays that she is pregnant is less likely to evoke his compassion than his anger. "How could you be so stupid or careless?" is closer to what young men in such situations will think today.

Behind most accidental pregnancies among youth are people who seek self-esteem and self-worth. The boys want to prove how masculine they are; the girls seek to reassure themselves about how lovable they are. In a sense, they are victimized by all of us because they do not know that which our society has refused to teach them —to understand their own sexuality and the uses to which they unknowingly put it to fill deep psychological needs.

As Dr. Klotz summed it up for the National Commission: "Sex education is meaningless the way it is taught in schools today." We must teach people the psychological attitudes underlying their sexual behavior. Dr. Noni Brar Koch, head of Hawaii Planned Parenthood, has said: "Hawaii's abortion law is wonderful but prevention is even better."

4. Another concern of traditionalists who believe we should teach and encourage premarital chastity is the possible effect of premarital sex on postmarital adjustment. If we become conditioned to a variety of sex partners before marriage, will we be content with only one partner later on? Many believe that premarital sex varietism inevitably leads to postmarital sex varietism. Some social scientists say that this does not automatically follow at all. It has even been suggested that having premarital sex experiences might *lessen* the need or desire to do so postmaritally. Older divorced people who were virginal at marriage twenty-five or thirty years before say that the drive to experience more than one sex partner during their lifetimes was among the reasons why they felt impelled towards divorce, in order to have guilt-free and socially acceptable sex variety, as so many do at least for a while, in our subculture of divorced and single people.

In any case, concern about premarital and postmarital sex will probably become moot. As humankind increasingly acts out the philosophy of sex for recreation and not procreation, and since in many relationships there will be no legal ceremony to provide a line of demarcation between the two, the question of their morality will likely fade away. As a matter of fact, the line of demarcation in future relationships will not be based on sex; it is more apt to be based on the date when a comarital couple who have been living together decide to make the arrangement legal. The words *premarital* and *postmarital* might then be replaced by the words *pre-legal* and *post-legal*.

All such values are matters of social style and custom, subject to change. A child born about now, reaching its twenties or thirties by the year 2000, will have lived in a world in which "genital fidelity" has ceased to be a viable human ideal.

5. Breakdown of family and marriage is another reason commonly given by those who are against the acceptance of premarital sex. To attribute the breakdown of family and marriage structure to premarital sex experience is to lock the barn after the horse is stolen. Such breakdown began long before today's young people were born. It began because we are a twentieth-century, technologically advanced society, teaching and acting out nineteenth-century concepts of husbanding, wifing, parenting, homemaking, and family togetherness designed for agrarian life-styles when family groupness and productivity may have meant the difference between eating and going hungry.

When we bombard twentieth-century human beings with clashing nineteenth-century messages and maintain the nonsense that young people are biologically and psychologically "children" not yet ready for sex knowledge, the resulting explosion gives us our high rate of divorce, of suicide both attempted and carried out, of fathers abandoning families because they cannot endure the demands, pressures, and costs of raising more children than they ever wanted or should have had.

"We are a nation of children who are raising children," the late Dr. Nathan Ackerman, noted family therapist, said of us. When a society says to young people, "We will treat you like children," we get exactly what we have programmed ourselves to get—chronologically grown-up people who act like children.

We need to write ourselves a new self-fulfilling prophecy, one which says that future generations of young people who engage in premarital sex will do so like responsible adults, and then take action to make the prophecy come true.

11

Extramarital Sex

The sexual revolution is freeing us from one more burden of hypocrisy, that of pretending we are obeying the Seventh Commandment—Thou shalt not commit adultery. We in the western world have long made pious proclamations in public against extramarital relationships while, privately, we were not only practicing them but even making them gloriously tax deductible under the guise of "business entertainment" on corporate income tax returns. Adultery for the sake of hospitality is part of our generous national character, and the wheels of commerce are regularly greased in the world's hotel bedrooms.

Extramarital sex, legally called adultery, has always been with us. The word "adultery" is related to the word "adulteration," which means "to make impure by admixture." Thus, legally, a marriage was made "impure by the admixture" of another sexual being into it. Throughout history adultery has had, at different periods and places, greater or lesser acceptance, but we Americans in a centuries-long cultural lag are just now getting around to acknowledging it. The fact is that at no time has adultery been condemned everywhere. In some primitive cultures, adultery was believed to serve a socially useful purpose.

Mass adultery—practiced in orgiastic ritual as some group sex participants do today—was performed at planting time in the hope of assuring abundant crops, the planting of human seed being associated in the primitive mind with the planting of agricultural seed.

You'll recall that the origin of the word "fuck" was from the verb *ficken,* meaning to plant seed.

Another reason for socially approved adultery was to cure the barrenness of women who did not conceive in their marriages. Such women were brought to church to copulate with priests who, as God's emissaries on Earth, supposedly had powers to bring forth children.

Still another reason for adultery had to do with the sovereignty of the family unit, especially among some tribes. A married woman belonged sexually to all men—her husband, his brothers, and brothers-in-law—within the family unit. Single men could have access to their brothers' wives, especially when the brothers were away on the hunt for food.

Another aspect of what we might call adultery in the modern world is polygamy, still practiced by some Middle and Far Eastern rulers. A basic reason for polygamy is economic. It helps to perpetuate one's financial and political control of a country. King Ibn Saud of Saudi Arabia, for example, had four legal wives, forty-three legally recognized sons, and forty-six legally recognized daughters.

While such potentates travel openly with their several spouses throughout the world, they never bring more than one wife at a time to the United States. Our State Department specifically asks them not to bring more than one spouse here, for fear of alienating American public opinion. When Ratna Sari Dewi Sukarno, fifth wife of the late president of Indonesia, came to the United States for a shopping trip, she steadfastly refused at State Department behest to discuss her marriage as one of several wives of the ruler.

We Americans are hard put to it to give up our monogamy myth which we have carried around like a Puritan pacifier sticking out of our childish mouths since our nation's infancy. Back in the 1940s, Alfred Kinsey reported that people who were interviewed for his sex research were more reluctant to answer questions on their extramarital affairs than on any other aspect of their sex behavior. He did manage to elicit the information that half of American married men had extramarital contacts occasionally or constantly. During the late 1960s, the National Statistical Institute said that it believed 87 percent of our divorces were actually caused by adulterous relationships, no matter what the legal semantics of divorce may have cited as the causes. In the majority of cases, wives learned of husbands' affairs and rushed to lawyers.

In his book *The Hypocritical American,* published in 1964, sex researcher James Collier reported: "Adultery is a commonplace in America. It has occurred in at least half of our marriages and probably in three-quarters of them. About ten per cent of married men copulate outside of their marriages as often as twice a month or more. A higher percentage, ranging up to about a fifth of all married men, commit adultery two or three times a year."

Marriage counselors believe that the majority of people who seek counseling nowadays have had at least one extramarital experience, and many counselees admit to having such experiences regularly. Those who have not had any sexual contact outside of their marriages often say they have wished to have such an experience. Only guilt feelings and the lack of a suitable partner held them back.

Nearly all married people, if we were honest with ourselves, would admit to having some fantasy adultery. Most of us meet people at parties or through business whom we find appealing, and with whom we fantasize having a relationship. For many, it remains just that—a fantasy adultery—but for increasing numbers, the fantasy becomes a reality.

Is the desire for sex experience with more than one partner an innate biological need of the human being? Dr. Russell Lee, former director of the Palo Alto Medical Clinic, says an emphatic *yes,* declaring: "Marriage is unbiological. Monogamous marriage is a bizarre and unnatural state. Marriage does violence to man's biologically ingrained instinct for promiscuity, his strong drive for freedom from restraint, his need for new and changing experience."

Lord Bertrand Russell pointed out that "marriage is a *social* institution, not a *human* institution," benefiting the society more than it does the individual.

Many social scientists do not agree with these judgments. Man, they say, has successfully been conditioned to accept sexual life with only one partner—after all, that is still the way of life for the majority of people in the world today, at least overtly, and that when man has extramarital affairs, he does so less from biological need than from deep psychological need.

Still other social scientists say: "Yes, man is polygamous but he is being conditioned to accept sexual life with only one partner. That's the price he is willing to pay for modern civilization, for some of the comforts and conveniences provided by marriage." As

Bruno Bettelheim has written in his essay *The Imaginary Impasse:* "A certain bondage comes with settling down, certain freedoms and satisfactions have to be given up to win some comforts and some measure of security."

When people do go outside their marriages for sexual experience, what needs do they seek to fill? In recent years, many studies on extramarital affairs have been conducted by sociologists, mental health agencies, writers, magazines, and marriage counselors. Nearly all reasons given by the interviewees, who come from a variety of economic, social, cultural, and ethnic backgrounds, fit into the following:

● It is an outlet for hostility and revenge, for punishment of a spouse. While he is with an outside sex partner, a person may think of his spouse: "Boy, I'm sure paying you back."

● Sheer boredom. The person seeks some excitement to relieve the monotony of life and spouse. Some men, impotent with their own wives, function well with another woman.

● An attempt to recapture the excitement, the lost mood of youth, the thrill of first love, to turn back the years, to feel like a kid again.

● As an expression of philosophical belief. "I am emancipated. I am Bohemian. Sexual freedoms go along with all other freedoms."

● Because of imbalance in sex drives between husband and wife. In order to fill sexual longings that a spouse is either incapable or uninterested in filling, the other will seek an outside relationship. Many spouses in this situation make an accommodation to the outside affairs of their husbands or wives, and feel relieved not to have sexual demands made upon them.

● Rebellion against marriage, wife, society—some of the same characteristics as rebellion against parents, the thrill of doing something not quite right, legal, or acceptable. Some people actively enjoy the excitement of arranging clandestine rendezvous, secretly parking their cars, and so on.

● Unfinished teen-age business. Sex activity or play was harshly forbidden in childhood and adolescence, and so sex becomes more of a turn-on when it is performed in a forbidden setting with a forbidden person.

● As part of adult growth towards maturity. Conversation lying in bed afterwards may be as important as the copulation to such individuals. This is the reason for much adultery today. Couples who married young and may have grown away from each other have a desperate need to find someone with whom they have rapport, and yet there may be compelling reasons why they don't want to break up their marriages, having to do with children, finances, professional standing, status in the community, etc. *The Significant Americans,* a study of extramarital relationships made by sociologists John F. Cuber and Peggy B. Harroff, reports that many executives who do not want to jar their business and civic positions, maintain the facade of a good marriage with wives who also enjoy their position in the community, and meet their personal needs in discreet extramarital relationships.

• The need for affirmation of one's worth. This, too, is a powerful reason for outside relationships. Many couples tear each other down, but there remains a great need for psychological "stroking," which can no longer be obtained in marriage but which is achieved in an extramarital relationship.

A major motivation for infidelity, says Morton Hunt in his book *The Affair,* is the need for self-esteem which comes from knowing you are still attractive to someone else. This is one more indication of our desperate need to change the institution of marriage. What little growth there is for many people in the institution of marriage as we know it today! What loss of human personality and of human joy we keep perpetuating when so many worthy human beings who have made untutored choices of mates early in life proceed for years afterwards to destroy each other's ego-strength.

• Another reason for adultery is that it is often the thing to do, to conform, on a business trip. Some men say they feel pressured to use the services of a call girl at out-of-town business meetings. They may agree, for business expediency, without having any overwhelming desire for the experience.

• The pull of the biological drive to experience more than one person sexually in a lifetime. As mentioned earlier in the discussion on premarital sex, many people now in their forties and fifties were, following social and religious expectations a generation ago, virginal at marriage. "I think I would die if I didn't experience sex with more than just my husband for my whole life," one woman says, to justify her brief outside affair.

- The need for sexual varietism in position and locale which one partner may find distasteful. Many a husband cites his desire for oral sex as a reason for going outside his marriage because his wife is unwilling to experiment with sex in different locales and with different parts of the body. This reason is apt to become less important as more people free themselves psychologically from the Puritanical sex messages of our past which said that sex was acceptable in only one position—with the man on top—and in only one locale—bed.

- Finally, a common reason for adultery is that plain old chemistry in which we get a yen for someone, yet we love our spouses. For some this becomes the actual adultery, for others it remains the fantasy adultery. Such chemistry, for which there is no logical explanation, often evaporates after just one opportunity to be with a person who does this to us.

Whatever their reasons may be for entering into an affair, it has been confirmed that when men have outside mistresses, they often select exactly the same personality types as their wives. Dr. John L. Schimel, quoted earlier, says that "adulterous husbands are usually driven by nagging wives into the arms of equally nagging mistresses." Such men may have a need for nagging women in their lives to carry out subconscious messages from their fathers which say that all women are demanding, nagging, or bossy. These men will then set up life circumstances and relationships to make their fathers' messages come true.

Single women who consistently get involved in affairs with married men also have psychological problems, according to Dr. Dieter Kern, a German psychologist. He believes such women seek out men whom they know offer them no future. Having spent years in "back street" relationships as a man's mistress, they tend also to be lonely suicidal types in their later years.

It was well into the sixth decade of the twentieth century that the American people developed, as a result of the sexual revolution, a toleration for truth great enough to stop them scribbling the graffiti of the scarlet letter *A* for adultery across people's reputations. We began to admit that extramarital relationships happen—indeed, often—and we began even to forgive those souls, once considered wayward, who indulged in it.

It is certainly an indication of our growing tolerance that when a popular actor, Anthony Quinn, fathered three children by one woman, while he was still legally married to another woman, his public acceptance did not diminish in the slightest. A New York museum even ran a film festival of his work, with no public protest.

Contrast this with our country's behavior nearly twenty years before that, when actress Ingrid Bergman became pregnant by Roberto Rossellini, Italian film director, while still married to Dr. Peter Lindstrom. She was villified coast to coast, her movies were picketed, bookings of her films were canceled, and she was the subject of Sunday sermons in churches across the land as a scarlet woman. Shunned and excoriated by the American public at that time, she was told she was not welcome back on American shores. Some United States legislators even tried to pass a law banning her.

About eighteen years later when she returned to the United States to appear in a play in Los Angeles, Miss Bergman said to a reporter: "The moral climate has relaxed since I was the subject of scandal eighteen years ago. It is a whole new generation and it certainly has changed everywhere."

Another indication of social change in attitudes toward adultery is evident in statements from religious groups. The conservative New York Board of Rabbis has urged people not to rush into divorce proceedings because of a single act of adultery by their spouses. The British Council of Churches issued a report in 1966 in which it declined to condemn all extramarital relations out of hand. "One rule cannot cover all possible situations," it said.

The mass media abound with examples of this growing acceptance and tolerance of extramarital relationships.

Many films now present outside relationships in a favorable or pleasant light with participants suffering no guilt or punishment. One film, *Secret Life of an American Wife,* even suggested that a woman's sex life with her husband could improve after an outside fling. All this would have been unthinkable a few short years ago when the movie industry's self-censoring board would automatically call for punishment of such wayward actions in films. A sex strayer was never permitted to go unpunished.

An ad to businessmen run by a typewriter company says: "Sneak away with your secretary some afternoon this week (and come look at our typewriters)."

A lingerie ad warns, "Darling, in romantic Pinehurst, the husband you steal may be your own!" Roadside advertising signs, exhibiting unusual irreverence toward the Father of Our Country, rhyme: "George Washington/He did sleep here/But with whom he slept/It is still not clear." Hallmark greeting cards has reported that among its best-selling cards is one that says: "Wanted your birthday gift to be just right, so a secret agent is keeping you under surveillance to find out what you really need. . . . He says you need an alibi for last Tuesday night."

And in unprecedented reportorial frankness, *The New York Times,* interviewing wives of World Series ballplayers who are out of town traveling a good deal, asks them: "Do you ever worry that your husbands might be unfaithful while they're out of town?"

A *Ladies' Home Journal* poll in 1968 reports that seven out of ten American wives no longer believe a single act of adultery should be considered grounds for divorce. Psychologist Albert Ellis tells a meeting of the American Psychological Association that it now appears that in our Judeo-Christian society, "healthy adultery is possible," and he suggests that it might help restore devitalized marriages if the partners did have occasional outside affairs, a report which a few years ago would not have been run by most of the country's newspapers but which now receives serious coverage in the nation's press.

Dr. Judd Marmor, one of the country's foremost psychoanalysts, tells a meeting of the American Psychiatric Association that "coveting the wife of another may be healthful. A thought of infidelity a day (without guilt) may keep the psychoanalyst away," he paraphrases the old saying about an apple a day. Dr. Marmor made it clear that he was not for or against infidelity, but that people should not feel guilty if they had such normal desires as experiencing outside sex partners.

The theme of all writings on adultery in popular publications is also changing. The theme used to be expressed in shocked titles followed by lots of exclamation points, saying "adultery is wrong, under any and all circumstances." Now such writings frequently pose this question: "Under what circumstances may adultery be justified?" The leading magazines feature on their covers such titles as "When Can Infidelity Be Justified or Forgiven?" . . . "Is Adultery Ever Justified?" . . . "Some Married People Must Have Affairs."

Those life circumstances in which adultery is increasingly condoned include intense loneliness, as when a spouse is overseas or in prison or institutionalized for a long time (our military bases provide free contraceptives to wives of servicemen, with everyone pretending not to notice that a wife often comes for contraceptives even when her husband is abroad); being married to a spouse with a long terminal illness (at one time a spouse who sought sex while a mate was dying of cancer was considered beastly; now such behavior is often understood and accepted by many people who feel sympathy for the person married to someone with a years-long illness); when a spouse is a chronic alcoholic or drug addict and is unable to function sexually; or when a spouse is completely uninterested in sex and refuses to seek therapy and there may be good reasons for keeping the marriage going.

Dr. Joseph Fletcher suggests in his book *Situation Ethics,* mentioned in the Introduction, that the loving ethics of a particular time, place, and situation, of a particular set of circumstances, and not archaic church law, should decide whether and when an extramarital relationship may be morally acceptable. The rightness of any act, he suggests, is in the whole situation at that time and not in any single factor or ingredient.

Underneath this condoning of outside relationships by an ever increasing part of our population is the strong belief most of us now hold that an adequate sex life is needed for physical and mental well-being, and that one should no longer be denied this birthright of sexual experience if one's spouse is unable or unwilling to function.

Studies on adultery reveal, surprisingly, that people are much more willing to condone it when it is done for serious reasons than when it is a casual one-night stand. It is apparently more acceptable if it happens for serious reasons of marital dysfunctioning rather than for a week-end lark. Of the one-night stand, or short-order sex, people are more apt to say of a married man: "What's the matter, he couldn't control himself until he got home?"

Studies also reveal that strong remnants of the double standard still exist at this point in time, although its strength is waning as women's freedoms grow. Women have been condemned much more than men on the grounds that a homebound woman does not meet as many people as her husband does and so, in order to have an outside affair, she has to go out actively seeking it, whereas for the man, it crosses his path in the course of his work and his life and he is all too human if he is tempted.

Eight out of ten people who have told interviewers of their extramarital activities reveal they have met such partners through their jobs. As more women go outside the home to work, more of them are engaging in such relationships. According to the Institute for Sex Research at Indiana University, one out of every three American wives has regular or occasional affairs. Most of these women are not interested in ending their marriages; they do it out of boredom and often because husbands do not engage in enough foreplay and lovers do.

As social attitudes towards adultery change, so are our laws changing to keep pace. Modernized divorce laws no longer include adultery as grounds for divorce. Divorce on the simple grounds of "irreconcilable differences" now exists in a few states and will likely soon exist in many more. In the past, possible charges of adultery against a spouse were a constant threat, especially if the person were in the public eye. Nearly all such charges are motivated more by money than by morals. They are traditionally used to gain financial advantage in divorce settlements.

Before the new California divorce law went into effect, a famous television personality was accused in a divorce action of "Adultery With Five John Does," as a newspaper headline put it. Such an item appeared in the *Los Angeles Times* on September 29, 1965. Ten days later, on October 9, there appeared in the same newspaper an item that the star had now reached a financial settlement with her spouse who then withdrew his suit charging her with adultery. He "now has no reason to believe his previous allegations were true," said the report.

Actress Melina Mercouri, commenting on adultery laws which have often led to huge financial settlements for aggrieved spouses, said; "If you take a European woman's husband, she has nothing. But if you take an American husband, you make the wife rich."

Convictions on legal charges of adultery are rare but their existence on our statute books means they can be used as legal threats. In some states, when a married person copulates with a single person, only the married person is legally culpable; elsewhere, they are both liable to prosecution. In some of our states, in order to prove adultery, you have to show that "intromission of the penis into the vagina," in legal terminology, has taken place. Technically, sex play and masturbation to mutual orgasm do not constitute adultery. Merely the opportunity to commit adultery—two people being alone all night in a house with the lights out—is enough to make them legally culpable in some states.

Attorney Louis Nizer, in his book *My Day in Court*, tells of a couple in New York accused of adultery who were photographed in the nude in the bathroom in the middle of the night by a private detective. The charge did not stick because the couple said the woman had a headache and they were in the bathroom looking for an aspirin.

Does all of the foregoing suggest that adultery may soon be openly countenanced and publicly admitted, as a result of the sexual revolution? Strangely enough, no, not at this point in time. While our behavior and our attitudes about *premarital* sexual activity seems to be converging, this is not yet true of our behavior and attitudes about extramarital activity. On the biological level, our future has begun. On the psychological level, our past has not yet ended. We apparently have some unfinished business to work through yet from our Puritan past.

The anguish of a great many people whose spouses commit adultery seems infinite. A faculty wife at Berkeley writes an open letter to campus coeds: "Please do not enter into affairs with our faculty husbands. I for one cannot do my best at home when I live in this kind of terror, and I know many other wives who feel the same way." Wives of New Orleans policemen pleaded with that city not to have policewomen ride in patrol cars with their husbands. "The job is hard enough on policemen's wives without knowing that their husbands are cooped up in an intimate situation with a woman for eight hours a day," said one wife. Helen Gurley Brown, whose writings casually advocate infidelity for the single girl, when asked what her reaction would be if she ever learned her own husband was having an affair, said: "I'd die."

There is a vital difference between adultery and other types of sexual activity; that is the fact that three people are involved in each act of adultery. One is necessarily left out, unchosen. Our self-esteem, for the most part, is so mixed with our sexual perform-ance in our sexized society that to be knowingly rejected as a sex partner in favor of someone else has a unique psychic pain all its own.

Because of this deep pain still associated with adultery, even in this time of growing public tolerance, many marriage counselors, in a change from the once commonly held attitude that confession was good for the soul, no longer advise a spouse to tell all. Many advise spouses to keep the affair to themselves and to become better mari-tal partners because of it. In the past the guilty partner, telling all, would free himself of the pain by transferring it to his mate. The teller would be healed while the other spouse often suffered. In an article in *Reader's Digest* entitled "The Limits of Infancy" Morton Hunt says: "Beware the urge to 'tell all'—it's far more likely to drive people apart than to bring them closer together."

In order for us to deal with this contradiction between our be-havior and our attitudes, we find that we now need to update our language to fit contemporary behavior. We need to redefine the meaning of the word *promiscuity* which, for many of us, once meant having sex with more than one person in one's entire life-time. No longer do many people consider a variety of sexual part-ners and experiences to be "indiscriminate mingling or association," as the dictionary and as history define promiscuity.

The patterns of sexual behavior we human beings practice today fall into these three categories, whether it be heterosexual, homo-sexual, or bisexual: consecutive—concurrent—conglomerate.

Consecutive describes serial monogamy, which is the sexual pat-tern of the majority of people throughout the world today. Mar-riage, divorce, and then remarriage are in fact serial monogamy, in which people have one sex partner, end that relationship, and start anew with a new partner.

In the interim between the ending of one relationship and the start of a new monogamous relationship, there may often be a peri-od of *concurrent* sexual practice. This is especially so in the world of single and divorced people. Morton Hunt believes from his wide study of adulterous relationships—concurrent sex patterns—that the extramarital affair "rarely achieves balance and equilibrium, but nearly always is a cause of change. Nearly every adultery rela-tionship ends in its own termination or in remarriage." Thus the concurrent adulterous affair winds up in consecutive serial monogamy.

A small percentage of the human population has always chosen, and no doubt will continue to choose, *conglomerate* sex experience in a constant change of sexual partners, sometimes known as "short order sex," or in group sex or mate-swapping.

The psychological dynamics of group sex are different from those of an extramarital relationship. In group sex, both partners know and approve of the experience which they join in together. The traditional logistics of adultery—three people involved, with two "chosen" and one left out—does not apply.

If we were polled for our choice of what sexual pattern we would most enjoy, one that comes closest to filling our physical and psychological needs, it is likely that the majority of us would opt for serial monogamy, a consecutive pattern, with an occasional guilt-free foray into concurrent sex—an outside sex act just often enough to provide the stimulation of variety and with no greater commitment than that. Oddly, that is a continuation of the pattern we are living right now. The only difference is that we would do it openly with social and interpersonal approval, without guilt, as part of the social norm.

We are having serial monogamy in a divorce-and-remarriage pattern. We will probably continue it even when we no longer go through the ritual of legalized marriage. Serial monogamy provides many comforts and securities which people do not want to give up. One husband probably expresses the sentiments of many men and women when he says: "It's nice to be able to play the field occasionally, but it's sure nice to have a home base to come back to."

In the future, especially when humankind's longevity increases and many of us live to be 80, 90, 100, or more, humanity will probably cease to expect genital fidelity for such a long lifetime, or to feel hurt or threatened by its absence. No matter what the setting of the relationship may be—communal or private—and no matter who the personnel involved in the relationship may be—man and woman, man and man, woman and woman—most people will probably find themselves gravitating towards serial monogamy with intermittent episodes of concurrent partners.

That would take care of both the human being's polygamous needs and our needs for comfort and security.

12

Group Sex

Part of the contemporary human's search for more intense sensory experience has led an estimated one to two million American men and women into conglomerate sexual activities. Variously called group sex, social sex, swinging, mate-swapping, or couple-hopping, this multisexual subculture has rites, rituals, and language all its own.

Another of the results of the sexual revolution is the emergence of group sex from a verboten activity associated with orgies and perversion to an activity which is being seriously studied by anthropologists and sociologists as a permanent subculture in which some part of the population will always be involved. Reflecting this increasing study of swinging by social scientists is the growing tolerance shown by monosexual individuals who are increasingly nonjudgmental of such practitioners. "If that's their thing, so let them," is the emerging attitude. As a result, many people who are no longer concerned that swinging will affect their careers or community acceptance, now openly identify themselves in newspaper interviews and on television shows as players of the group sex game, and marriage counselors report that more clients unashamedly admit their participation in group sex as part of the sexual revolution's brave new freedoms.

Ms. Carolyn Symonds, writing an M.A. sociology thesis for the University of California on this phenomenon in our culture in the 1970s, divides multisexual relationships into two basic types: Recreational Swingers and Utopian Swingers.

She classifies as Recreational Swingers those who seek the experience in the hope of finding new excitement and stimulation in tired marriages; those who are tired of the clandestine rigamarole of extramarital affairs and want themselves and their spouses to knowingly have outside sexual relationships with no commitments; and those who feel the excitement and sociability of sex parties might help cure them of impotence or nonorgasm.

Recreational Swingers meet in large or small groups by prearrangement on a weekly, monthly, bimonthly, or biweekly basis, sometimes in private pairs and trios, sometimes en masse, to engage variously in heterosexual, homosexual, and bisexual activities. The word *swinging* irritates some. The married ones prefer to call it *comarital sex*.

Grouping is a great social leveler. Their nakedness often covered by the protective cloak of anonymity, participants might range from presidents of corporations to pressers in dry-cleaning plants, from Ph.Ds to high school dropouts. Men and women who might scorn social contact with others when clothed may find themselves, when naked, taking part with them in the same "pretzel," "flesh pile," or "daisy chain," as the assorted postures of group sex are known to the initiates.

Utopian Swingers are more apt to find their way into group or communal marriages which often have an idealistic goal of greater fraternity and brotherhood and seek to cure the sick institution of marriage by experimenting with new ideas and new ideals. One notable group begun by Larry and Joan Constantine mentioned in the chapter on companionate marriage, frequently appears on the programming of such professional organizations as The National Conference on Family Relations to present arguments in behalf of group marriage and extended families as solutions to family breakdown. Utopian Swingers, a name they dislike—they prefer the descriptive *group marriage*—are looked upon with respect by many social scientists who believe they are dedicated and courageous people, pioneers in the marriage styles of the twenty-first century.

By far greater in numbers than those in group marriage, Recreational Swingers, also known as Organizational Swingers, are often strangers who meet through coded advertisements in swinger magazines and central clearing offices with postal box numbers. They may be screened in advance, are known mostly by first names, and may come from distant cities. Wealthy or prominent persons who may be known by sight in their own communities may fly to distant cities, sometimes in private planes, for a weekend of group sex with strangers.

A smaller number of swingers prefers to operate in "closed" groups whose members do not advertise. Couples who enjoy each other's company socially as well as sexually may meet periodically in each other's homes, with their children circumspectly trundled off to relatives for the night or weekend.

Charles and Rebecca Palson, a husband-and-wife team of anthropologists who joined swinging groups out of personal and professional curiosity and reported their findings in a piece entitled "Swinging in Wedlock" in *Trans-Action* Magazine found that a few of these couples form close and enduring relationships, host each other's children, celebrate birthdays and take vacations together, and have some degree of emotional involvement and long-term friendship within their closed swinging group.

But in the average closed group the dropout rate is high and recruiting new members is a constant problem, deciding who will do the recruiting, who might be invited, and how best to approach new couples so they are not offended or repelled. "Part of the fun of the group for me," says one man, "is sitting around gossiping about whom to invite. We're like a bunch of kids, laughing over the reactions we anticipate getting from people we know if we walked up to them and invited them to swing." Recruiting among single men and women is discouraged in closed groups because singles cannot always provide a person to even out their numbers and because singles may be looking for a mate to marry, threatening the existing marriages.

Whatever their modus operandi may be, the mores of group sex, often unstated, are that the woman is expected to take care of contraception. Occasional pregnancies do occur, with the woman sometimes not sure who fathered her child—her husband or a group partner. It is not considered "cricket" to charge a group sex experience with having caused a pregnancy. A woman's menstrual period or a vaginal infection at a time when a party has been scheduled raises the question of whether the husband may go without her. Based on the rule of "each one must bring one" to even up their numbers, many parties will not permit one spouse to show up if the other is indisposed.

A typical group sex party begins with socializing and drinks as at nearly any social gathering. Gradually, those who wish to do so may start to undress or to fondle another while clothed. A woman at a large anonymous swing has the implied right to say No to a man who makes an overture (beginners, unaware of this implied right, have been known to hide in the bathroom to avoid men who don't appeal to them). The interaction may be either "open"—that is, sexual activity going on simultaneously among many people in the same dimly lighted room and where the groans, sighs, and moans of orgasm are often a turn-on for others in the room; or a "closet" arrangement where one or more couples pair off in separate rooms. An open door to a room means others may come in and join the sex mix; a closed door means "stay out."

While group sex is the antithesis of what we have been traditionally taught is the way to a deep and abiding relationship between a man and a woman—monogamous devotion—there are couples who say that swinging not only enriches their marriage but actually helps to hold it together. The excitement of sex with strangers reflects itself in the excitement of their sex lives together between outside liaisons; swinging has brought a whole new source of secretly shared pleasure that makes them dearer to each other. "To one degree or another," the Palson research team found, "many swingers naturally develop towards a more secure kind of marital relationship, a tendency we call *individuation*,"—growth in the marital bond of an individual couple.

But many swingers, unable to deal with feelings of jealousy about spouses in sexual activity with others, or with increasing fears of their own inadequacy when they see the sexual prowess of others, find that the experience only results in making the mattress of marriage even creakier. Indeed, the growth of group sex is giving rise to new specializations in the field of marriage counseling—counselor to group or communal marriages and counselor in the problems of swingers.

The problems bringing a group couple to a counselor's office stem most often from one partner wanting to initiate or to continue participation and the other wanting to avoid or end it; or one of the partners becoming emotionally involved with a group sex partner —which is not playing the game according to its unspoken rules.

Much as group participants may disclaim ever feeling jealous, in more introspective moments many admit to the inevitability of such feelings. It is their inability to deal with such feelings that signals the beginning of the end of group sex for some. One or the other is just too threatened. Confirming how difficult it is to deal with such feelings, "The Man and Woman Thing," a report of idealistic family experiments which appeared in *Look* Magazine for December 24, 1968, says: "Most of these family experiments that shared bed partners broke up during the four months of our coverage."

In statements made by swingers to interviewers, one can discern a pattern of disenchantment and disappointment and often of pressure from a spouse to continue an activity in which the other spouse has lost interest. *Newsweek* Magazine in its June 21, 1971, issue reported on group sex throughout the United States, in general, and on one couple who run a human swap meet, in particular. The husband said: "Maybe swinging doesn't always save a marriage, but our marriage would be stifling without it." His wife is reported as disagreeing on whether swinging can help save a tired marriage. "I don't think it's the answer."

Underneath the image many groupers try to convince themselves of—that it is fun and games—is the reality that it often may also be fears and qualms. Fears that children, friends, relatives, neighbors, bosses, or co-workers might turn up among strangers meeting for sex haunt many. Fears of being raided by police or infiltrated by police agents are constant. Venereal disease, while easily treated, is not easily tracked down when participants use only first names or false names and come from other cities.

According to studies of swingers, it is usually the husband who initiates the group sex with his wife (a magazine headline asks: "How Can I Convince My Wife To Go into Swinging?"), and it is frequently the husband who wants to end their participation. Unavoidable physiological facts of life inevitably make many men dissatisfied with swinging. A woman can function sexually whether or not she is aroused. A man needs first to experience the physiological phenomenon of erection. Dr. Gilbert D. Bartell, associate professor of anthropology at Northern Illinois University, in his book *Group Sex: A Scientist's Eyewitness Report on the American Way of Swinging* reports that only about one-fourth of male participants are able to function effectively at sex parties. Three-fourths are unable to function more than once during a party; some not even that one time. Their experience then becomes one of voyeurism, watching others.

A woman, after attending her first such party, a typical one with a dim room full of mattresses with writhing couples, trios, and quartets, wrote a report on her experience for the *Los Angeles Free Press*. It concluded:

"Chances are that you will attend three or four more parties. You will feel more relaxed at the next ones and eventually try most of the things you have heard, dreamed, or read about. You will forget to ask names and may not even think twice about sleeping with someone you don't know anything about, much less have any feeling for. You will find that you still have sexual fantasies and that V.D. is easily taken care of. Chances of lasting friendships are rare. You will still have most of your sexual and emotional hang-ups and maybe a few new ones. The hang-ups of the people you will meet may be worse. You may be more sexually aware and you certainly will be jaded. With relief, you will go back to sex on a private basis."

Confirming this, a report on the film *The Swappers* concludes that "prolonged exposure to it seems to lead most of the jaded couples in the film down the primrose path to marital fidelity."

And so for many participants, group sex thus becomes a temporary quest that may last for months and often not more than a year or two, in the unending human drive for variety of sensual experience.

Some who deal with marriage problems as researchers and counselors predict that group sex will reach its peak and then decline because the younger generation will have conducted its sexual experimentation and exercised its sexual freedoms at a much earlier age. Also, it will have had acceptable forums like sex education classes and rap sessions in which to talk about sex. One counselor says: "I get the feeling that group swingers are finishing their unfinished teen-age business and getting their fill of acting out the sexual fantasies and talk denied to them while they were growing up. The younger generation isn't going to need swinging to fulfill itself.

They've already experimented with a variety of partners, so what is group sex going to do for them? Now many youth, in fact, want a one-and-only good human relationship, not just a sexual one."

What human beings seek in sexual experience is a feeling of oneness with another human soul, the greatest of possible pleasures both physical and spiritual, combined into one. Far from filling the drive we have for this transcendental feeling—what psychologist Abraham Maslow in his study of the orgasmic experience of the self-actualizing person described as the ecstatic "oceanic feeling" of being at one with the universe—group sex lowers us to a nadir of human estrangement and alienation.

At the instant it is possible to be closest to another human being, strangers find themselves with strangers performing in a sexual stadium, often for an audience. Dr. Laura Singer, a New York marriage counselor, says this deep fear of closeness to another human being is the very reason some people get involved in group sex. It is significant that some group participants avoid the intimacy of kissing. Many choose not to entrust the sensitive, personal orifice of their mouths to strangers. They permit mass-produced pseudointimacies from the neck down but, also significantly, they resist stimulation (both sexual and intellectual) from the neck up. Several studies of swingers report that many lead bland, circumscribed lives, uncommitted to civic or social change or activity, unsympathetic to social activists, uninterested in intellectual exploration.

Dr. Alexander Wolfe, a New York psychoanalyst, also believes that sexual conglomerates are unlikely to find the satisfactions they seek. "We seek in a variety of sex partners," he says, "the personal gratification and reassurance of our worth that it is difficult to find elsewhere in our lives and our work." Sexual Don Juan personalities, male or female, whether they've exercised their sexual athleticism privately or in group sex, often wake up the morning after still disliking themselves despite frequent sexual experience with a variety of partners. One's self-esteem derives from a whole lot more than orgasm.

Further suggesting a reason for a possible decline in group sex is the attitude toward it of women liberationists who angrily consider it a strong manifestation of male sexist supremacy. "It's the same old bag," says one liberationist, "of females parading themselves and being selected by men on the basis of male-determined standards of physical attractiveness."

The Palsons state that some women enter swinging with the desire to please men and that a woman swinger will often "judge herself in terms of her desirability and attractiveness to men." Sex chauvinism is also suggested in their report that should a husband have erection problems and obviously be miserable, the group's mores consider it wrong for a wife to ignore his condition and, even if she herself is having a good time, the wife may be expected to go to her husband's side and even to leave the party with him.

Nevertheless, anthropologist Gilbert Bartell suggests, an increasing number of people are becoming interested in experimenting with swinging, and he predicts swinging will grow in popularity and become a permanent part of the American culture. Eventually, he says, 15 per cent to 25 per cent of American married couples at any one time will probably be involved in swinging, with new ones trying the experience as others drop out.

The Palsons think that acceptance of swinging may be related to economic trends, periods of prosperity giving people more money to spend on such extramarital activity. Group sex can be expensive, entailing entrance fees to parties, weekend trips to other cities, child-care expenses at home, the cost of ads in swinger magazines, or of providing refreshments in closed groups when private homes are rotated for parties.

"Given economic prosperity as a necessary condition for increasing sexual freedom," they write in *Trans-Action* Magazine for February 1972, "it is quite possible that with economic difficulties . . . the number of available acceptable sexual alternatives (such as swinging) will decline and swinging may all but disappear from the American scene."

That applies to Recreational Swinging. Utopian Swinging, a small idealistic group who share sex along with other activities in a group marriage or a small and loving fraternity of human beings, may turn out to have a larger place in our future especially since people will live longer and will choose not to maintain monogamy for a long lifespan.

The following letter, describing one small utopian arrangement, confirms the pattern of monogamy with an occasional foray into concurrent sex as the one most likely to be commonly practiced in the future. It was sent anonymously to a speaker who had said that extramarital relationships were painful because there is usually one who is left out, unchosen.

> For many months, at intervals of four to six weeks, we have been spending relaxed weekends with another couple, also in their early fifties. Our mutual esteem has progressed from intellectual to affectionate to sexual, and, speaking for ourselves, has revitalized our happy marriage. For both of us unpromiscuous people, this relationship has provided an outlet and release which is at this point in time important to the continued health of our marriage. Also, it gives each of the four of us the pleasure of a loving relationship with a second warm and understanding individual. Besides that, the wives are compatible and have many common interests; also, the husbands.
>
> We have allowed this relationship adequate time to develop, so that no step in its progress has come as a surprise to any one involved. We set standards for the experience with our loving friends as we set them for ourselves as a couple—plenty of private time and pleasant surroundings. There are no children to be maneuvered. We can count on sleep, and/or food, and/or liquor, to be part of the party. (And I put liquor last because we consider it the least important of the three enjoyable necessities.) This couple has been married even longer than we have and it is the first such experience for them also. This has all been done in the spirit of love, rather than tee-hee-hee experimentation. We enjoy it, they enjoy it, but we are not interested in being statistically important.

The numbers of such people could become statistically important in the American future, constituting an ideal group marriage in which the couples live under their own roofs enjoying their privacy and join together with joy and love when they wish to.

While multisexual relationships, recreational or utopian, are entirely illegal at this point in time, the sexual revolution has seen the start of jousting against the barricades of tradition. Almost certainly during the twenty-first century, monosexual relationships will no longer be the only form having legal sanction. Multisexual relationships, whatever form they may take—group sex, group marriage, three individuals, two or more couples—will find social and legal acceptance. New laws begin when enough people start breaking the old ones.

PART IV

SEX AND
PARENTHOOD

13

We Are All Sex Educators—
and Students

On the basis of the way human beings live and behave through-out the world, a parent who withholds sex education from a child is making a choice to cripple that child. The parent is giving the child a subliminal injunction to be inadequate in its dealings with other human beings. And since the pattern of our sexual relationships is often reflected in the pattern of all our interpersonal relations, chances are that the child reared to be inadequate in sexual knowl-edge will carry this same inadequacy into other areas as well.

Human evolution has gone past the point of no return so far as giving sex education to young people is concerned. The choice is not whether to give it but how best to give it so as to create the op-timum joy, pleasure, and responsibility within the individual and within the society.

Every sex act has both a private and a public sector, the private sector being one of responsibility to one's self and one's partner, the public sector one of responsibility to the whole community of humanity. The sex act is the most responsible act we ever perform. Irresponsibly performed, each sex act carries with it the possibility of creating an unwanted human being.

There is a parallel here to the human being's primary drive, the one for food and water. To best equip a child to live its life fully and to complete its human experience, we have an obligation to teach it all we can about food nutrition. The new knowledge the sexual revolution has brought forth makes it imperative that we also equip a child with all the knowledge we can about sex. Otherwise parents give a child a half-birth—a biological birth but not a psychological birth. We endow it with physical equipment and no information about how not to be a victim of that equipment.

That much-debated question, "At what age and at what grade in school should we start teaching sex education?" confirms how naive and uninformed we are. Sex education starts at birth with the recording made on the infant's nervous system of the spank that helped start it breathing. The infant's first experience with physical touch is likely to have been an unpleasant one.

Our personalities and attitudes are imprinted in us, recorded like a tape recording on our nervous systems, by the time we are four or five years old—the years of "personality implanting." How we are apt to feel all of our lives about our sexuality and about our bodies has been designed for us by our parents and others in our environment long before we start to any school, even nursery school. Alfred C. Kinsey believed that attitudes affecting adult sexual behavior were already formed in the child by two or three. "If a child is more than three or four months old," he told audiences, "parents have already lost valuable time and opportunities."

Every one of us constantly gives out sex messages. By our behavior, our laughter, tonal inflections, vocabulary, our style of dress, cosmetic makeup, hairdos, displays of affection, the braggadocio or innuendo with which we discuss sex or laugh at sex jokes, the pleasure or discomfort we feel in touching others, all reveal how we feel about the sexual side of ourselves. "It is hard for man to accept himself if he doesn't like his own body, or if meeting the needs of his body arouses fears, guilt, shame, or anxiety," says psychoanalyst Dr. Alexander Lowen.

The briefly clad teen-aged boy and girl in open display of lovemaking on a public beach are giving sex education to the toddler playing nearby. The mother who turns her cheek for daddy's kiss because "you'll smear my lipstick" is giving sex education to her child. The father standing at the toilet bowl urinating when his infant son crawls in is a sex educator.

Parents' attitudes about whether or not to take a youngster into their bed for cuddling give the child sex education. A locked bedroom door, differentiated from times when it is unlocked, gives sex education. A home in which sex is unmentionable and sexual curiosities may never be voiced is giving a subliminal message that sex is "dirty" and not to be talked about. Children constantly give each other sex education in playing house or playing doctor.

Every one of us constantly also receives sex messages. No person in the United States of any age can watch TV, see billboards, magazine and newspaper advertisements, or read magazines, without being subjected to endlessly repeated conditioning which says that to be sexy is the optimal goal, whether you are a person or a product.

"I really bought it because it's sexy," says a woman in an automobile ad.

"Guaranteed to look sexy for a year," a bathing suit ad promises.

"Put on Spring's sexy new mouth," says a lipstick ad.

"The sexier chutney," proclaims an ad for a meat condiment.

"Why do slim, sexy redheads eat yogurt?" asks a food ad.

"How to have sexier feet," advises an ad for a foot spray.

On TV, a wife who brews better coffee is rewarded by having a physically affectionate spouse. The young girl who drinks the right brand of soft drink is rewarded by having the boys flock around. Buy our motorcycle, the male is told, and you'll get a girl to ride off into the woods with you. The woman who uses the right shampoo can get a man to sniff around her appreciatively. Clairol hair tint's question, "Does She or Doesn't She?," with its sexual double entendre (considered one of the most successful slogans in all advertising history because it has almost become a part of the language), is seen on billboards and in advertisements from coast to coast.

Underneath most television commercials and printed advertising is the subliminal hint that if you use the product you will either "do it better in bed or have it done better to you in bed," as one candid advertising executive puts it. We are constantly being conditioned to equate our worth with how well we function in bed, as do*er* or do*ee*.

For young people there is an additional subliminal message which only adds to youth's confusion and belief that we are a hypocritical people. To the adolescent this conflicting message says: Be sexy but don't engage in sex. Cheek-by-jowl with Be-sexy advertisements are Don't-engage-in-sex articles, warning youth of the dangers (never the pleasures) to be encountered in sexual experience, such as romantic heartbreak, disillusionment and disappointment, guilt, impaired sexual functioning later on, and so on. We keep telling college girls to retain their virginity while college girls keep giving us the feedback, reported in many polls, that they are engaging in sex, enjoying it, and are guilt free about losing their virginity. Virginity is no longer a marketable commodity.

Marriage counselor Ben Ard, a professor at San Francisco State College, sums up the attitude toward sex existing in the United States at the start of the sexual revolution: "Conformity of United States youth to adult advice and practice perpetuates one of the world's sickest cultures as far as sex is concerned. The American sexual tragedy is that our Puritanical sex views create untold havoc in our love, marriage, and family relations."

Getting oriented to the aftermath of the sexual revolution first requires that we give parents themselves sex education. Nearly all parents, no matter how much or how little formal education they may have had, seem plagued by the same questions when it comes to talking sex with their children. What to say, when to say it, and what words to use. This is not surprising. Hardly anyone raised in contemporary America received adequate sex education and we certainly never had training in techniques of passing on sex knowledge to others. Even medical schools training those who deal most intimately with the human body have rarely given sex education to future physicians.

In no other subject have we all been expected to be such experts on the basis of so little training. Moreover, our confusion is compounded by the barrage of varying opinions from child-rearing experts, many of whom diametrically differ from each other. "It's okay for your children to see you nude. It's okay to take young children into bed for cuddling," are the opinions of one school of child rearing. "Never let your children see you nude. Never take your children into bed with you, it's too erotically arousing," says another school of child rearing. Just as some parents may begin to feel they are doing the right thing, along comes a new opinion to raise doubts in their minds.

The majority of us have learned what we know about sex, a good deal of it inaccurate and mythological, in the same way: from gossiping and conjecturing with equally ignorant peers; from playing doctor; from "dirty" books surreptitiously borrowed or bought and stealthily read. All of this is what columnist Art Buchwald calls the "soda fountain school of sex education" in which thirteen-year-olds gather in the local candy store after school and tell the eleven-year-olds what "it" is all about and the eleven-year-olds believe every word.

Small wonder, then, that many of us of all ages can say, along with Alexander Portnoy, the hero of Philip Roth's *Portnoy's Complaint:* "I am marked like a road map from head to toe with my repressions. You can travel the length and breadth of my body over superhighways of shame and inhibition and fear."

Whether the school, the home, the church, or the community center should be the primary source of sex education has been among the hotly debated questions of the sexual revolution. Political conservatives and liberals differ on where and when sex education should be taught, the conservatives believing it should be taught only by the parents in the child's own home, and the liberals believing it should be taught at every grade, beginning with nursery school.

The battle was joined in January 1969 when the bulletin of the John Birch Society, a conservative organization named after a young American OSS captain killed in China, printed a call-to-arms by Robert Welch, head of the society, for a movement to restore decency to American education.

For some years, scattered school systems throughout the country had been offering a variety of courses with such names as Family Life Education, Marriage and Family Living, Homemaking, Preparation for Marriage and Parenthood. Some of these courses entirely eschewed any discussion of sex; others included limited information on the reproductive process, talking about what happened *after* sperm and egg joined up but not at all about *how* they did so. The *verboten* fact no one dared ever mention, among the reasons why students laughed off these courses as "human plumbing courses," was that sex felt good.

Now, Robert Welch wrote, our nation's most urgent requirement was for "organized nationwide, intensive, and angry and determined opposition" to sex education in public schools. Sex education, he believed, was a Communist-inspired plot to destroy one whole generation of American youth, to convert the generation "into debilitated, directionless, and unprincipled wastrels of their cultural inheritance." By so doing, the Communists would have a weakened, busily fornicating populace which cared more about pleasure than patriotism.

Taking up the cudgels of morality, the Reverend Billy James Hargis of the Christian Crusade declared that he, too, believed that sex education was "part of a gigantic conspiracy to bring down America from within." The Communist Manifesto apparently included a hitherto secret section known only to Robert Welch and Reverend Hargis—"Overthrow by Orgasm." The latter told a rally in Boston of conservative Americans: "I don't want any kid under twelve to hear about lesbians, homosexuals, and sexual intercourse. They should be concerned with tops, yo-yos and hide-and-seek." Some American youth answered by saying it *was* concerned with hide-and-seek—"under the bedcovers."

Many observers of the political scene believe that conservative organizations have seen in the sensitive land of sex education a fertile landing ground on which to attempt to gain political control of boards of education, of school curricula, and educational policies.

In the months following January 1969, in many communities, even the mild version of sex education then being taught was vigorously attacked and expunged. Sex education became the major cause for the defeat of members of boards of education, of the oustings or resignations of principals, teachers, and administrators across the land. Anaheim, California, a pioneering community in family life education, saw the election of political conservatives to its board of education and the resignation of its school superintendent. A teacher in North Carolina was sued by the parent of a thirteen-year-old girl who saw the film *Human Reproduction* in school, on the grounds that with this film, the teacher was "disseminating obscene, lewd, and vulgar materials." Dismissing the suit, a judge declared, "I wish I had seen this film when I was in school." An Iowa minister objected to the use of such "filthy language" as "sperm, uterus, fertilize, pregnant, and reproduce" in sex education courses. Pickets marched outside the annual meeting of the International Business Machines Company, excoriating them for manufacturing sex education materials for classrooms.

Divided even among themselves, some parents in the antisex education movement believe sex education to be acceptable if parents are allowed to approve of the texts used. The Schmitz law in California, for example, named after a one-time state legislator openly a member of the John Birch Society, requires that parents approve of sex education texts: since a consensus among parents is hard to achieve, the subject of sex education is increasingly skirted in California schools at this point in time, with the likelihood that the election of a liberal state regime will result in that hampering law being rescinded.

Other parents believe sex education to be entirely unacceptable, in any way, shape, form, or manner, no matter what texts are used. Still others say that sex education classes should be given *only* for parents, who would then teach their own children at home. This viewpoint is shared even by some prosex education advocates who believe that parents need up-to-date sex education as much as their children do. Accordingly, among the recommendations of both the Presidential Commission on Obscenity and Pornography and the National Commission on Population Growth and the American Future is that the United States government support and encourage a massive sex education program for American adults.

To put this American controversy into historical perspective as we enter the last third of the twentieth century, it must be pointed out that while the antisex educators have made waves in the waters of human progress, they are not holding back the tides. Out of desperate societal need, out of personal and family trauma and anguish over unwanted pregnancies and out-of-wedlock births and abortions, sex education in our schools is expanding.

Fifteen months after the first attack against sex education, the Associated Press reported in March 1970 that there were sex education gains across the nation, stating that it now existed in one form or another in every state and was increasing. Inevitably, sex education will be included in all academic curricula from nursery school on up and in all early childhood TV education and elsewhere. Even the Vatican has decreed that Roman Catholic seminaries put more stress on teachings about sex. The great sex education controversy is passing into history.

The growing consensus among parents is that the subject must be a part of all education in all grades beginning with a child's earliest school experiences. When nursery school toddlers play house, pretending they are mommies and daddies, could be the time to start inculcating them with the knowledge that two children are considered an ideal family size. During this time of women's liberation and population control, youngsters who learn typing might well be taught this up-to-date version of the traditional learner's sentence: "Now is the time for all good men and women to come to the aid of our country by choosing to parent no more than two children."

On one aspect of sex education most conservative and liberal parents alike are in agreement. No matter what their political persuasion, they care about the attitudes of the person teaching their children in this sensitive area.

Who should be our teachers of sex education and what qualifications should such a person have? Even Sweden, far more experienced than we are in such matters, has difficulty in finding good teachers of sex education. Eliminating people who might seek to become sex educators as a way of getting their "kicks" concerns many of us. Dr. Stanley D. Wagy of the Family Health Association of Cleveland once told of rejecting an applicant: "At the mention of the word 'sex' her eyes lit up in a distinctively pathological manner that quite frankly scared the hell out of me."

A teacher's own moral values also concern parents, many of whom believe it is impossible for a teacher to separate his or her own values from clinical information. Will a teacher who is a "swinger" in personal life be advocating swinging for students? Will a much admired homosexual teacher be implicitly "selling" homosexuality to the students? Will such questions even matter if the child's attitudes toward sex have already been firmly implanted at home since infancy?

A discussion of teacher training in the SIECUS Winter 1968 newsletter suggests that an important element for anyone training to teach sex education would be an awareness of his or her own feelings about sexuality. Many teacher-training programs now require trainees to attend group sessions to explore why they want to teach sex education and how comfortable they are with their own sexuality. More and more colleges now offer summer training programs for sex educators and some colleges have begun to offer degrees in sex counseling and education.

Good sex teachers, says Margaret Mead, are people who are "able to stand up in front of a mixed group of people—a diverse set of parents, a bunch of adolescents—and talk simply and clearly without embarrassment" about sex relationships. Teacher-training specialists suggest that any teacher or counselor who relates well with young people and has their confidence can be trained as a sex educator and would probably make the best teacher.

What we are taught in school is merely a start on the sex information we need throughout life. What interests us at a particular time in life is that which is appropriate to our biological development at the time. A kindergarten child is not interested in a geriatric sex problem but he is interested in playing with his own genitals and wants approval for this pleasurable experience.

Our need for sex knowledge never ends. As we enter each new stage of life, physiologically, maritally, parentally, geriatrically, we find that each period needs its own updated information.

Certainly the highly sexually charged adolescent needs different information from the aging male who is experiencing impotence. The divorced woman who is dating different men, each of whom may seek to get her into bed, needs different information from what she required as a married woman. At a time of high remarriage rates, we have vastly increased numbers of step-parents finding themselves sexually attracted to a stepdaughter or stepson. The growing number of cases of incest going through our courts are more likely not to involve a child's own biological parent making sexual advances but a child's step-parent doing so, and of a resentful, jealous spouse bringing legal charges.

Sex education for the elderly is a new concept. Until now we have believed that the sex drive ends by or during the fifties. As an old joke goes, "What at age twenty-five we called virility, at age sixty-five we call lechery." Now we know, according to a bumper sticker: "Even dirty old men need love."

While the frequency and intensity of the sex act certainly wanes as we get older, sex desire itself never ends, and people function sexually even into the nineties and hundreds if they are free psychologically to do so. However, the ejaculatory contractions are apt to be weaker than in earlier years and wives of older men often say that they cannot feel by penile contractions whether he has achieved orgasm.

A birthday card for men says of their age and their sex drive:

30 to 40	Tri-weekly.
40 to 50	Try weekly.
50 to 60	Try weakly.

The facts of social change also demand updated sex education. Population control, for example, requires that we change our philosophy about sex and womanhood. Historically we believed woman had a need both to bear and to rear. We are now revising that belief and saying that the female has a biological drive to gestate and bear a child but not to rear a child. The joys of motherhood are often mythological. Women have been told—by men—that they were supposed to find this a sublime experience. Honest women will publicly admit that many of the so-called joys of motherhood are mostly in male minds. At a time when less of a woman's life will be spent in childbearing and child rearing, what can we offer woman as a substitute for her biological drive to gestate? Sociologist Philip Hauser urges us to teach women to find satisfactions other than biological, and this requires a whole new evaluation of sex and marriage, of work outside the home to structure the time of the woman no longer occupied with babies.

Even our sex education vocabulary needs updating. Over and over people use the word "sex" when they really mean gender. Differences between male and female sexuality may be infinitesimal. What we mean when we talk about "differences between the sexes" are differences between the male and female genders. And, as pointed out in an earlier chapter, it is only recently that we have learned to define the several components of gender—chromosomal, gonadal, hormonal, external genital, and internal genital.

Because every one of us is a sex educator, every one of us therefore carries the obligation of all good teachers constantly to update our own knowledge and attitudes as new information becomes available through research and as new freedoms achieved by the sexual revolution are woven into our lives.

"Our society must update . . . cultural and religious ideas of human sexuality," Dr. William H. Masters and his wife, Virginia Johnson, the sex researchers, have said. "Otherwise we guarantee a continuation of the present high rate of marriage and family failure."

Whether our children will exercise their sexuality within the same context of marriage and family as we have known it in the past is unlikely. But if we give them an endowment of good feelings about their bodies and their sexuality, and if we instill in them a sense of both personal and public responsibility for their acts of intercourse, then it won't matter what the familial forms and life-styles may be in which they exercise their sexuality. Whatever they do, it will be as warm, loving, self-accepting, responsible human beings.

So how do we go about educating the sex educators—ourselves? Almost inevitably there will be in our future a nationwide chain of sex clinics to which parents and other adults can go for education and for counseling with their sexual problems. Masters and Johnson have proposed sex therapy centers for which seminar leaders would be trained.

Colleges can help educate the sex educators by requiring a course in sex education for every diploma granted. Medical schools can require internship as sex educators for every premed student. This has already been done experimentally with great success at the University of California Medical Center in San Francisco, where students have gone out into the community to discuss "family life" with schoolchildren.

Ideally, sex clinics ought to be located in store fronts because studies have shown that public facilities are much more widely used if they are visible from the street and people don't have to go up in an elevator to get to an office. Also, stores would encourage spontaneous walk-ins of troubled people who might otherwise be reluctant to seek sex counseling. Many vacant stores dot our land because of businesses moving away to suburban shopping areas. If the government were to allow the owner of such a store to make its free use as a sex clinic a tax-deductible contribution to public health, thousands of stores could be made available overnight.

Government agencies concerned with population control, private foundations, leaders of industry who make frequent speeches about the business community's obligation to work in the field of mental health, all could provide funds to staff such clinics. We already have in existence many facilities to which sex counseling could be added immediately. More and more senior citizen centers are being opened in stores fronting on main streets where public transportation is easily available. Maimonides Medical Center has "storefront psychiatry" in Brooklyn, one of 200 such centers with federal support under the Community Mental Health Acts of 1963 and 1966. Suicide prevention centers, student counseling services in colleges, YMCAs and YWCAs—all of these could bring sex clinics into immediate existence by adding a specialist in sex counseling to their staffs.

Today we take the existence of public utilities like police and fire departments, free public libraries, free schools, public transportation, all for granted. Some day we will also be taking for granted and benefiting from such "social utilities" as storefront mental health centers and sex clinics brought to us by our sexual revolution.

But first we will have to educate the parents and adults of America, most of whom seem not to know that they themselves already are sex educators.

14

How to Talk Sex with
Our Children

An acronym of the word *SEX* tells how we give sex education:

S —what we *s*ay,
E —the *e*xample we set by our actions,
X —the e*x*trasensory perception, or
"radar rearing," that children get from
the atmosphere in the home.

How our children communicate with us about sexual feelings and
curiosities as adolescents is determined by how we communicated
with them as children. Today, young people from all educational
and economic and cultural backgrounds make similar statements:

"I was never allowed to talk about anything like that."

"My folks always seemed embarrassed if I raised the subject, as
if they were eager to have it over with, so I stopped asking."

"My mother said, 'That's something you should discuss with your
father.' "

"I think my parents know less than I do. Sometimes I wonder
how I ever got born!"

So, how, then, do we handle children's curiosities and questions
in order to have them grow up feeling good about themselves and
their sexual feelings?

As we know, children's attitudes about sex and their bodies begin
at birth; children only a few months old, as soon as they develop
the motor skills to do so, engage in a version of masturbation, pleas-

urably touching their genital areas and exploring their bodies. Sex questions appear as early as the second year, almost as soon as speech appears. Studies of children's sex questions reveal their areas of curiosity, in order of frequency, to be: origin of babies; intrauterine growth of babies; process of birth; the organs and functions of the body; physical sex differences; relationship of father to reproduction.

As many parents have experienced, children ask many questions over a long period of time before they get around to the one involving the father's part in reproduction: "How does the daddy's sperm meet with the mommy's egg?" Most children obviously need to build up a prior body of knowledge before this question occurs to them. Few children, of course, use the word *sperm*. They are capable of using it properly; the environment just hasn't taught it to them. Adult advisers for the children's television program *Sesame Street* told producer Joan Ganz Cooney that they did not think children generally could be expected to know the names for their body parts. Ms. Cooney did not go along with this evaluation and she found, after a study, that the capacity of children had been underrated. "The adults were hung up on the body parts business," she declared, "but the children are not."

The absence of accurate information or of a climate in which it can be obtained gives rise to incredible fantasies and fears. Studies of childhood sexuality reveal these ideas in the minds of many small children:

A mother has a baby by eating something special and giving birth through the anus.

Giving birth is fearful because the mother's stomach gets cut open.

Babies are born trembling and crying with fear.

A baby exists fully developed somewhere "out there" prior to being born and the parents order its delivery.

A baby is made by a daddy urinating inside a mommy.

Girls are punished for misbehavior by the loss of their penises.

The unwillingness or discomfort of many parents to discuss sex with their children, plus Nature's unfortunate design in placing orifices of reproduction so close to orifices of elimination, has created much confusion and fantasizing in the minds of children that sex is "dirty" and related to bathroom functioning. A common fantasy small children have is that of being sucked into the toilet bowl as punishment for playing with their genitals. One child believed his mother had a penis in her rectum because she sat down to urinate. Most children are never permitted to see body orifices of their parents, of their mothers especially, and they ascribe procreative functions to eliminative orifices. One can imagine what it can do to a child's self-esteem if he starts out early in life believing that he himself and feces both came out of the same defecatory opening.

Two researchers, Dr. James E. Moore of the Communications Institute of America, and Diane G. Kendall, a counselor, reporting on "Children's Concepts of Reproduction" in the February 1971 issue of *The Journal of Sex Research,* found, from the vocabulary with which children answered their questions, that "it is obvious that few families [even well-educated ones, since their study utilized the children of university parents] teach their children the words found in dictionaries" for body parts or functions. "It is as easy for a young child to learn and say the words *womb* and *vagina* as it is the words *stomach* and *bottom*," they declare.

The two questions children most need to have answered are the same two questions about which parents seem most uncomfortable:

"How does the baby get inside the mother's uterus?"

"Where did I come out of you?"

A teacher of sex education has found from her experience with her own son and daughter that brief and truthful answers and actions work admirably. To the first question she said: "A daddy puts his penis inside the mother's vagina and it feels loving and good and warm. Most of the time mommies and daddies do it for love. Once in a while they might decide to make a baby with their love. Some people do it only for love and choose never to make a baby, and that's good too.

"Lots of people have sex," she added, "without loving feelings —maybe because they're angry, or maybe they want to punish somebody. That's not a good way because it can make a baby who isn't wanted and loved."

That other inevitable question she answered by lying down on the floor, opening her legs, and pointing to the opening, saying: "That gets bigger when the baby is born. Most babies come out head first. Once in a while a baby comes out buttocks first; that's called a breech birth." She also pointed to the separate openings for urination, defecation, and birth. When her son, then aged four, asked about touching the genital area she said matter-of-factly, "No, that's a private part. I'd prefer that you not touch it."

Whatever the words we parents use, the important message we are getting across is the double-level message below the surface which says to a child: "I respect you and the questions you ask. Your curiosity is understandable. You are not bad, dirty, or naughty because you have such curiosity. You can trust me to be honest with you."

The customary way in which children do something about their sexual curiosity is by playing doctor. Many parents are upset by this kind of play, mostly because they are burdened with guilt about having played it themselves. Many adults have been severely beaten or reprimanded when they were caught playing doctor as children and so they are intensely uncomfortable about the idea.

The mother mentioned above handled it by *joining* the play. "I was variously the hospital superintendent, the nurse, or the dietitian," she says. "My hospital had a rule that 'shots' could be given in the upper thigh, not the buttock, and pants were not to be taken down. Periodically I'd walk into the room and ask 'How's the patient, Doc?' Then, without letting the play go on too long so that it shouldn't become overstimulating, I would take orders as the dietitian for hospital meals—lemonade or milk and cookies."

Her children early learned that this kind of play was acceptable and didn't have to be sneaked behind closed doors. Bedroom doors were always open when they played doctor so the hospital "superintendent" could make her rounds.

Underlying much parental anxiety about how to handle this whole matter of sex is the fear that if sex is portrayed in too favorable and pleasurable a light, children will become overly stimulated and seek sexual experience earlier than the culture permits. Here, too, as in many other areas of living, being able acceptably to talk out feelings often results in their not being acted out precipitously. Parents can acknowledge that sex feels wonderful and still teach that it is not acceptable in our culture to do anything about it until the teens. Just as parents can convey the idea that masturbating feels wonderful but that it is among the functions we humans perform in private.

Having a child walk into a room full of guests while playing with its genitals is among the common experiences of parenthood. It is easy to interpret the difference in the effect on a child between a parent who becomes flustered, embarrassed, or angry and roughly removes the child and a parent who quietly guides the child back to its own room, saying: "I know that feels good but it's one of the things people do in private."

For most adolescents, masturbation is their major outlet for release from sexual tension. This is often a tension- and guilt-filled time for many young people. Parents can help reduce some of the tensions by respecting their children's privacy, by knocking on doors before opening them, and by not making any comments, jokes, or innuendoes about telltale stains on bedsheets. Empathize with the fact that young people are caught in a bind between their powerful natural drives which say they are ready for sexual experience and societal taboo which doesn't permit them sexual expression. Indeed, the Rene Guyon Society, named for the French philosopher, believes that societies should permit intercourse at any age children are physiologically capable of it and that this will be the style of human behavior some generations hence, in an age of sensory humankind, when we have totally conquered unwanted pregnancies.

Sex is ideally a two-gender human expression. Children, no matter what their gender, should be given sex information by either, or both mother and father, and should feel comfortable while discussing sex with either one. Daughters and fathers, mothers and sons, should all be able to discuss sex. Telling a daughter she should "go talk to your mother about that" or telling a son "that's something boys discuss with their fathers" perpetuates the notion that there is something not quite nice about the whole business.

This genderizing of sex education is common in our schools. When a film on menstruation is shown, this is often the scene: Girls get signed okays from home to see it. Boys are curious but are told they may not see it. When girls come out of the classroom or auditorium after the film, some boys are hanging around and they ask leeringly, "Whatja see?"

Boys have mothers and sisters and someday they will have wives or girlfriends or companionate mates who menstruate. Boys see ads for sanitary napkins and tampons and boxes of them in stores.

Seeing such a film, learning of premenstrual tensions and menstrual hygiene, is part of sex education and serves to make both male and female more sensitive and responsible. By separating boys and girls for sex education, we encourage sexual irresponsibility.

Children can handle reality. It is being shielded from reality by parents who think they are protecting children from truths of life that children can't stand. It's not the dealing with reality that often hurts—that becomes a growth experience which increases a child's self-esteem. It is the child's uncertainty and insecurity when reality is withheld that is often destructive. Withholding reality becomes a put-down message from parent to child which says: "You're too little and too young to deal with it or even to know about it." That gives a child a message to *stay* too little and not to grow up. Growing up isn't an approved form of behavior in such a family.

Children easily adapt and understand and like it when parents say, in effect: "There may be some unpleasant or harsh facts of life but every one learns to handle such things. I know you are capable of dealing with them, too." A child gets a good feeling of being admired and respected by parents who do this.

Parents who have not up until now felt comfortable discussing sex with their children and who are uneasy about introducing the subject after many years of silence are finding it an effective starting point to say something like this: "I never had sex education. It did not exist when I went to school. We were not allowed to talk about it and I have not been comfortable with it. My own knowledge is still inadequate. I would like to feel comfortable discussing sex with you. Will you help me to feel comfortable?"

Today's generation of young people have had more new information, more stimuli bombarding them, more new events in a shorter space of time than any other group in history. As much new information probably becomes available and is transmitted around the world in a single day as became available during a whole decade when most of us were young. There is much important and exciting information we can learn from our youth if we will listen actively and creatively to them, and open our minds to them.

This acronym of the word *LEARN* offers a helpful guide to ameliorating parent-child tensions not only in discussing sex with our children but in all other areas as well.

L—*L*isten. Look them in the eye and give them your undivided attention.

E—*E*mpathize. Much of the school curriculum is boring, out of date, unchallenging; textbooks are full of dull jargon and unclear writing; classes are too large. How much patience would we grown-ups have if we had to sit through what our children sit through in school?

A—Acknowledge/Accept. Acknowledge their feelings and accept them even if you don't agree with their feelings. Many parents give young people a message: "Don't *have* your feelings, they are not acceptable to me." Telling people not to have their feelings is like telling them not to breathe. They can't help what comes in to their nervous systems. When you make it acceptable to have *their* differing feelings, then you are creating an atmosphere in which it is also acceptable for you to have *yours*.

R—Respect. Children are *people* who happen to be younger than we are. Dr. Jerome S. Bruner, Harvard University educational psychologist and a specialist in the learning process of children, maintains that ten-year-olds are capable of adult reasoning, logic, abstract thinking, decision making, and of knowing the consequences of their decisions. Unfortunately, our culture provides small opportunity for young people to put all this mental ability to work; we infantilize our young people—and many of our grown-ups, too—long beyond the years necessary. Some ten-year-olds throughout the country are now doing college-level work in an experimental social studies curriculum, "Man: A Course of Study."

N—Nurture. Everyone, young or old, is seeking some nurturing which says: "I love you and accept you, even if I don't agree with all your behavior . . . even if you don't get A's on your report card . . . even if you need a bath . . . even if your hair is long . . . even if you masturbate . . . even if you sometimes use four-letter words . . . even if you don't want to go to college . . . even if . . . even if . . . even if . . ."

Admitting our fallibility, not pretending that we always have all the answers to everything, and demonstrating that we are open to learning from a younger generation whose education, based on more up-to-date research, is more recent and more valid than ours, very often works well to establish the beginnings of communication between parent and child. Some young people may be startled and suspicious at first by this sudden unaccustomed humility from previously know-it-all parents, but they respond once they realize parents' sincerity.

Margaret Mead, in her book *Culture and Commitment,* says that one of the great, permanent cultural changes occurring during our lifetime is that humankind's tradition of the older generation teaching the younger generation will no longer apply. Henceforth, due to the rapidity of the information-and-knowledge explosion, each younger generation will teach the older. An older generation that resists this constant updating of knowledge will find itself hopelessly behind the times, locked in constant battle with the younger generation. Parents need to *join* rather than to *challenge* progress.

How exciting it can be to realize that the sexual revolution has brought beautiful freedoms to our children to enjoy their human experience. And how much better off many would have been if such freedoms had existed for us. Human lives can soar if the sandbags of past ignorance are thrown overboard.

15

Dirty Words

To get an idea of how our attitudes about language are formed, imagine yourself a small child. Every one encourages you to speak, they mouth words for you to imitate, they give approval for sounds you make. Mastering new sounds and finding that they produce things, people, food, reactions, is like playing God. You utter sounds and they work like magic. How powerful you feel.

Then one day you utter a new sound. Lo! That sound brings you a scolding, angry faces and voices, perhaps a slap, maybe a poisonous-tasting substance forced into your mouth to wash out your "dirty" words. How confusing. For most sounds you're lauded and rewarded. Suddenly for one or two sounds, you're punished. What's different about those punishment sounds?

What you do not yet know is that those particular sounds, a combination of letters put together to form a word, are associated with some human activity called *sex*. You don't even know what sex is.

But you've been handed a beautiful weapon with which to bug people. Parents and other grown-ups don't like certain sounds. So any time you're sore at them and want to hit back, you utter those forbidden combinations of letters. Oh, boy. Right on cue. Listen to those grown-ups get uptight.

Eventually, as you get older, you begin to get an inkling of what human behavior those *d-i-r-t-y* words are associated with. Recorded on your nervous system is the information that talk about sex, about your own body parts, about the functioning and pleasures of

187

your body, is all *bad*. Your physical being is certainly worthless and a source of problems. It feels good, but it's not nice to say so. You can't be too nice a person if you enjoy feelings and things about your body that everyone says you must not talk about.

And so another child has been started on the road to sexual difficulties as a grown-up. Imprinted on him are feelings of guilt for enjoying his body sensations, and shame for being such a bad person as to like all that.

That's exactly how most of us grew up. What does all this say to us as parents?

First, all children experiment with new sounds. Mastery of new sounds and words is a thrill for a small child. To a child who speaks what are called "dirty" words, it is no more than one more combination of vowels and consonants that his mouth, tongue, and lips are capable of forming and enunciating clearly. Expect a child, in his verbal explorations and experimentations, to produce some sounds you don't approve of. To the child that often is a verbal growth stage. Winston Churchill's mother once wrote: "Winston is going back to school today. I do not feel sorry, for he is certainly a handful. Not that he does anything naughty except to use bad language."

Second, don't give your child a verbal weapon to use against you. Repeat the words back calmly, matter-of-factly, without any shock reaction, preferably within the context of a sentence. The double-level message you are giving is: "You can't use words to bug me or to hit back at me. I'm not buggable."

Third, the whole matter of dirty words, for an older child, can be turned into an interesting exploration into etymology. Explain to your child that some words are not acceptable at this point of time in our country even though they are perfectly acceptable elsewhere. Names like Shitara and Dymshitz, which include in them one of our *verboten* words, are common in other countries.

You might discuss why those particular words are unacceptable. What has happened to them through the years that they should be frowned upon now? In Elizabethan days, many of today's forbidden words could be spoken aloud in the theater and were even used in polite society. What has caused the change? An admirable book for pursuing the subject is *The Magic and Mystery of Words* by J.

Donald Adams, a collection of short essays along with a chapter on the origins of four-letter words.

Fourth, it can be fun to use forbidden words. Let your child have his fill, right in front of you. Tell him, as a minister told his son, to say and write the words over and over until he is sick of them or starts to laugh. Take any word you wish and say it over and over and over and over again. It soon begins to sound funny and you'll probably start to laugh. The child is desensitizing his nervous system to the excitement and shock value of the words. It probably will never again be much fun to use them.

Classes in sex education for adults who are training to be sex counselors and teachers of sex education use exactly this technique to desensitize people's shock reactions to dirty words so that they can more comfortably deal with students and with patients who use them. In a pioneer course in sex education for adults at the University of Minnesota, Prof. Gerhard Neubeck starts the first class by having men and women say aloud over and over to each other words like *penis, vagina, intercourse* associated with the body and with sex.

Fifth, acknowledge that it is human to let off steam or to make jokes by using those words. The most dignified and proper persons easily find themselves uttering an angry obscenity when a maniac driver comes close to sideswiping their car.

The late wife of diplomat Averell Harriman jokingly told her husband that a world leader didn't know his "arm from his elbow," as a newspaper obituary of her edited the common expression. Canadian Prime Minister Pierre Trudeau, angered by a parliamentary critic, formed an obscenity with his lips, but did not say the word aloud.

Obscenity is even used as part of officialese when international diplomats wish to communicate in coded language. Former British Prime Minister Harold Wilson has told how he and President Lyndon B. Johnson used "salty language" by agreement, as a way of indicating that they themselves and not civil servants had actually prepared secret dispatches.

Sixth, know that language is a constantly growing and changing thing. The frequent use of four-letter words on stage and screen means that throughout the world people are being desensitized to their shock value and many words through frequent usage will soon cease to be considered obscene. Even an actress like Katharine Hepburn, whose professional image has been one of great dignity, uttered a four-letter word in her Broadway role as Coco Chanel. "No-No Words Are Now Yes-Yes" sums up a commentary by *New York Times* film critic Vincent Canby, on the vocabulary now being commonly used in movies.

That we are en route to greater freedom of vocabulary even in publications intended for reading by the whole family is evident in such examples as the use of the word "erection" in a *Los Angeles Herald Examiner* piece on a therapist who runs nude encounter groups; the use of the word "urine" rather than, as in the past, "human waste products" in a *Los Angeles Times* report of people who live on houseboats and pollute the waters; the word "ass" referring to the human anatomy and not a donkey, used in an advertisement on the book page of *The New York Times,* quoting a remark by comedian Groucho Marx; the use of phrases like "mental masturbation" and "intellectual orgasm," quoting Representative William Clay of Missouri as he attacked a national political figure on the floor of the House of Representatives; and of the expression, "Boy, I really got horny," used in an interview with an actor on *The New York Times* Sunday film page.

John Kenneth Galbraith, our former ambassador to India, in a speech assailed politicians who had "the mobility of a man who was up to his ass in prestressed concrete," a statement which was quoted verbatim in many newspapers throughout the country.

That four-letter word *fuck,* while it is heard and seen in many films and plays, in many novels and in the radical and college press, has not yet been accepted into television, academia (books and dictionaries are still banned by some schools if they contain the word), by family newspapers, and by news magazines. At a discussion among publishers in 1969 about acceptable contemporary language, Henry Grunwald, editor of *Time* Magazine, said he did not think *Time's* audience was yet ready for four-letter words.

As the shock value of taboo words wears off through their repeated usage it is likely that four-letter words will soon be finding their way into frequent print. This has already begun in mass circulation magazines like *Esquire* and *Playboy.* When that happens man, in his perverse way, will undoubtedly bring forth new words to make taboo.

Not long ago the word *pregnant* was taboo on United States television. It is an example of how illogical we are that while a character in a television soap opera was not permitted by censors to say that another character was pregnant, newspaper ads and television commercials for an automobile had a man saying admiringly about the car, "She's really stacked." In England, until recently, the word "bloody" was so taboo that a book of etiquette urged hosts not to serve lady guests meat that was too "ensanguined."

Discussing the psychology of scatology in the book *Four-Letter Word Games,* Dr. Renatus Hartogs and Hans Fantel say that we use obscenity to deal with our fears—their boldness makes us feel brave when we are scared, giving us Dutch courage—with our shame about bodily functions, and with our rebellion against authorities like church, state, parents, and teachers.

Society labels as obscenities those gut-level, nitty-gritty words which expose social and human hypocrisy, greed, and lies. Obscenities are notably short, mostly one syllable, and to the point. Longer polysyllabic words are often euphemisms serving to cover up and take the sting out of social injustice, bigotry, cant, and cruelty. What we have labeled obscenity and try to make unpalatable is much more of a true "telling it like it really is" than the polite parlor euphemisms we insist be used instead. To make language *verboten* thus becomes an attempt to repress feelings which people express with the forbidden vocabulary. It has never worked and it never will.

The Reverend Howard Moody, a Baptist minister, writing an article "Towards a New Definition of Obscenity" in the Protestant magazine *Christianity and Crisis,* says that what is truly obscene is material, sexual or not, that has as its basic motivation and purpose the degradation, debasement, and dehumanizing of persons. Among obscene words, says Reverend Moody, is " 'nigger' uttered by a bigot."

In 1969, the 181st General Assembly of the United Presbyterian Church heard a strong plea by Dr. Purnell H. Benson, director of the Business Research Center at Rutgers University, that the church encourage the open use of sex words in sex education classes. He said:

"Our youth are talking in a new idiom. Some of us feel restless about it but we need to get used to it. The untenable attitude of the Victorian language is largely responsible for the breakdown in our communications with the young about sex. We want to help them see that sexual response of husband and wife is a God-given means for husband and wife to show their unity and affection and emotion to each other. It is quite impossible to do so if the words 'penis' and 'vagina' are omitted from our vocabulary or if any other words by which sexual feeling is described are avoided by us."

Humankind, searching for techniques to reduce tensions between person and person, between nation and nation, might consider the value of encouraging people to use whatever vocabularies their psyches need, as a means of reducing violence. Professor John Cohen of England says: "The man who first abused his fellows with swear words instead of bashing their brains out with a club should be counted among those who laid the foundations of civilization."

Humankind would find it better to opt for four-letter language than for four-weapon—bombs, guns, napalm, rockets—wars. More of us ought to remember as adults that childhood saying, "Sticks and stones can break my bones, but words can never hurt me."

16

Nudity

At this stage of our evolution, we human beings have not yet made peace with the fact of our physical being. Humans are born naked, but throughout most of the world they are buried with clothes on. It may be in this nonacceptance of the physical side of human existence that many of our psychical ills begin. As suggested earlier, human beings do not yet fully accept themselves if they don't like their bodies or if they feel psychological discomfort about its functions.

We are en route right now to freeing ourselves from one more thou-shalt-not of our past: our negative feelings about our bodies. The past few years have seen the greatest public exposure, literally and figuratively, of the nude human body in history. While much of it has been vulgar and tasteless, the net effect on the human psyche as well as on the human physique is apt to be a wholesome one.

In order for each family to decide a comfortable policy about nudity for itself, it is necessary to put nudity into historical and sociological perspective.

Our natural state, as mammals, is to be naked. But we have always covered ourselves. Thomas Carlyle described man as "the only clothed animal." What needs do we fill by covering our nudity?

Most obvious, of course, is our need for protection against the elements. We cover our nudity for practical purposes of climate control. Neither the Arab in the burning desert nor the Eskimo in the Arctic wasteland could long survive without the protection of burnoose or parka.

Outside of covering our bodies to preserve ourselves, we first began to cover ourselves because of shame and superstition. Man's earliest wardrobe—a fig leaf—was designed to hide his genitals, that shameful part of the human being associated with his baser nature, his sex instinct.

Throughout history, different cultures have selected different parts of the body to feel shame about. An essay on *The Future of Nakedness* by John Langdon-Davies reports: "If you were to surprise a woman in her bath in various countries of the world today, here's what would happen. A Mohammedan woman would cover her face. A Laotian woman would cover her breast. A Chinese woman (before the Revolution) would hide her feet. In Sumatra the woman would conceal her knees. In Samoa she'd cover her navel."

Concealment is usually for either of two purposes. The concealed part is associated with what is shameful in man's nature and is therefore to be hidden, as in the genitals associated with sex. Or it is to be concealed because it is connected with man's nobler nature and is therefore to be kept preciously to one's self and not dissipated by overexposure. The Samoan woman hiding her navel, for instance, does so for the latter reason. The noble navel is the primary source of life, of nourishment of the unborn, and therefore to be hidden from the casual eye.

Undoubtedly the deepest need of all that we fill by covering our nudity is psychological. The only chance many of us get to show any individuality or to establish or maintain our positions in the social and financial strata is when we put our clothes on. Henry Thoreau said: "It is an interesting question how far men would retain their relative rank if they were divested of their clothes."

Nudity can be not only a great leveler in the human hierarchy but it can also be a great demoter. In the movie *The Detective* Frank Sinatra objects when a detective is questioning a suspect whom he has forced to disrobe. "Why's he naked?" asks Sinatra. "That'll make him confess quicker," the detective answers, explaining that's how the Nazis would interrogate their victims.

It has been an astonishingly short time—dating only from 1965—since the contemporary era of public nudity began. In March of that year the film, *The Pawnbroker,* was given a seal of approval by the Motion Picture Association of America only after much contention over two flashes of nudity: a prostitute baring her breasts and a shot of the pawnbroker's wife in a Nazi camp.

As evolution goes, scarcely a second of time passed before almost every movie or play had its "obligatory" nude scene. So rampant did nudity become that within four years, by 1969, Actors Equity and the Screen Actors Guild were forced to draw up guidelines covering nudity on the job and at theatrical auditions, partly because a new kind of voyeurism saw show business hangers-on calling many auditions for nude roles in shows they somehow never got around to producing.

Those same few years have seen an unprecedented acceptance of nudity in advertisements, in the mass media, in nightclubs, and even on the TV set in the family living room when *The Bill Burrud Show* presented a documentary favorably showing a family weekend at a California nudist camp, including a nude Sunday morning religious service. A British publisher, stating that he was keeping up with the times, published an illustrated edition of the Bible, the first in history to show a man and woman in nude embrace.

That same brief period has seen the changing of many laws in regard to nudity. County ordinances and state laws against nudist camps have been overthrown throughout the country. Topless and bottomless bars and restaurants constantly seesaw between legal acceptance and rejection, often depending upon who is in public office or plans to run for office on a purity platform.

For many years nudist camps were associated in the public mind with licentiousness. The public image was of carousing orgiastic sex, an image only dissipated when Dr. William E. Hartman, then head of the sociology department at California State University, Long Beach, and a research associate, Ms. Marilyn Fithian, revealed in 1967 the results of their two-year study into 150 of the country's nudist parks.

Contrary to popular mythology, members of nudist colonies were mostly whole families from the upper financial and social strata, often were politically conservative not liberal, and the camps were highly moral places with strict rules against drinking or physical touching. Husbands could attend only if accompanied by their wives. Obscene language or lewd behavior were grounds for instant loss of membership. Because there was stigma attached to the practice of nudism, and because many members had jobs in which they dealt with the public, such as clergymen, policemen, and teachers, last names were not given and only first names used. Many nudists did not know the identities or home cities of fellow members.

The director of a large nudist camp said: "We've always insisted on certain principles and standards. Nudism has been accepted as a family activity, a wholesome, esthetic escape practiced in harmony with a definite code of ethics and proprieties adhered to by all."

One of the questions in the Hartman-Fithian study dealt with happiness in marriage as a result of nudist membership. Nearly half said it had increased their marital happiness; one-fourth said it had increased frequency of intercourse in their marriages. Half said it had had no effect on the frequency of sexual relations; 2 per cent said there had been a slight decrease.

In the several years since that study was released, the acceptance of nudity by the public in films, on stage, in advertisements, has seriously affected the membership of American nudist colonies. Some of them are going out of business as former members apparently no longer feel the need to go away to hidden preserves to enjoy outdoor nudity.

"It's the sexual revolution that's killing us. The pornographic movies, the topless-bottomless bars, the dirty magazines, they're making nudism in America passé," was the summing up of a nudist camp manager who hired a professional promoter in an attempt to keep his club from closing.

While commercialized nudity in films and on stage has already begun to decline, it is likely that young people will continue their practice of nudity as a form of social and political protest. Toward the end of the 1968 presidential election, nudity was increasingly used by them to call attention to their causes.

In New York City, young people stripped off their clothes, donned masks of the candidates and pranced nude on the steps of the Board of Elections. They said they were demonstrating "the bare facts about the candidates and showing equal disrespect for all." Later that year, several persons stripped and handed out copies of an open letter proclaiming "Anatomic explosions are better than atomic explosions." Students at Reed College, protesting a bookstore rule that shoppers must leave their coats at the door as an antishoplifting measure, came to shop and did leave their coats at the door but had nothing on underneath.

Nudity as a form of fund-raising has also come into use. Parents at the Laurel Hill Cooperative Nursery School in San Francisco had their most successful fund-raising ever when they put on a tour of homes and art studios which included nude models and dancers, and one highly successful turn-about idea of having a fully clothed model being painted by a nude artist.

Prurience about the human body seems to be largely an American hang-up. Other Western cultures, as well as some Oriental and Eastern cultures, routinely have beaches for nude bathing and some have public coeducational baths, as in Japan. A West German resort offers its patrons their choice of nude and non-nude beaches. The former are called *freikorper kultur,* free body culture, and the latter are called textile strands because patrons wear fabric to cover themselves. The chain of Club Mediterranee resorts throughout Europe routinely includes solariums for nude vacationers. In Holland nudity has even helped candidates to get elected to public office. In 1970 a protesting political group calling itself Gnomes of the Orange Free State campaigned for the Amsterdam City Council by posing nude in trees and dancing nude at political gatherings. The group, somewhat to their own surprise, won five seats.

It is in the light of this vast and rapid social change since most of today's parents were children and their attitudes about nudity were imprinted on them that we need to examine attitudes for today's family unit. Parents who pass on prurient attitudes of shame about the human body may be illy preparing children to live in the world of the future. Equating nudity with good health rather than with sex is a simple way to foster wholesome attitudes. Being naked and having an air bath all over your body not only feels good, it is one of the ways in which sensible people maintain good health.

Benjamin Franklin, who enjoyed swimming and sunning in the nude, would happily proclaim, "Let the skin breathe!"

It is important, however, for parents, even those who are comfortable with nudity, to know that children's attitudes seem to go in cycles as they grow up. Many apparently go through periods of comfort and discomfort with nudity, which may be caused by prurient attitudes they observe in the community and in the homes of friends.

Should children say, "Cover up, Mom and Dad," it's a good idea for parents to go along with what children are comfortable with, at that point in time. It's likely to change soon. The cue that a child is once again comfortable being nude often comes when he or she walks from bedroom to bathroom without clothing.

Even when children are comfortable with nudity, they often worry that mother and father will show up nude in front of visiting friends. Parents can easily relieve children's minds of this anxiety by reassuring them they would not do so.

How we feel about nudity, our comfort or discomfort with the facts of the human body, is likely to be related to our mental health in general. Teen-aged girls, raised in homes with no nudity, who accidentally saw fathers' or brothers' sexual organs, had ambivalent feelings of disgust and pleasure. Children who routinely see parents' bodies and genital parts from infancy suffer no such upset.

Anthropologist Margaret Mead has proposed that limited nudism may well offer a possible solution to prudery and neuroses that lead to sex crimes. "In the long run," she has written, "it may be that the acceptance of a limited range of social situations in which children can run free and adults can enjoy relaxation without wearing clothes will be the end result."

And, as pediatricians and wise mothers of small children know, the end result of children running free without clothes is the elimination of diaper rash for which the best prescription has always been: "Warm sunshine on bare bottom."

Whether or not to permit nudity at meal times is a matter of a family's esthetic tastes. "We don't," one family reports, "both for esthetics and because plastic seats on kitchen chairs are sticky to sit on, especially in hot weather!"

17

Pornography

Blatant, commercialized, ugly and dehumanized sex is everywhere. No child can watch television, look at billboards, use a public library, pass a newsstand or the signs outside a movie house, walk past counters of contraceptive supplies in a drugstore, wait in a doctor's or dentist's office full of magazines, without being exposed to human sexuality. Mail-order catalogs, newspaper advertisements, magazines with fulsome ads for brassieres, lingerie, and sanitary napkins—any and all can be sexually informative and stimulating for pubescent boys and girls. It is impossible to shield our children from sexual information, helpful or harmful. We can only help them to deal with it.

Many highly inflamed opinions about pornography, pro and con, have been formed with no scientific backing. Studies of the effects of pornography on our behavior had rarely, if ever, been made until the several recent studies, mostly done at colleges and universities, which were authorized by the Presidential Commission on Obscenity and Pornography while it was gathering information for what turned out to be its controversial report, issued in 1970.

On the basis of these studies, a majority of the Commission's eighteen members, most of whom had been appointed by President Lyndon B. Johnson, concluded that exposure to such printed matter, ugly though it may be, did not have a detrimental effect on character or moral values or cause sexual deviancy. On the contrary, the report suggested, many sex offenders such as rapists and child molesters had had no exposure to pornography while growing up and many of them came from homes in which it was forbidden to talk about sex. The report recommended there be no laws prohibiting the publishing and dissemination of such materials to adults and that such existing laws be rescinded. It did recommend, however, that there be laws controlling the distribution and availability of such material to young people.

A minority opinion of Commission members, including President Richard M. Nixon's one appointee, maintained that exposure to pornographic publications and "stag" movies and art did stimulate sexual criminality, sexual delinquency among juveniles, and deviance. Many of the public said this represented their point of view, too. In October 1970 President Nixon rejected the Commission's report and "its morally bankrupt conclusions and major recommendations."

Some studies authorized by the Commission and their findings included these:

(a) Repeated exposure to pornographic materials results not in titillation or stimulation but in boredom. A group of young men over twenty-one at the University of North Carolina were monitored electronically to record their physiological responses as they looked at stag movies and still pictures and read pornographic books. The more they were exposed to these materials, the lower were the responses of their nervous systems.

(b) A marketing study of pornographic materials in Denver conducted by the University of Colorado School of Business showed the majority of purchasers to be white, middle-class, married men between thirty and forty-five years old.

(c) Young girls are often sexually aroused by popular and rock-and-roll music and by love scenes in movies and on television, according to a study conducted by Ms. Patricia Schiller, executive director of the American Association of Sex Educators and Counselors and teacher of sex education at Howard University. Her study questioned 487 girls at a Washington, D.C., school for unwed mothers and 91 college coeds. The college girls found movies most sexually stimulating, followed by books, records, and television. The younger girls listed television first and records second, many of them revealing that romantic scenes they were watching with boys on television led to sexual intercourse and their pregnancies.

For the majority of adults of good will in the United States today, who do not want censorship and yet deplore the excesses and brutalization of the pornographer's product, the whole matter of pornography evolves into a question of how do we best handle it with young people without impairing the rights of many adults who apparently enjoy this kind of literature.

Arguing against censorship, Avrum Stroll, a University of California philosophy professor, has pointed out that censorship is inconsistent with self-government. The freedom to inquire, discuss, and debate is an essential base for self-government. Censorship implies incompetency on the part of the population to look after itself.

"However distasteful certain materials may be," he has said, "—in literature, television, films—to some, they have an educational value. You can't impose censorship on the young, for it is only when they are allowed to choose within their own terms of experience what is of value and what is not, that they become mature citizens."

Those who are against censorship of pornographic materials say that people with a great interest in suppressing them are those with psychosexual problems of their own who, repressed about expressing their own sexuality, give their deep interest in sexual matters a noble guise by being searchers after pornography. "They certainly get to spend a lot more time looking at it than the rest of us do," has been said of them by many mental health professionals.

On the other hand, those who are concerned about pornography believe it to be a dehumanizing influence on human personality, devoid of love, tending to make human beings somewhat less than they truly are and could be, and thus a regressive influence on civilizing humankind.

An important fact to be examined is that the vast majority of adults today who had some exposure to pornography in their own adolescence are not sexual perverts, sadomasochists, or homosexuals. The vast majority are heterosexuals who care very much about establishing happier sexual relationships with our own spouses. Underneath all the research and writings pouring out in contemporary society is the healthy theme of increasing sexual happiness in marriage. We may be more in danger of harm from the low level of literary craftsmanship in such materials—some of them are written in what might be called the exclamation point school of writing—than we are from the sexual language and images evoked in such books.

But balancing the harmless exposure to pornography experienced by many of us is also the important fact that the sadomasochistic scenes and acts frequently portrayed today were no part of the "dirty" publications of our youth. Our reading was indeed sexy; it was not violent. The social climate then was much less conditioned to violence than it is today, with beatings, chains, whips, people tying up, torturing, and flagellating each other for sexual pleasure, all of which are commonly portrayed in today's pornography. A commercial film made by one of our largest motion picture studios portrayed the bloody head of a woman rolling about on the floor after being cut off by a crazed lover, and a rifle being fired down the throat of another woman.

So outrageous have become the excesses of violence of the pornographers, whether the output is on pulp paper or slick film, that even political liberals and ardent civil libertarians find themselves agreeing with the so called "variable obscenity" theory which imposes different legal standards for printed material available to children and that offered to adults. Poet John Ciardi has written of the collected works of Marquis de Sade: "Sade drives me from my earlier position that my children were free to read any book with my blessing so long as they would discuss it with me. I am not willing to have them read Sade this side of their adulthood."

At present the legal status of pornography indicates a hands-off attitude by government toward adult sexual interests, behavior, and reading matter, with some controls on the availability of such material for young people. In October 1970 the same month that President Nixon issued his denunciation of the Commission on Obscenity and Pornography, the United States Court of Appeals ruled that consenting adults may send obscene material to one another through the mail for their personal and private use. Incidentally, a good deal of what goes through the mails is not printed material but aids to copulation such as artificial penises and vaginas and vaginal vibrators, the latter increasingly being used by the growing numbers of older single women in our population who, far from being wanton libertines, are women sadly living in a period of time when females in their age bracket far outnumber available males. For many of these women, their only source of sexual release is such masturbatory devices.

William B. Lockhart, dean of the University of Minnesota Law School and chairman of the Commission, predicted that its findings would ultimately help form a more enlightened society that knows the truth. "In the long run," he has said, "the public will decide."

Ervin Gaines, director of the Minneapolis Public Library and chairman of the American Library Association's Intellectual Freedom Committee, suggests that pornography is a persistent art form which has been found on the walls of a house of prostitution in Pompeii 2000 years ago and which crops up daily in our lives in the form of graffiti and dirty jokes. "Pornography must be important or it would not be so prevalent. It has some meaning in our lives that we do not understand." He suggests that some libraries collect it so that it can be preserved for the benefit of future scholars and historians. Since then, a collection of pornography has been donated by a Los Angeles attorney to the library of California State University at Fullerton "to help clarify the murky area between literary freedom of expression and the commercial exploitation known as pornography."

Pornography has always been with us and it is likely to continue to be with us, either legally or illegally. Young people have always found ways to get access to it and they will no doubt continue to do so. It seems to be almost a law of nature that anything that is forbidden only becomes more desirable and sought after. If we do not provide an acceptable setting where children can discuss sex—in the classroom, in the home, in the church or community center— then we are sending them to the pornographer to get their information. John H. Gagnon and William Simon, sociologists and former staff members of the Institute for Sex Research, writing in the social science magazine, *Trans-Action* (July-August 1967) make the point that not giving classes in sex education encourages children to turn to pornography for information denied to them elsewhere.

A possible guide to parents for discussing pornography with their children may be found in a statement from Donald Barr, educational philosopher and headmaster at the Dalton School in New York, a father of four who, deploring the brutal sexuality of films, has said: "A man . . . who puts his pocketbook above the needs of his audience, especially the vulnerable children . . . is an immoralist. He is peddling the subtlest forms of sickness and perversion, subtle because they are shown at the local movie house in the guise of the commonplace."

Pointing out the difference between obscenity and violence in

Shakespearean plays and in today's pornographic films and literature, Dr. Barr makes an important point: "While he (Shakespeare) is showing these things he also has commentators who stand by and say, 'How revolting. This is no way for people to live.' This is the element . . . missing from much contemporary art. When adolescents see movies like this and no one protests, they feel their sickest impulses are being fundamentally authorized."

Our illogic is well illustrated by the report by a *Los Angeles Times* film critic who told of sitting behind a mother and small son watching the movie *The Moment of Truth,* about a bullfighter. During scenes of the goring of horses with blood spurting from their necks and shoulders, from which the reviewer, sickened, "turned away, again and again," the mother and son sat unflinching. When a frank love scene came on the screen, "the mother reached over and placed a hand across her son's eyes."

One family's solution to the subject of pornography, utilizing Dr. Barr's guideline, was to deliberately bring pornographic magazines home and to look through them with their teen-aged children, talking about how ugly and sick and devoid of love and humanity it was. The parents talked about the low level to which some people stoop in order to make money. "We use pornography as a lesson in human values," these parents say. Parents who provide an atmosphere in which sexuality can be talked about, questions asked and answered, curiosities acceptably expressed, books brought home and talked about, need not feel concern about the poison of pornography.

Parents will find it helpful to make a distinction between sordid pornography and what is called erotic art. Many artists throughout history, from Michelangelo to Picasso, have painted and sculpted great art having to do with human sexual expression. In the public mind the two—pornography and erotic art—are inextricably mixed. There is a vast difference, however, between the sculpture of human figures in sexual embrace on religious temples in India, and the scenes of sexual violence and degradation pictured in most pornographic magazines and books. Also, as was mentioned earlier, and as the Commission on Obscenity and Pornography mentioned in its report, fine erotic art, enjoyed by husband and wife in the privacy of their bedroom, may be a good visual aid to help tired marriages.

PART V

SEX PROBLEMS OF THE SINGLE PARENT

18

Dating and Mating

The year following the end of World War II saw the start of a new phenomenon on the American scene. During 1946, as servicemen returned from overseas and found that their wives had made new alliances, or hasty wartime marriages were regretted, we experienced our highest divorce rate.

In the generation that has passed since then, there has come into existence a vast subculture—the world of the once married—with manners, mores, customs, and problems uniquely its own. Most of its members come from those who are divorced; fewer, but still a great many, are widowed.

Each business day, Monday through Friday, nearly 3000 individuals begin divorce proceedings in the United States. Most of them have children. Each day, more than 10,000 human beings—6000 divorcing parents and their children—enter new life styles as single parents with children. At any one time, though their numbers fluctuate as divorced ones remarry and the married get divorced, there are believed to be more than five million formerly married men and women raising more than seven million children under the age of eighteen in single-parent families.

Sooner or later, when the initial shock and trauma of their new status have ameliorated, these single men and women become concerned with the logistics of dating and mating. Where and how to meet new people, and once they have been met, where, with whom, and when to engage in sexual relations are questions that plague most single parents. Underneath much probing is their concern about the effect on children of their mating and dating.

Due partly to the double standard which has permitted greater sexual freedom to the male, and partly because wives usually have custody of children and so do not have the same privacy for sex as do ex-husbands who live alone, women as divorced parents are more beset with problems.

That the mores and the double standard of the past die hard, even in this era of freedoms, is indicated by the inner doubts of some divorced women as to whether they should have sex at all. A counselor who conducts group therapy for divorcees is astonished at how many of them question the propriety of their having sex. "A surprising number are still committed to the idea of sex being acceptable only in marriage," she says. At a discussion among older divorced men and women, when the talk turned to sex, one woman called out, "We're all single people here. What are we doing talking about sex?"

Once a woman has answered this major question (ultimately most of them do choose to have sex) her answer gives rise to a great many dilemmas. Whether to have sex after a date when children are asleep in the home; whether to carry a diaphragm and vaginal cream in her purse "just in case"; whether to take pills even though she does not then have a sex partner or wait to take pills until she finds a partner, even though that enforces an interval during which she must take pills to build up immunity against conceiving; what the children might tell their father about her dating; whether an embittered, punitive ex-spouse might try to get custody of children on grounds that her sex activity makes her an unfit mother—these are dilemmas most divorced mothers find they have to work through.

The pervasive double standard makes some children feel that it's all right for father to go out with many women, but that it's not quite nice for mother to do the same with different men. A divorced mother has told, with some bitterness, that when her children become angry, they threaten to tell their father of her frequent dating. It is also the mother who has to deal most often with children who are hostile to men friends when they call for her.

For nearly all divorced people, finding new social outlets follows the same pattern. The man, a new face on the single people's scene, is sought after and wined and dined, often to the shock of his ex-wife who can't imagine what other women see in him. The fact is, there are more of her than of him. (For generations after a war, women continue to pay militarism's price; every country whose men are decimated in war has a permanent disproportionate number of women who live out their lives without men.) The woman will be invited by married friends for a while until the wives begin to feel threatened by her singlehood as too enticing to their husbands. Eventually, the divorced find they need to make their social lives in the company of other single people. They soon find less in common with married friends. And such friends, soon exhausting those among their acquaintance to whom to introduce the single man or woman, are not a source of supply of new romances.

To fill this need for a large segment of our population there has emerged a big business, the singles industry, which provides ways in which single male and single female of any age and status—never-married, once-married, parents or childless, separated or widowed —can meet.

Hotels offering special weekends with computer matching, discussion clubs, sensory awareness groups, nudist colonies, college extension courses, nature lovers, ship cruises, human growth centers, apartment complexes, yacht outings, ski clubs, chartered flights, all exist as part of the singles industry. Every weekend, in every major city, there are dances for singles. Parents Without Partners, organized in 1957 to help single parents cope with children, is often attended even by singles who don't have children. On a week-end night the country, coast to coast, is one vast Single Mingle or Single Swingle, as these activities are known. Even senior citizens' clubs are attended more by singles than by marrieds.

Newspapers abound with ads from computer matching services; single people's directories run ads offering "a dignified way for respectable men and women to meet." Computer services, who are among heavy advertisers, have not yet had wide acceptance in all strata of singles. Many find them too costly and unreliable, with not enough people yet registered to give a single searcher a good choice for his money. Some services charge hundreds or thousands of dollars; many will not register a woman over forty-five. As one disappointed user complains, "You can't computerize a person's smile, the expression in her eyes, her sense of humor, or just that chemistry that makes something inside of you go 'bong!' when you see a particular person."

Nevertheless, it is not the *technique* of computerization which is lacking at this point in time; it is the cost and the fact that not enough of the population is registered. Leo Davids, sociologist at York University of Ontario, Canada, foresees a time when mate selection for all will be much more scientifically and satisfactorily handled through computer mate-finding, in which basic information such as total years of schooling, aptitude and I.Q. scores, areas of intellectual interest, religiosity, leisure and recreation preferences will give people a pool of other people with similar preferences to date, rather than their spending a lot of waste motion on the chance element in mate selection. When this comes to pass, technology can greatly increase the possibility for human happiness. How much easier it will be for two people who can do yoga headstands, speak French, enjoy folk dancing, and abhor television to find each other through computer mate-selection than for them to have to play "dating roulette" in the hope of finding such people.

Whatever the techniques for meeting people, the newly divorced person shortly finds someone with whom to have sex. These early sex experiences after divorce often have great significance to men and women. Both seek to affirm their self-esteem, their desirability, their sexual skills, after a period of being put down and torn apart that marks the end of most failing marriages. Many engage in frequent and almost frantic sexual experience during the first months of divorcehood. A psychiatrist calls this "the erotomania of the newly divorced."

Morton Hunt reports in his book *The World of the Formerly Married:* "It is common, almost standard, for the man to make an overture—verbal or physical, jestingly or seriously—within the first few dates and, in many cases, on the first or second date."

The recently divorced woman, if she is not asked, often suffers depression and lowered self-esteem. On the other hand, if she is asked too quickly, she is upset also. "It makes me feel like a thing, not a person," many divorcees say.

They are both ambivalent and uncertain and anxious. The theme of sexual behavior for the man almost always is: "Let's have sex so we'll get to know each other better." He wants physical intimacy to precede psychological and emotional intimacy.

The theme for the woman is: "Let's get to know each other better, then we can have sex." She wants the emotional intimacy to precede the physical.

It takes a while with this kind of experience and with enough dating for a man to realize he can still be a man and not have to prove it by sexual overtures on every date, and for a woman to realize she does not need to permit herself to be used, that she can turn a man down and still count as a person. Within a year after divorce, the majority of people are psychologically ready to reenter a sexual pattern of serial monogamy, one relationship at a time, with perhaps a brief concurrent pattern should they find themselves wanting to end one relationship and start a new one.

The tribal customs of dating men and women are amazingly similar to those of teen-agers. Two women, gossiping on the telephone, evaluating the character and behavior of their male dates, sound remarkably like adolescent girls. One girl whose mother berated her for staying on the phone such a long time, surreptitiously made a tape recording of her divorced mother's conversation on the telephone and then played it back, much to her mother's embarrassment. She and her daughter sounded alike. Older men boasting of their sexual prowess and conquests sound like teen-aged boys.

Many problems in diplomacy and human relations arise in this subculture. How do women friends handle it if a man dates one of them, then finds he's attracted to her friend? What if two women drive together to a single people's activity and one gets invited out for coffee or a cocktail by a man but the other doesn't? A group of intelligent divorcees in Los Angeles has resolved such dilemmas by their agreement that none of them will feel rejected or abandoned should a man date one and then another. Also, if they go places together and one is invited out, she is free to accept. The other will drive home by herself without feeling abandoned. "Any one man might not interest any of us after a date or two. We don't want to risk breaking up rewarding friendships among the women for the sake of a date with any one man. Should a relationship become serious, we're delighted for the man and woman."

The ego-pain of a man who constantly asks women for dates and is turned down is as great as that of any adolescent. "I suffered terrible psychosomatic symptoms whenever I started to dial a woman's number for a date when I was first divorced," one man recalls with distaste. "If she accepted, I was relieved. If she didn't, I felt dejected."

Within five years, despite much forswearing of ever again being willing to enter the institution of marriage, most divorced men and women do remarry. During this time, most begin a monogamous relationship which could be but not always is en route to another marriage. The problem then arises of whether or not the divorced woman's steady beau or fiance should stay over and sleep in the same bed with her. Should her children be permitted to cuddle in bed with them? What if that relationship should not end in marriage and later there is still a different man with whom she has established this kind of relationship? What does all this say about sexual mores to the children of divorced parents? The divorced husband, living alone, is freer for a variety of sexual liaisons without his children being privy to father's behavior. However, he may become that steady beau in another single parent's bed.

Part of this same dilemma for a woman is how much to tell her children when she goes off for a weekend with a beau to a hotel where they may be registered as Mr. and Mrs. If an emergency were to arise at home, would the children know where to reach her and under what name? Our laws are so far behind actual behavior that in some states it is still illegal for an unmarried man and woman to register as Mr. and Mrs.

It is impossible to provide simplistic answers to the problems of the single parent in regard to sexuality today. How much to tell children and how open to be about one's dating and mating depends on a great many factors in the parent-child relationship. How accustomed is that family to leveling with each other about intimate feelings and anxieties? A mother who is comfortable saying to her children: "I'm lonely without a man. I miss a man's attentions and sexual companionship," is a mother who will not need to hold back on her whereabouts if she spends a weekend with a beau. A mother who likes to pretend that sex doesn't exist will find herself fabricating her whereabouts and many other facts about her life as a single parent.

A mother who can level and say to her children, "I'm torn between a desire to spend more evenings with you and a need to be out with adult men and women" is the same mother who can level and say to her children, "I worry sometimes that my dating around as a divorced woman might not set a good example for your lives."

It is undeniable that young people today have been exposed and conditioned to men and women staying with each other without marriage. It would be hypocrisy to think otherwise. In a class in a Los Angeles school, the teacher found that half of the children came from divorced homes, and that many of that group had men either living in their homes or staying overnight sometimes with the mothers. Like these facts or not, these are reality for today's children at a time in human development when we are dropping old patterns of behavior without having yet defined the new ones.

Once again it may be helpful to consider the philosophy of Joseph Fletcher. As we have seen, Dr. Fletcher advocates that human behavior be guided by situation ethics. He asks: "What is most loving and protective of our fellow human beings at a particular time, place, and situation?" Such a code of ethics may help single parents determine what and when to tell their children. It provides a parent with the option to say, at some future time: "I told you what I did then because I felt that to be right at that time. Now I have had more experience and more knowledge and so have you. We are both older. I believe you are readier to handle this kind of information now than you were at that time."

It is worth being reminded, again, that children can handle reality, including the reality of the ambivalent and uncertain feelings many divorced parents have about their own behavior. It can become a growth experience for a child to hear of a parent's uncertainties, and it may help a child to make a wiser decision about mate-selection in the future if he concludes: "I see what pain my parent is going through. I will learn from this and try to select a mate when I grow up with whom I am better suited so that I, too, don't have to go through this painful experience."

19

Long Courtships

Unfortunately many divorced people who remarry do not benefit from the experience of having had one marriage end in failure. Increasingly, these second marriages are also ending in failure. Obviously, something is deeply amiss in our society when we have so few provisions to help save many good human beings from the pain of successive marital failures. Half of the murders in this country are committed by husbands or wives at times of marital stress, divorce, or separation.

We attack the problem through counseling after a couple is already in the legal maws of divorce machinery and harsh actions have been taken and harsh words spoken, rather than insisting on the same counseling before allowing them to marry. People are not stupid; we are victims of an educational system that is deficient in what it teaches us about one of life's major decisions—marriage.

We have all been asked, during our adolescence, by a sadly deficient and obsolete educational system, to make the two major decisions of our lives at a time when we have not been alive long enough even to know what it is we desire—what kind of person we would be happiest marrying, and what kind of occupation we would be happiest preparing for. We are asked to make these major decisions on the basis of no practical experience but rather on the ideal of romantic fantasy derived from mythology. What we want in our tempestuous teens is not what we want in our more thoughtful thirties. An old saying goes, "Washington is full of great men and women they married in their youth." We could extend that beyond the confines of Washington and say: "We are a nation full of good people and the spouses we selected when we were too young."

One way to begin to deal with the problem is to start the social custom of long courtships before marriage, especially for second and subsequent marriages. Such courtships should create conditions as close to marriage as possible, including sleeping and living together. Prince Charming who kisses Cinderella good-bye at midnight is not the same person who awakens with tobacco smoke on his breath at 7 A.M. The divorced man who charms the children of a woman's first marriage with his skill at backyard barbecuing is not the same man as the stepfather who comes home from work annoyed that these same children haven't raked up the leaves around the barbecue.

Some people propose that this long courtship be undergirded with the social expectation and custom that people of all ages would attend adult education programs to update their knowledge and feelings about marriage, and to unfasten the bindings of obsolete notions from a past in which most women did not go out to work, when large families were needed to work the farm of an agrarian society, and when girl children were considered undesirable handicaps because that meant daddy had to get up dowries to get them married off. These are the notions still underlying much behavior in marriage, parenthood, and family life today.

At the time a couple decided to make their marriage legal, they would be required by law to present a diploma or certificate reading: "This man and woman have completed a marriage education program which entitles them to marry legally. This is the contract with which they are entering marriage." The certificate would then state what the couple believed their contract to be.

One such contract, which might well fit many couples today when an increasing number of women work and earn their own money and thus relieve their husbands of the need to support them financially, might read something like this: He will be supportive and understanding and cooperative about her career and its demands on her time and energy. In exchange, she will help provide him with a more interesting life-style through her work and her contacts than he might otherwise have had with a woman who was not career oriented. Moreover, the fact that she earns her own money relieves him of the burden of providing full financial support of their marriage and, hopefully, will enable him to extend his own longevity without having so many financial pressures on him.

A Dutch-treat concept of marriage, in which a working male and a working female each pay their own way and split expenses down the middle, is already growing among liberated young couples. The economic benefit to a male of woman's liberation is incalculable, when he is freed from the burden of having to support another grown human being. Why are so many men thick-brained about the benefits to be gained if only they would knock off some of their male supremacist mythology, pitch in unashamedly with the housework and other drudge work and enjoy the benefit of a working woman who supports herself and shares the expenses!

Does it seem unreasonable to establish such requirements for marriage? We constantly do that every day in other areas of life. We are accustomed to being told that a particular job requires an M.A. degree plus two years of practical experience. Why can we not inculcate into marriage some of the same practices we already have about many jobs?

Demographer June L. Sklar even suggests a "financial solvency" test for couples to curb early marriages which wind up on welfare. Later marriages, Dr. Sklar says, would result not only in a reduction of fertility levels but also in a better-educated population, fewer abandonments of families by fathers, and fewer divorces.

"Love flies out the window when poverty comes in the door," an eighteen-year-old wife writes to columnist "Dear Abby," telling how she wishes she had not left a comfortable home with mother and father at the age of sixteen to rush into an improvident marriage. At every conference with the youthfully married, the theme of most of the people present is one of: "I'm sorry I married so soon. Why didn't somebody pressure me to stop me? Why didn't somebody teach us better? We should have gone together for a longer time."

While such ideas seem visionary when first proposed, we are already en route in our society to a legal requirement that would delay youthful marriages. The State of California has adopted a law giving the courts authority to order counseling before marriage when one of the partners is under eighteen, and enforces a thirty-day waiting period between applying for a marriage license and being able to use it. Other states are likely also to pass much-needed legislation that would extend the required waiting time between taking out a license and being permitted to marry. New York State has already extended its waiting period from three to ten days. Other countries, notably the Soviet Union, now require a thirty-day wait. It is finding that more than one in ten couples never returns to get married. Colombia requires a thirty-day course in marriage education and a diploma before couples can marry under church law.

A pixie-ish marriage bureau clerk keeps a permanent sign which she hangs on her office door every noon: "Out to lunch. Time to think it over and change your mind."

Laws demanding longer waiting periods and required counseling at all ages and stages of life, and social custom encouraging long courtships, are two ways in which we can begin to deal with the high rate of marital unhappiness and human misery abroad in our land.

The best teacher is example. If older people contemplating second marriages start the custom of long courtships and make of it a time of both education and evaluation, it is likely young people will follow suit. Long courtships will certainly not guarantee the solving of all marital difficulties, but they provide time in which a couple can learn and become adept at using techniques that will help to solve difficulties as they arise.

We can probably, in our advertising-oriented world, even sell long courtships like a product. Charles Revson, cosmetics tycoon, uses as an advertising slogan for his skin-tanning product, "A suntan and marriage—two things no woman should ever rush into."

More of our states are now empowered to demand counseling as part of the divorce procedure. Why don't we change our timing and demand the counseling as part of the marriage procedure?

As we humans become more self-determining and permit the state to have less say-so about the living arrangements in which we choose to relate to each other, noncredentialed pair-bonding arrangements will grow. Eventually the idea of courtship may fade away. There will be no legal ceremony for many people to mark the end of the courtship and the beginning of legal marriage.

All this is one more indication of how the sexual revolution is giving us freedoms we are not yet taking advantage of. We can now have a socially acceptable sex life without feeling the need to rush into marriage, as we once did. We have to learn how to use this freedom to grow with and to achieve happiness with. We can turn it into an asset.

20

Why Marry at All?

The large majority of divorced parents, especially older ones, do not intend in a subsequent marriage to bring more children into the world. They have enough trouble coping with the problems of his and her children from previous marriages without adding *their* children. As nonparenthood becomes more acceptable, fewer divorced parents are producing offspring in second marriages.

If there are no children of this new union who need legal and societal protections, why then should divorced parents involved in a new alliance choose to marry at all? Why not just continue to live together in a companionate arrangement permanently?

Because, liberated as we may seem to be, and in spite of the many companionate arrangements which apparently now exist, there still are tremendous social, financial, occupational, and legal pressures to have that document properly recorded in society's archives, stating that a legally recognized authority has joined a man and woman in a legally recognized and sanctioned social unit.

Employers, insurance companies, educational institutions, landlords, and governmental agencies not only do not give official recognition or approval of nonmarital living arrangements but look askance at them. A policeman in New York City and a clerk for the Federal Bureau of Investigation in Washington have had to fight to be reinstated in their jobs after they were dismissed because they were living with women to whom they were not married. Credit rating bureaus almost automatically recommend that credit not be extended to people living together; automobile insurance companies will not knowingly insure such couples.

A couple living together and working for the same employer, a conservative savings and loan corporation, found themselves in a fantastic number of small deceptions every day. They did not feel free to put both names on the mailbox. They avoided outside socializing with fellow workers and being in a car pool with them. They were cautious about answering incoming phone calls at night. One of them cleared out when the other's parents came to visit from out-of-town. (Temporary clearings-out when the older generation visits are common scenes among young nonmarrieds.)

Another couple who were divorced from first spouses and eager not to be legally married a second time found it just too difficult to buck the system when they took a year's sabbatical from their jobs as public school teachers to travel abroad. "It was just less of a hassel to get legally married in terms of medical benefits, job seniority, draft status, forwarding addresses, accident insurance, and our passports," they said.

An older divorced couple who were at first content with a companionate arrangement finally found it desirable to be legally married so that the wife could some day inherit the husband's union pension and social security payments and be included in his union medical plan. Still another couple learned that one year after their second marriage was formalized, the husband, who was on disability social security, could also get social security for his stepchildren so long as they were full-time students.

Most laws on our statute books implicitly discourage unmarried arrangements by giving benefits or protection only to legal spouses. Couples living together, should they want to include companionate mates in health insurance plans, are uneasy about having to lie when they answer the question "legal spouse?" on insurance forms. The machinery that would give civil, legal, and financial rights even to unmarried men and women who live together is apt to take many years yet either to grind out new laws or to remove old ones. Many test cases are needed to establish the civil liberty to be single and yet to receive the same benefits married people do.

Our income tax structure certainly gives preference to the married. In 1966 the Brookings Institution, which makes economic studies, declared that we have a soak-the-singles tax structure in which the widowed, the divorced, and other single people pay higher taxes than married persons with the same income. Individuals like Vivian Kellems, Connecticut industrialist, and groups like the National Association of Single Taxpayers, battle constantly to change tax laws which discriminate against the unmarried. Among the many inequities is that a single parent who has physical custody of a child cannot claim that child as a dependent while the parent who makes child support payments—which are in most cases far below the child's actual expenses—can claim the child as a dependent.

There are two areas in which it is to the financial benefit of couples to live together and remain legally single. One is where a woman is getting handsome alimony and would lose it if she were to remarry. However, there are fewer of these so-called "alimony bums" around than rumor and male propaganda would have you believe, as more ex-wives go out to work and support themselves, and as judges are limiting the number of years for which a divorcee is awarded alimony.

The fantastically high alimonies we read about are few and far between. If you follow up a few years later on these publicized divorce agreements, you find that they are rarely still in existence or being carried out because the woman may have remarried, the ex-husband's financial situation may have changed or he is much in arrears. Most divorcees are having a financial struggle.

The other area of financial benefit is where a widow may be getting a pension either from her late husband's job or social security and would forfeit it if she remarried. Residential communities of older people around the country, such as in St. Petersburg, Florida, have many couples living together without marriage because they find their combined incomes to be larger that way. It is ironic that many of these people who may have been shocked in their youth by the companionate marriage espoused by Judge Ben Lindsey in the 1920s now find themselves living in the same kind of situation they once excoriated. Thus do the realities of life force us into changed attitudes.

Such nonmarital styles among the elderly will undoubtedly increase as we have more senior citizens in the total population. It is an indication of growing acceptance of this arrangement that the woman moderator of a Los Angeles television program, a senior citizen herself, has come out publicly and said that she believes living together is a fine idea for older people, although she disapproves of it for young people, especially those with children.

When there are no children around, as in these colonies of older people, it is far easier to maintain unmarried arrangements with inner comfort and peace and many of them are agreeing, "What do we need to be married for?"

But when there are children living in the same household with the man and woman, pressures do arise for the pair to marry. One couple who thought they could make a go of it as unmarrieds found it terribly upsetting to the woman's children from her first marriage. "What will we tell our friends when they ask who Tom is?" they asked their mother with concern. "He's not your husband. He's not just a boyfriend. What *is* he?" Asked on school questionnaires to list members of their households and their relationship to each other, children are frequently upset by not knowing how to describe mother's companionate mate. Other children have asked their mothers not to be lying in bed with their companionate-mates when neighborhood children and playmates visit, thus creating one more subtle pressure to be married.

The experiences of young mothers of out-of-wedlock babies are still another indication of pressures to be married. For a while many young mothers were choosing to keep their out-of-wedlock children and attempting as single parents to raise the children themselves. But many of these unwed women have learned that while in some countries babies born outside of marriage suffer no stigma and receive full rights, benefits, and legal recognition, they certainly do not at this point in the United States. "It's Tough To Be Illegitimate" is the headline on a report of the legal difficulties of such children. In some states children cannot inherit property, or recover workmen's compensation for parents killed on the job, or legally demand support from fathers.

Out-of-wedlock mothers are legal pariahs despite the freedoms brought to us by the sexual revolution. Even those who may not care so much about whether the parents are married do care about the deprivations frequently experienced by such children, financial deprivation as well as emotional deprivation of being raised without a father figure in their lives.

And so there has already begun a backlash in which single women are finding it too difficult to be unmarried and are giving up their children for adoption or are choosing, after all, to get legally married. Homes for unwed mothers report that they are now getting one- , two- , and three-year-olds back for adoption because the single mothers couldn't make it on their own.

Despite the Brave New World halo of heroineship with which some young women enter this experience, the reality is that there is still no great public acceptance of the mother raising an out-of-wedlock child. A public housing project in New York has tried and failed to evict unmarried mothers because other tenants didn't want them as neighbors. Even Vanessa Redgrave, the British actress, who is rearing two children out of wedlock, has acknowledged, "I guess it is hard sometimes to be an unwed mother. But people like Mia Farrow and myself are celebrities so we are forgiven. [Miss Farrow subsequently married Andre Previn, the father of her twins.] . . . The unmarried mother who works in an office or any other ordinary job is called a woman of sin."

Confirming public pressure on unmarrieds to be married, a group of clergymen, polled on the types of problems for which their counsel is most often sought, report the problems of unmarried mothers to be the most numerous. In August 1972 a group of young unwed mothers started an organization in Chicago entitled Mothers Alone, Inc. to fight for greater legal and societal recognition for themselves and their children.

From the foregoing it is apparent that there are many reasons why single parents choose to get legally married. This is particularly true for women. In a male-dominated society, many women do not now and never in their lifetimes have had equality of opportunity to make a living or to accumulate social security benefits on their own. Financial security in their old age still derives very much from a male. What a commentary it is on our primitive stage of humanitarian development and social justice that a woman can put in a lifetime of hard physical drudgery homemaking and child rearing and it does not contribute one whit to her financial security in her old age!

Let us introduce laws and social security benefits that equalize a woman's security and we are sure to see many women now getting married who will choose *not* to marry once they can make it financially on their own. It is significant that the greatest number of women who speak out openly of their uninterest in ever being married are successful career women who have financial security. "There's nothing marriage can do for us that we don't already have," they state.

Actually, we seem to be heading toward a future in which a query about one's marital status may not even be considered a proper question to ask. Here, too, the rapidly growing practice of addressing a woman as Ms. denoting neither marital nor single status, is a step in that direction. The question "marital status" may well disappear from printed forms, voting ballots, questionnaires, and other documents as the single state becomes an acceptable lifestyle. Some states have already agreed to register female voters as Ms. and not to ask if women voters are married. Medical insurance forms are beginning not to ask a woman who comes for an abortion if she is married or single. Married or not, every one will enjoy equal benefits, rights, privileges, and opportunities.

It would be ironic if such an antidiscriminatory style of human relationships in which one no longer needed to marry because of legal, societal, or financial pressures, actually worked to strengthen legal marriages. Because we would no longer *need* to be married, those who *chose* to be married would do so out of deep conviction about the institution. Our legal marriages could then be fewer—but firmer.

While we are in transition to the future, most couples still are choosing to marry. We have a high divorce rate but more people than ever before are also marrying. The trend is for them to marry at later ages and we are likely to see the age at first marriage go higher here in the United States as it already has in such countries as Sweden and the People's Republic of China, where average age at first marriage is the late twenties or early thirties. But among the age group thirty-five years and over, according to the United States Census Bureau, the percentage of those who marry increases continuously in an upward spiral.

This suggests that no matter what the nature of a society there will always be many who choose to marry legally. Humankind has not yet devised any method greater than the total bond and commitment of marriage between a man and a woman that is potentially as conducive to enhancing our lives as there is to be found in a good marriage.

"Marriage within the American social structure means a success," says pastoral counselor Ben T. Cowles of Pasadena, California. Often, to marry becomes the ultimate self-enhancing experience which says to the community: "I am worthy of another person making a commitment to me before all of you."

The human being has a deep need for the nourishment to be derived from healthy roots, firmly planted in life's commitments, from which we can draw spiritual and physical sustenance. It is undeniable that these roots often do not exist when couples live together. When such people encounter difficulties in their relationship, they are quicker to blow up and say, "Let's end it, we're not getting along." The legal documentation of a marriage certificate has the psychological effect of making many couples try harder to work through their differences than if one or the other can say, "We have no legal ties, so I'm going."

For some, living together thus becomes a kind of copping-out, a running away from the working through of human differences, and thus a deprivation of the growth we experience when we stay and work through the problems of a committed relationship like marriage.

In Ignazio Silone's novel *Bread and Wine* a character says: "In all times, in all societies, the supreme act is to give oneself to find oneself." That well applies to marriage. Giving of oneself to the marriage bond can also be the finding of oneself.

PART VI

THE FUTURE OF SEX

21

Sex for Recreation,
Not Procreation

Man on his voyage through the endless terrain of time encounters bumps of turmoil. These bumps of turmoil often turn out to have been bumps of transition to calm periods. Our present turmoil is likely to be the bumpy unheaval of humankind passing through one more calibration on its evolutionary scale on its way to the next higher stage of human development. Philosopher William James has said in his essay *The Energies of Men* that so far in human existence man has brought into use only a small part of that of which he is yet capable.

Our emergent philosophy of sex for recreation not procreation is likely to have been one of the requirements for mankind to go on to a higher plateau of evolutionary growth. Just as women's liberation is likely also to be a requirement before humankind can grow forward.

The question facing us is not: "Do we permit these changes to happen?" but rather: "In the course of evolution, their happening is inevitable. How do we best implement into human experience the changes they bring?"

What changes will sex after the sexual revolution bring to us? What are our patterns of behavior, our sex codes, our ethics, our customs, and styles of the future apt to be like? Highly variegated. We have gone from sexual Puritanism to sexual pluralism in less than a generation.

We can find a correlation between the multi-styles of dress today in which anything goes—mini, midi, maxi, uni—and the multi-morals of our sexual styles—hetero, homo, bi—in which anything also goes. The moral uniform of the nation is no longer a stiff-necked tuxedo; now it's bare chest and flowered blue jeans.

For some of us, the growing freedom to have sex only for fun rather than for fertilization is not bringing liberation. Our widespread open discussion of sexuality has become a burden to some, a kind of tyranny in which we are trying to live up to unreasonably high expectations of sexual performance that it is impossible for most to achieve.

We are becoming a nation obsessed with sex mechanics, so hung up on techniques and searching frantically to determine sources of orgasm as vaginal or clitoral that we are playing one huge national game of Sexual Report Card.

We may be reaching more climaxes but we are not reaching more peaks of joy as we push onward, ever onward, to reach a higher Gross National Product of orgasms, lest we be faulted as sexual underachievers. "We are not a sex-starved people," says psychotherapist Paul Bindrim; "we are an emotion- and warmth-starved people."

Hopefully, we will soon have done with this obsession with quantity and we will mature toward a concern for quality which will permit us to care more about the psyche and less about the physique in the sex act.

Our new philosophy of sex for recreation will find us increasingly accepting its concomitant—the philosophy of pleasure. Hedonism, so long abjured by man, will join equalism—equality between the genders—as two of humanity's main themes of existence.

Present research into the human brain will probably strengthen hedonism. In experiments at research centers throughout the country, pleasure or "reward" centers in the brains of monkeys have been stimulated by electrodes, forecasting a time when we will be able to achieve the kind of sensation we now experience in orgasm simply by manipulating the pleasure centers in our brains.

One can envision a time when, in a widely accepted custom befitting the philosophy of pleasure, a busy executive will take a few minutes out of a hectic day and recharge himself or herself physically and sensorily by attaching electrodes and enjoying an electronically induced orgasm. Such a "pleasure break" could become as routine as a coffee break is today.

Further adding to human pleasure, brain wave control augurs the end of sexual problems, pain, and malfunctioning. Learning to control his brain waves, an impotent man can easily will himself to have an erection and to maintain it as long as he wishes; a nonorgasmic woman can will herself to reach climax. A woman suffering dyspareunia, painful intercourse, or painful menstruation, can eliminate the pain, as can the woman in childbirth. Some experimenters foresee the day when a woman will be able to control her own fertility through brain waves. A heart patient, uneasy about having sexual relations because of an accelerated heartbeat, can will himself to lower the rate of beat during intercourse.

For some men, sex is becoming more like hard work. As women are freed from fear of pregnancy and from Puritan messages about female sexuality, they are also freed to make more sexual overtures. In the past the male would make an overture when he was capable and desirous, when he could experience erection. Now when his initiative is no longer the sole one in the sex act, many men find themselves called upon and found wanting. Among the side effects of both the pill and the intrauterine coil is a growing tendency for women to become sexually desirous more often and for men not to be able to perform as often as women would wish. A team of British doctors has found that for some of their patients the coil acts as a sex stimulant. Dr. Robert Kistner of Harvard Medical School reports in his book *The Pill: Facts and Fallacies about Today's Oral Contraceptives* that many wives now feel sexually liberated while some husbands feel sexually enslaved.

Now that we are free to talk more openly about women being multiorgasmic, many of us are learning about this sexual capacity for the first time—we have never even heard of it before—and men find they have the added burden of trying to provide multiple orgasms as part of their sexual productivity.

It has been suggested that many men are finding the need for sexual performance such a burden that they are becoming uninterested in sex. Dr. Ralph Greenson says "sexual satisfaction is becoming more important for women and less important for men." He observes a "growing indifference and lethargy toward sex in American men, the young as well as the old." This may explain why we have so much open sexuality—we need it to keep telling ourselves how sexy and masculine and virile we are—trying to convince ourselves of what we are not experiencing and may not even desire.

This burdensome effect of sexual liberation on men is summed up in a cartoon showing two men, businessmen types carrying briefcases. One is saying to the other: "You think you've got troubles? My wife just bought a book on sex education."

Accepting the idea of pleasure and our right to experience it, we will see as a result of the sexual revolution the growth of sensuality seminars in which people attend classes to learn how to free up and get more out of their sensual natures. We have barely touched the surface of our capacity for sensual experience.

Paula Newhorn already conducts a Center for Sensory Development in Los Angeles in which she teaches men and women to free themselves of inhibitions and hang-ups by showing them how to exercise their genital muscles, the techniques of heightening sensation in erogenous zones through light and heavy stroking and massaging, how to use fabric and textures such as chiffon scarves and feathers for tactile turn-on, how to be comfortable with the noises and sounds of orgasm and the sex act, and how to defuse "loaded" words associated with sex—all designed to add to the human pleasure potential.

As we pursue our pleasures, some of us may care less about sexual privacy. Marshall McLuhan, writing on *The Future of Sex*, suggests that young people, considering sex to be merely one more of life's sensory experiences and just not that all-important, may go to it when and where the urge strikes them, no matter who happens to be around—which is not much different from what has been happening for a long time in some tribal cultures in which children have been exposed to the sex act all of their lives.

If this were to come about, humankind would be the poorer for it. As humanity proliferates and the bombardment of people-pollution on our nervous systems becomes more severe, we will increasingly need the privilege of privacy as our refuge from the madding crowd. Rene Dubos points out that "man needs to be by himself; he reacts to continued oversocialization with all sorts of frustrations, repressions, aggressions, and fears which soon develop into genuine neuroses." To give up one of our last oases of privacy, the sex act, could be disastrous to the human spirit.

As we grow accustomed to the idea that sex is mostly for pleasuring ourselves, it is likely that we will figure out a way to carry out that pleasurable intention without having to worry about its side effects—unwanted pregnancy. We will want some sure and easy method of mass contraception. Scientists have suggested that we consider adding infertility chemicals to our food and water. Those who wished to have children could then take a fertility agent to counteract the infertility chemical, in exactly the same way that some women now take fertility pills to help them conceive after they have been on birth control pills and become infertile.

We may well see a time when a couple will need society's permission to have a child. In 1969 a group of scientists warned President Richard M. Nixon that they considered voluntary birth control to be "insanity" for the future of this country and of the world. They urged that we begin to consider the idea of enforced birth control for the future and the denial, through increased taxes or sterilization, of a couple's right to breed more human beings than they can provide for, emotionally as well as financially. People unfit to be parents would be screened out, parent training would be widespread, and licensing of parents would become an accepted social custom. California State Senator Anthony Beilenson has already introduced bills, the forerunners of similar legislation that will someday be introduced into other state legislatures, that would not allow income tax deductions for more than two children. U. S. Senator Robert W. Packwood of Oregon proposes income tax relief for a maximum of three children on a sliding scale: $1,000 for Child 1, $750 for Child 2, $500 for Child 3. Some social scientists suggest that the government impose a heavy "diaper tax" after two children.

Involuntary limiting of families is repugnant to many. But whatever form it takes, parenthood-by-permission may become an inevitable part of our future. Even those who object to it as being undemocratic may some day find themselves coming out for such a system in self-defense against those who turn out babies they cannot provide for and which wind up as society's wards being supported by the rest of us.

Mr. E. R. Whitmore, Jr., prosecuting attorney of Chelan County in Wenatchee, Washington, writing a Letter to the Editor in which he comes out for involuntary sterilization, says that "the responsible people in society are going to have to control the irresponsible before they are overwhelmed by sheer force of numbers."

Over half our states now have laws permitting involuntary sterilization but these apply only to persons institutionalized for mental defects or mental illness. In some states, habitual sexual deviates with a number of convictions for sex crimes may also be legally sterilized.

Sterilization does not inhibit sexual activity or desire; it inhibits only the capacity to procreate. Involuntary sterilization for excessive, irresponsible procreation of babies who are abandoned, battered, or neglected, would come about through court order as the result of judicial decision, and would impose heavy fines and/or jail sentences or sterilization on such parents.

Arguing strongly against legally enforced population control, Harriet F. Pilpel, attorney for the American Civil Liberties Union, says that sex education and widespread availability of contraception to all age groups have not yet been with us long enough for us to know whether or not they will be effective in teaching people to voluntarily limit the numbers of children. "I am convinced that if we really make freedom of choice possible with respect to human reproduction," she says, "there will be no need to resort to compulsion."

Long before we start regulating the right to breed, however, we will certainly be giving full legal support to any woman who chooses not to breed. Abortion will be legal everywhere in the United States and will some day become an office or home procedure through injection of a hormonelike chemical, prostaglandins, known as PGs, or through the use of the vacuum aspirator in which a vacuum syringe is inserted into the cervix and the products of conception drawn out.

Such "do-it-yourself" abortion procedures will be wholly in the personal or private realm with no laws applying. A woman will be able to go into a drugstore and buy a vacuum aspirator or a saline solution with which to douche, without a prescription. Pregnancy test kits are now for sale in Canadian drugstores, enabling a woman to determine herself with a simple urine test at home whether she is pregnant.

Finding out whether she is pregnant and determining what to do about it will be entirely within the province of a woman's civil and human liberties, with no law and no male, be it husband or physician, telling her what she may or may not do with her own body.

When sex alliances no longer carry the obligation of the past to beget children, we will find ourselves caring less about who mates with whom. Among the sexual styles arising out of our new freedoms will be an acceptable and widely practiced style of relationship to which we might give the name *chronosex*—sex between the generations without regard to one's chronological age.

Up until the sexual revolution, this kind of alliance was certainly practiced but not widely accepted. There has always been much implied criticism of older men or women mating with young people.

Actually, nature has designed with great imbalance in the sex drive of male and female. We now know that the male's great drive peaks in his teens and twenties while the female's great surge may not come until her thirties or forties. Armed with this knowledge and with a liberated culture accepting of such sexual styles, more older women are likely to mate sexually with younger men, as they traditionally have done in some European countries where it has long been the custom for an older sophisticated woman to "initiate" a young man into the mysteries of sex. Older men, for whom it is a physiological fact of life that their waning sex prowess is often restored, at least temporarily, in relationships with young women, may now find social acceptance for such "Lolita" arrangements.

The word *chronosex* is only one of the new kinds of words that will undoubtedly come forth in the future. All social change brings forth new vocabulary. We already have *fetology,* the study of fetuses and of genetic engineering; the word *hyponatology,* the art and science of lowering birth rates; the word *envirotecture,* the study of man in relation to his environment. *Sexological* education will refer to a combination of biological and psychological sex education. The word *sexicity* may become a new adjective to describe a person who has sexual felicity, skill, or know-how.

Our future walks toward us from its place on the horizon. Some of us will cower before it; others will greet it with outstretched hand. To be alarmed by change makes of it a tyranny. To be enchanted by change makes of it an adventure.

22

Future Styles in Procreation

During the summer of 1816, poets Percy Bysshe Shelley and Lord Byron, and Shelley's wife. Mary Wollstonecraft Shelley, whiled away rainy days on vacation in Switzerland by making up horror stories. Two years later Mary Shelley published the results of their idle pastime, a novel, *Frankenstein,* a chilling tale about a Swiss scientist who imparts life to a homemade man formed of parts stolen from mortuaries and dissecting rooms. The monster, angered because he cannot live and experience love as humans do, eventually kills his creator.

The idea of an artificially created human has thrilled and terrified man ever since. It continues to do so now as the idea enters the realm of possibility. Procreation in the laboratory, starting not with a fully grown creature who is given life as in *Frankenstein,* but from the embryonic stage, is already on the drawing boards of the wondrous human capacity to create.

Our foreseeable future will probably include these several types of procreation: impregnation and gestation as we have always known it; artificial insemination, and artificial inovulation, methods already being practiced; and test tube procreation and genetic engineering—known as "cloning"—methods far from perfected but already begun in man's odyssey of procreation.

Artificial Insemination. More than 100,000 youths in the United States today are the result of artificial insemination, a method only about a decade old. As recently as 1967 Oklahoma became our first state to recognize offspring born through artificial insemination as the legitimate children of their mothers and fathers, entitled to all rights of inheritance, support, and recognition. Many of our states do not have such laws and children born through artificial insemination have dubious legal rights which have not yet been tested in the courts of those states.

Artificial insemination may be achieved by either of two methods. A.I.H. stands for Artificial Insemination Husband, and involves the use of semen from a woman's own husband who because of health reasons or penile flaccidity or other problems is not able to complete ejaculation into the vagina.

A.I.D. stands for Artificial Insemination Donor, meaning that the sperm comes from a donor to a sperm bank who is not known to the couple. A.I.D. gives rise to many legal questions, the main one being whether a wife has legally committed adultery by allowing another man's sperm to be injected into her. In a test case in New York State in 1967, a physician attempted to obtain a divorce on the grounds that his wife had committed adultery by being artificially inseminated without his knowledge or consent. He himself had been sterile for many years. The jury decided it was not an adulterous act on the wife's part.

Another case that same year, this one in California, involved a husband who as part of divorce proceedings brought by his wife, refused to give financial support to a child born to her through A.I.D. After much legal seesawing in courts which first upheld the father and then overturned that decision, the man was held legally liable to pay support for the child because his wife had been inseminated with his approval.

The use of artificial insemination as a procreative method is likely to increase as the result of epidemics of venereal disease which are making more people infertile. The wife of a man made infertile because of V.D. will be able to conceive with A.I.D.

As this method increases so will legal and psychological problems. To help avoid entanglements, artificial insemination agreements now provide that the wife, the husband, the physician who performs the procedure, and a judge must all sign the agreement. To strengthen the child's legal protections, the father is often asked to state that his agreement constitutes legal adoption of the resulting child.

Many fathers of children so conceived find emotional difficulty in dealing with the relationship at times of marital or child-rearing dissension. There is a tendency, some fathers admit, to point out the misbehavior of *"your* child" to a wife. One wife who has had A.I.D. says she makes it very clear that "My husband *is* our baby's father. Fatherhood is more than genes and chromosomes."

Artificial Inovulation. This very new method of procreation, also known as "proxy pregnancy," involves the removal of a fertilized egg a few days old from a woman who is unable to gestate herself, usually for health reasons such as a heart condition, and its implantation in the womb of a "host mother" who then bears the child. This was the theme of a 1971 film, *The Baby Maker.* A well-known embryologist at the University of Birmingham in England has offered a fee of $4800 to any woman who would carry a baby for another woman as part of his experiments.

As with all scientific advances, artificial inovulation will inevitably create a host of new legal, ethical, and moral questions. For example, what if the host mother find herself emotionally unable to give up the baby she has carried for nine months and refuses to turn it over to its biological mother? If an artificially inovulated child learns the identity of its host mother, can it make any legal claims in proceedings involving inheritance? Should the host mother suffer a miscarriage, would she be liable to a lawsuit by the biological mother on grounds she did not take good care of herself during her pregnancy and thus did not keep the terms of their agreement? Should the host mother change her mind about the gestation and get an abortion, could the biological mother accuse her of murdering another woman's embryo? What if the child should be born defective and is rejected by the biological mother? Would the mother providing the embryo have a right to sue for injury or death to a fetus if a host mother were hurt in an accident?

Some future time may see all such matters being brought into our courts. Human advances and progress have never come easily.

Test Tube Procreation. Human embryos have already been kept alive briefly in test tubes in the United States, England, Italy, and elsewhere. Before long a scientist will conceive a baby in a test tube and successfully place it inside a woman who will bear the child, in a combination of test tube procreation and artificial inovulation.

This was the prediction of Dr. James D. Watson, Nobel Prize-winning biologist from Harvard, testifying before a Congressional subcommittee on science in 1971.

This achievement will probably be followed by the growth of ovarian and testicular tissue outside the human body and its successful transplantation into a test tube, rather than a woman's body, for its entire nine-month gestation. (While the phrase "test tube baby" is a dramatic one that captures public fancy, the reality is that a tube could not provide sufficient growth space for the developing fetus. The actual container would look more like an artificial womb.)

The moral and ethical questions, if an embryo is created in a test tube and grown to full term in glass, are fascinating to contemplate. Would a scientist, growing a human under glass, have the right to interfere with its continued growth to humanship by further experimentation?

The human aspects are also fascinating to contemplate. Babies created under glass could mean the end of the professions of obstetrician and obstetrical nurse. Hospital labor and delivery rooms would become obsolete.

It seems probable that most women would choose to have their babies grown in laboratories. Childbirth has been measured as the highest source of pain on the human pain meter. No man who could ever have experienced the pain of childbirth would blithely insist that the female has an innate need to gestate and experience childbirth. That is among the myths perpetuated down through the ages by men, not by women. Freed from the pain and the physical inconvenience of gestation and delivery, what would that mean to the human female? Would she then seek to end menstruation as an unnecessary inconvenience? Dr. Edgar F. Berman, a Washington, D.C., physician, caused a furore among women liberationists when he said that the hormonal and behavioral changes caused by the monthly cycles disqualified women from holding high public office. What if woman had no more monthly cycle, being able to store up eggs in advance in the deep freeze to create as many babies as she wanted in her lifetime?

Genetic Engineering. Some day we will be able to custom design through genetic manipulation the style of baby we want. Dr. E.S.E.

Hafez, an experimental biologist at Washington State University, foresees the day when a woman can stroll through a genetic laboratory and select the kind of child she wants from one-day-old frozen embryos, guaranteed free of all genetic defects and described with tags as to gender, eye color, hair color, and probable I.Q. The frozen embryo would then be thawed and injected into her or into a host mother.

Beyond that, the science of cryogenics, of preserving for long periods through freezing, will enable us some day to clone whole human beings, to reproduce carbon copies of great, creative individuals even long after they are dead, through maintaining frozen sperm banks of semen and cells from geniuses. "For musical reasons, it might be nice to have a whole conservatory of Beethovens," says a report in *The New York Times* on our genetic futures, but what would be the effects on society of so many people with Beethoven's temperament? Unscrupulous scientists could clone an army of tyrants as well as of geniuses. Would a world full of geniuses thrive, or does there exist an ecological balance for humans as well as for nature? Does humankind require brawn, as well as brain, to survive?

When we can clone human beings, we can also create humans who have four or six or eight parents, not just two. Genetic experiments with mice have already produced one offspring with the characteristics of four parents. If we have an offspring with multiparents—multimoms and multidads—will we have more parents fighting over filial affection and obligation? Who is then legally responsible for such a child? If the generation gap is so huge between offspring and one set of parents at present, what frightening possibilities of dissension might there be between an offspring and several sets of parents?

Arguing on behalf of cloning, theologian-philosopher Joseph Fletcher has said: "There is nothing sacred about conventional reproduction. It seems to me that laboratory reproduction is 'more human' than conception by ordinary heterosexual intercourse. It is willed, chosen, purposed, and controlled and surely these are among the traits that distinguish Homo sapiens from others in the animal genus. I cannot see how either humanity or morality is served by genetic roulette," which we now have in human reproduction.

So alarming are all these awesome possibilities that many scientists, among them Dr. James Watson, mentioned earlier, and Lord Louis Rothschild, a physiologist, are pleading for a worldwide commission for genetic control. When we can grow babies in test tubes and when we can clone human beings, "all hell will break loose, politically and morally, all over the world," unless we institute controls, says Dr. Watson.

While we are off on our flights of fancy into the future, some scientists are hard at work in the here-and-now of procreation. Each year, in the United States, a quarter-million families are saddened and financially burdened by the birth of babies who have inherited incurable diseases, irreversible retardation, and malformations. Geneticists are working hard to perfect and enlarge techniques that can prevent or at least ameliorate the anguish experienced by such couples as the parents of the children who have rare genetic diseases like *xeroderma pigmentosum,* in which a boy is destined to live his entire lifetime only in the dark because the slightest exposure to light from the sun causes his skin to break out in ugly malignant tumors; or another incurable skin disease called *epidermolysis bullosa dystrophica,* in which the only cloth a child can tolerate next to its skin is pure white silk. Any other textile causes the child's skin to break out all over in blisters. "The doctor has told us," the mother of the latter child reports, "that if we can combat infections and pneumonia, he might live to be twelve years old."

Genetic counselors can now identify many defective fetuses *in utero,* in plenty of time for them to be aborted. Before long, it will become routine for couples planning to have children to go to genetic clinics for testing in the same way that we now routinely have blood tests during pregnancy.

Other scientists are at work to learn more about the procreative process. Incredibly, with all our knowledge, man does not yet know what happens at the instant a baby starts its way down through the birth canal. What happens in the female uterus at that instant to trigger the birth process? This is still a mystery to us.

And while we are doing all that genetic engineering in the distant future, it might be nice to contemplate having human beings born in a more advanced stage of biological and physiological development. For example, ducks swim and horses walk within minutes or hours after birth. No other species is helpless after birth for so long a time as the human species. What a boon to humankind if infants could take care of their own middle-of-the-night feedings or didn't even need them, or could change their own diapers or were born already able to control their sphincter muscles and thus didn't need toilet-training!

23

Future Styles of Population

As long as man has existed he has been plagued by nature's riddle—will an expected child be a boy or a girl? Man has sought
through superstition, fortune-telling, old wives' tales, the signs of
the zodiac, amulets and charms, to know in advance of birth whether a woman's swelling abdomen housed a girl or boy child. Everywhere, studies have shown, men prefer that their children, especially a firstborn, be male.

Among the privileges accruing to humankind is that we will
soon be able not just to learn the gender in advance but even to determine ourselves what we want the gender to be. Man will thus
have taken one more giant step forward toward controlling human
destiny in his eternal struggle to improve on nature.

Already, the gender of unborn children can be learned with almost 100 per cent accuracy by about the twelfth week of pregnancy, by the insertion of a needle into the mother's womb, the withdrawal of amniotic fluid, and the analyzing of cells shed by the
fetus. At present this test is being done only where there is medical
need to know a child's gender, as in the case of hemophilia which
afflicts only males. The skill and the know-how exist, should we
need to make use of it.

But even this test may not be needed when we are able to predetermine the gender we wish to create. Pioneering work by Dr. Landrum B. Shettles, reported in his book *Your Baby's Sex: Now You Can Choose,* indicate that the timing and position of the sex act, the acid-alkaline content of the vagina, and the depth of penile penetration, may all help determine whether it is a boy or a girl.

Professor Charles Birch, head of the Sydney University School of Biological Sciences in Australia, anticipates that husbands may one day decide their offspring by taking pills, "pink for a girl, blue for a boy," he says, only half in jest.

Assuredly, by the year 2000 and probably before then, man in one way or another will be in complete charge of determining the gender to be born. The riddle of birth roulette will have forever ended.

When we can do this, what will be the effects of gender determination on our population?

Among the rewards is that we can do away with a growing problem of imbalance throughout the world in which we have many more aging women than men. Millions of women are destined to live out their latter years without male companionship because of earlier deaths through disease and war of the human male. Practically every nation involved in World War II finds itself with a disproportionate number of elderly females today. Dr. Victor Kassel, a Salt Lake City specialist in geriatrics, has suggested that polygamy should be made legal after the age of sixty so that one man could be shared in a companionate arrangement by more than one woman. Humanity would soon figure out how many boy babies to conceive in order to even up the balance between the genders in their later years.

But gender determining will have profound risks, too. Dr. Amitai Etzioni, Columbia University sociologist, believes that gender determination will have widespread social, moral, and political effects. Because more men than women consistently vote Democratic and because women are by far the greater consumers of culture, more regular churchgoers, and the keepers of the conscience, charged with the moral education of children, he says that "a significant and cumulative male surplus could produce a society with some of the rougher features of a frontier town." History has shown us that in all-male communities such as frontier towns and gold-mining camps where the gentle-izing influence of women was lacking, acts of violence often become accepted solutions to personal and social problems. It is significant that in our own recent history, it was the *Women's* Strike for Peace, not Men's Strike for Peace, that influenced American military policy.

"Racial and class tensions might be aggravated," Dr. Etzioni further believes, "since the lower classes and minorities are more 'male oriented' and would almost certainly choose to turn out far more male children. A greater boy surplus in lower status groups will prompt these boys to seek girls in higher status groups." Turning out too many boys might also increase homosexuality.

What all of this suggests is that we urgently need a new "ism"—equalism—under which would-be parents are educated about the desirability of female as well as male offspring. Liberated woman no longer needs a dowry; she may not even be interested in marriage. Economic reasons for history's downgrading of female offspring no longer exist.

Our future styles of population will also be much affected by family size. The nobility of parenthood, in which large families were lauded, has ended. Protestant theologians, meeting at the School of Theology in Claremont, California, in April 1970 on the "Theology of Survival," indicated that Christianity has played its part in provoking the current environmental crisis, and that any solution to it would require major modification of current social and religious values. Among the values to come under attack was "the right of couples to have large families."

Our future is likely to limit the size of a family through laws, societal pressures, education, and through the pocketbook. Social scientists increasingly point out that the two-child family is happier, more emotionally stable and better off financially. Dr. Judd Marmor reporting on the effects of overcrowding in a family, says that some emotional deprivation is inevitable when there are too many offspring and there just aren't enough hours in the day for a mother to give the nurturing, the time, and the attention to each child that it might require for ideal growth, especially for skin-to-skin cuddling.

Studies by Dr. Augustus F. Kinzel at the United States Medical

Center for Federal Prisoners in Springfield, Missouri, and by Dr. Kurt Richter of Johns Hopkins University, and Dr. Edward T. Hall of the Illinois Institute of Technology all indicate possible correlation between overcrowded living conditions and acts of violence. Those living in too close "body buffer zones" are more likely to become involved in violence, a possible explanation of why slums have more violent crimes than less crowded areas.

Furthermore, the cost of child rearing is becoming prohibitive not only to society but to the individual family. The price of parenthood from the time a woman conceives through birth, pediatric care, nursery school, babysitters, schooling at all levels, food, housing, clothing, recreation, summer activities, and "miscellaneous" has been modestly estimated as averaging upward from $50,000 to rear a child with some small degree of comfort and privilege in contemporary America. Many families spend a good deal more than that per child. A man, thinking seriously about how much work he has to put out to support each child for twenty or so years, might well consider whether it's worth that much hard work to express his masculinity by turning out babies.

Sentiment against large families has become so powerful that when some couples were in the news in recent years because of multiple births due to fertility pills taken by the wives, they were flooded with letters from the public excoriating them for their "selfishness" and for being "murderers of society" by inflicting their greedy wish to have more children on the world when they already had children.

Based on predictions by some demographers, should we have two children per family our population will take on unfavorable characteristics that will breed a whole new set of problems. Where population control is successful, a side effect is that the population becomes progressively more elderly, as it has in Japan. The elderly are not the major consumers or purchasers in society, but they may control the political and legal machinery and often tend to be more conservative. Fewer children being born also means that fewer schools and teachers are needed. Already we are experiencing a surplus of Ph.D.'s.

Dr. Rene Dubos believes that two children per family would not leave enough children in the population for adults to see and interact with. "Already there are not enough children for adults to see. In some cities you walk around and never see children," he has said.

By present indications and forecasts by population experts, what is in store for us in the population style of our future is a lot more elderly, more males, smaller families, and fewer teachers who have fewer youth to teach. The lines of political battle will be more sharply drawn, with a larger segment of conservative elderly trying to run things for a smaller segment of rebellious young.

24

The Sensory Human of
the Future

Where will our philosophy of sex for recreation and not procreation, our new ethic of existence which cares for quality not quantity of people, lead us? What will all this mean to humankind in the near future and, beyond that, to our descendants generations from now?

Let us see what an historian of the future, say, ten generations or about three hundred years from today, might write about us. Or perhaps the report would be one written by a bright schoolchild as a history project, a boy or girl who was eugenically bred to be a creative, disease-free, nonviolent, cooperative humanist? What might our historian or our brilliant student write about the times and the traumas through which we are now passing? Let's take a look at ourselves in historical perspective and find out what history's verdict on our era might be. The report follows.

About halfway through the twentieth century on the planet Earth, the most revolutionary idea ever brought forth in humankind's existence exploded like an ideological atom bomb. This idea said that the sex act for purposes of procreation was now about to end. Henceforth, sex would be acceptable mostly for pleasure. This reversed everything humanity had ever been taught. Many of the "eternal verities"—the sacredness of motherhood, the desirability of large families, the acceptability of sex only in marriage—all went sliding down the chute of time. What sparked the ideological change was man's growing realization, at that point in time, that the planet whose interior decorator he had been was nothing but an overcrowded, dirty, spheroid slum tenement. I say "man" advisedly; woman had not up until then ever had any decision-making authority of any great consequence or duration.

Until that time, the theme of human sexual behavior had always been to be fruitful and to multiply, to fill up the Earth's empty spaces with more people. Societies needed more people to produce more population to produce more gross national product that would support a state's aggrandizement and expansion. The sex act that resulted in pregnancy was lauded as pure; motherhood was woman's divine calling.

Because increased population was in the interest of the state, the state controlled people's sexual behavior through laws, social custom, folklore, mythology, and religious injunction. Any sex act or human relationship or form of release from sexual tension—oral-genital sex, masturbation, male-with-male, female-with-female—which subverted the state's goal by denying the possibility of procreation, was declared to be illegal, immoral, and sinful. Sex was approved only when it carried the possibility of socially sanctioned pregnancy.

A citizen's body belonged not to him but to his government. This was especially true in the social and legal position of the female. Woman was the chattel of the state and her husband. She had no rights whatever as to whether or not she wanted to bear and rear children. For many centuries, woman wore the shackles of chauvinism around her body as she wore the symbol of her slavery—the wedding ring—around her finger. The ring had, in fact, derived from the custom of a master identifying his slaves through rings in their noses.

The laws of the world mostly approved of sex only when it encompassed these factors: man-and-woman, face-to-face, the man above, with no contraception to interfere with nature's process. These were the factors most conducive to procreation. Even a change in physical position—the woman above—was often illegal because that meant that the life-creating sperm could too easily flow back down out of the vaginal canal and thus would find more difficult its ordained task of fertilizing a female egg. (As the drawings on the ancient walls of Pompeii showed, men and women of all times ignored this law. The human need for variety of sources of pleasure has frequently taken precedence over the human wish for law-and-order.)

In a perverse kind of human arithmetic practiced by that early man, the whole of a woman's body counted for much less than did the quarter-pound of skin, tissue, fiber, and muscle dangling between a male's legs a couple of inches outside his torso.

That same half-century saw the ending of the sexual double standard and the introduction of equalism as a human standard. The words "male" and "female" were removed from statutes, legal forms, job advertisements, to be replaced by the word "person" or "human." The abbreviation Mrs., denoting a married woman, was declared discriminatory against women who chose not to marry and was replaced by the title of Ms. meaning Miss or Mrs. The designation Mr. had never denoted marital status; now neither did Ms.

What many people had long suspected was confirmed at last. The former lack of creative output in music, art, poetry, literature, philosophy, scholarship, by the female, which man had long attributed to her intellectual inferiority, was due only to the fact that the female, busy with the demands of baby making and child rearing, had never before had time to devote to creative pursuits. Freed at last from the primary use that had been made of her personhood as procreative apparatus, the female now began to be lauded for the first time more for her mentality than her mammaries.

In a complete reversal of all previous human experience, individuals who chose never to bear children, once looked upon as pariahs and social outcasts, now were hailed as ideal citizens. Inspired by a college valedictorian who announced to the world in ringing tones that she chose not to bring children into the sick society, many now decided to forego parenthood entirely. Instead of nurturing their own biological offspring, they chose to nurture the many unwanted children born out of wedlock who might otherwise languish without loving.

As evolution brought our ancestors closer to the twenty-first century and the new freedom of sex for pleasure began to be incorporated into their behavior, they became the early ancestors of the Sensory Human we all are in this century.

Cadres of men and women became skin nutritionists in sensory groups, sometimes called touchy-feely groups, teaching people how to feed their skin hunger by stroking each other lovingly. People so pleasantly stroked found it hard to become angry and to make war on each other.

As industrial parks, office-residential edifices, and educational institutions like colleges were constructed, the law required them to include sandboxes, swings, seesaws, jungle gyms, and mud pits on their grounds for use by grown-ups, so that even adults, no matter what their ages, could swing high in the air, build sand castles, pat wet mud, and otherwise enjoy, guilt-free, their physical beings and continue throughout life the sensual delights of their childhood.

These experiences in playpens for grown-ups and in feeding skin hunger so satisfied early Sensory Human that they no longer needed chemicals, known as drugs, to enjoy the sensory experience they had long been deprived of by the Puritanism which said you were being sexually seductive if you touched other people in warmth and love and affection. It was during this same era of which I write that humankind first learned to separate sensual need—for touching and stroking—from sexual need—for orgasm. Folk dancing became the global pastime, providing one more way in which people could acceptably move and touch a wide variety of fellow humans in warmth and affection. This was, of course, the origin of our annual Folk Dance Olympics in which our winners come not from those who best each other but from those whose minicomputers, affixed to their bodies, reveal that they have touched in dancing the greatest numbers of fellow humans from the greatest numbers of countries throughout the globe.

It is with some amusement that we delve into historic archives and learn about the language customs of that era. Just how primitive and uncivilized that man of long ago was in his humanistic orientation can be judged by the language he chose to forbid. Popularly known as four-letter words, both law and custom said that words associated with the body processes of digestion, elimination, and procreation could not pass the lips of the refined and dignified.

When you stop and think about it, how illogical our ancestor was! Many words associated with the act of love he made ignominious while words associated with the act of hate he ennobled. He could get whole armies to march and slay by exhorting the four-letter word "flag." We wonder what he would think of our own forbidden words of today—kill, maim, hurt, bomb, jail, war—which are becoming extinct in the human lexicon through disuse?

It was during the 1970s that a little-known philosopher, Irving Laucks, a scholar at the Center for the Study of Democratic Institutions in Santa Barbara, California, the Mount Olympus of twentieth century thinkers, accurately forecast the future when he maintained that humankind was entering its third major stage of evolutionary development, which philosopher Laucks described as:

First evolutionary stage: Primeval Man
Second evolutionary stage: Acquiring Man
Third evolutionary stage: Cooperative Man

Dr. Jonas Salk, physician-inventor of a vaccine that had forever wiped out that dreaded ancient scourge—poliomyelitis—said much the same thing on November 3, 1970: "Mankind is in the midst of a transition from an epoch of competition to an epoch of cooperation. This new era is about three generations away."

As history confirms, these gentlemen were right. Man was indeed passing through in the stormy latter third of the twentieth century one more calibration on his evolutionary scale, en route to our present era.

The forward sweep of history selected that half-century, from 1950 to 2000, as the time in which humankind would be forever freed from its sexual ignorance and prurience. Many people suffered much as they fought for changes in laws and in human rights. Women marched to the sound of the drummer of freedom, demanding their rights to their own bodies. Persons both male and female went to jail, fighting for the right of all to free access to contraceptives. Women throughout the world in order to force changes in repressive laws, courageously laid bare their illegal actions in having had abortions. Many youth were freed from their age ghettos and allowed to become the masters of their own destiny, to seek a variety of medical help without having to ask parental approval. A pioneer like Margaret Sanger, who began planned parenthood clinics in the early part of the twentieth century, was spat upon and physically beaten and jailed because she dared to gather women about her secretly in darkened living rooms to whisper the illegal tidings about how their worn-out bodies might achieve the spacing of their children.

The travail of such noble forebears did honor to all those who came after them. Ever since their time, humankind has maintained its right to do with its own body what it will. The sexual-civil-liberties code which began at that time, stating that no form of sexual expression may be legally proscribed unless it is done with force, violence, without the consent of both parties, to the mentally retarded, or to minors incapable of knowing the consequences of their actions, is now so ingrained a part of human existence that it is hard to imagine a time when there was no such sexual-right precept and human beings were made to feel shameful and fearful about the exercise of their sex drive.

It is because of such courageous forebears that we now lead the good life available to us on the planet Earth with space, air, water, and food for all. It is as a result of their efforts that we succeeded in amending the United States Constitution to insist that liberty and justice were not enough of an inalienable birthright; henceforth each person's birthright must also include space, air, water, and food. The world has never known such flowering of human personality. The standard by which a person's worth is judged is not, as it once was in that long-ago time, how many babies he could turn out but how cooperative he can be in the human community.

We thank them for the freedoms they carved out for us.